Prime Cut

Prime Cut

Livestock Raising and Meatpacking
in the United States
1607–1983

By
Jimmy M. Skaggs

Texas A&M University Press
College Station

Library of Congress Cataloging-in-Publication Data

Skaggs, Jimmy M.
Prime cut.

Bibliography: p.
Includes index.
1. Meat industry and trade—United States—History.
2. Cattle trade—United States—History. 3. Stockyards—
United States—History. 4. Packing-houses—United States—
History. I. Title.
HD9415.S58 1986   338.1'76213'0973   85-40742
ISBN 0-89096-249-9

Manufactured in the United States of America
First Edition

for
Seymour V. Connor
professor emeritus of history
Texas Tech University

Contents

Illustrations

Preface

This study began several years ago when my valued friend and col-
league H. Craig Miner, professor of history at Wichita State University, indirectly suggested I undertake something of this sort. The
actual scope of the project was proposed by Dr. Albro Martin, then
editor of *Business History Review* and now Oglesby professor of the
American heritage at Bradley University. I shall long be indebted to
them.

I am beholden to many friends and colleagues because of this
work. Dr. Stephen K. Stoan, head of reference at the Ablah Library, Wichita State, and his entire staff tirelessly helped me pin
down obscure facts; Pauline F. Jopling, of the government documents section, cheerfully found much data for me; Thoburn
("Buck") Taggart, interlibrary-loan librarian, patiently made the library holdings of much of the United States available to me; and
Dale R. Schrag, former head of circulation at Ablah Library and
present director of libraries, Bethel College, North Newton, Kansas, and Kathy A. Downes, present head of circulation at Ablah
Library, courteously allowed me to develop what must have seemed
to be a temporary branch library at my home. Too, Dr. John C.
Gries, associate professor of geology at Wichita State, true friend
and fellow eclectic, happily shared his treasure trove of assorted
Americana with me. They made my task far easier than it might
have been otherwise.

Other friends were shamefully imposed upon: Dr. David J.
Murrah, director of the Southwest Collection at Texas Tech University, Lubbock, tolerated my many long-distance requests for infor-

mation and unfailingly filled them all. Dr. T. Lindsay Baker, curator of science and technology, Panhandle-Plains Historical Museum, Canyon, Texas; Donald E. Green, professor of history at Central Oklahoma State University; Dr. Harmon R. Mothershead, professor of history at Northwest Missouri State University, Maryville; Dr. Gary L. Nall, professor of history at West Texas State University, Canyon; and B. Byron Price, director, Panhandle-Plains Historical Museum, generously shared their unpublished research findings with me, and many others academic acquaintances far too numerous to list individually—most of whom are noted in the bibliography—have greatly influenced my thinking over the years through their publications, correspondence, and conversations.

I especially grateful to Mr. Anthony Lutty, International Secretary-Treasurer of the United Food and Commercial Workers Union, Washington, D.C., for information not readily available elsewhere. Mildred ("Millie") and Samuel H. ("Sam") Marcus, she charming and he the emeritus chairman of the board of Excel Corp., Wichita, generously permitted me to reproduce several photographs from their personal collection. Dr. Bob L. Blackburn, director of publications and education, Oklahoma Historical Society, allowed me to reprint a classic meatpacking photograph, and the efficient and capable staffs of several archival repositories greatly assisted me by locating other illustrations: Rebecca Herring, assistant archivist, and Lisa Shippee Lambert, library assistant, Southwest Collection; Claire R. Kuehn, archivist, Panhandle-Plains Historical Museum; and Nancy Sherbert, curator of photographs, Kansas State Historical Society, Topeka.

Since I am a bifurcated academic—that is, one who is housed in two separate academic departments and colleges of a university—I have received generous amounts of direct support for my scholarship throughout Wichita State, without which this work might have languished forever, unfinished. Dr. Paul J. Magelli, former dean of the Fairmount College of Liberal Arts and Sciences and, now, president, Metropolitan State College, Denver, provided research moneys, as did Dr. Lloyd M. Benningfield, dean of Wichita State's graduate school. Dr. Douglas Sharp, dean of the College of Business Administration, and Dr. Gerald McDougall, chairman of the Department of Economics, Wichita State, released me from teaching duties during the spring semester, 1984, so that I might complete this manuscript. And my loyal friends and colleagues in American studies: Dr. Gregory S. Sojka, chairman, encouraged this work at every turn, all the while scheduling my classes to suit my particular research and writing needs; and Dr. James H. Thomas, associate professor, assisted me in innumerable ways.

Numerous persons typed drafts of the manuscript. Lauri Dickerson, Martha Hiebert, Fran Majors, Connie Wheeler, and Anne Zuercher translated my nearly indecipherable script into legible prose, all the while patiently tolerating my frustrated outbursts whenever I seemed stymied.

Professor Martin and Dr. Margaret Walsh, then visiting professor of history at the University of Kansas and now senior lecturer in economic and social history at the University of Birmingham, England, read the entire manuscript for different reasons at successive stages of its development and offered cogent, helpful criticism, for which I am profoundly grateful. Yet, in that acknowledgment I do not imply their—or anyone else's—endorsement of this work, for the three of us disagree on some significant aspects of interpretation, if not ascertainment of fact.

Indeed, while I wish to acknowledge those who played a part in this undertaking, I alone accept responsibility for it. Blame for whatever may be wrong with this book is rightfully mine, and credit for much of that which is right—the latter of which I hope reflects positively upon Seymour V. ("Ike") Connor, my friend and mentor, whose scrupulous dedication to history, to truth, inspired it.

Prime Cut

1

A Microcosm of the American Economy

The red-meat industry is a microcosm of American economic development—a case study in imperfect markets. From colonial times to the present a multitude of farmers and ranchers have produced a prodigious supply of slaughter animals for processing by a relative handful of generally large-scale meatpackers to feed an increasingly dependent albeit discerning urban population. The linkages in this meat chain—in which millions of suppliers and millions of consumers have been connected by merely thousands and eventually only hundreds of processors—give the industry an hourglass configuration, the constriction point tightly gripped by a few firms allegedly prone to price-fixing and product adulteration.

The history of livestock raising and meatpacking from 1607 through 1983 is replete with scandal, government intervention, and mutual recriminations among a myriad of interest groups, none of whom believes that the public sector behaved properly. More than most other sectors of the nation's economy, the interstate red-meat trade encompasses the national experience, from the taming of a raw, unsettled frontier, which eventually gave rise to a complex agrarian supply base, to the evolution of industrial colossuses as competitive as any other American enterprises.

Toward the end of the nineteenth century the historian Frederick Jackson Turner called attention to the "rancher's frontier," a leading wave of the westward-washing tide of American settlement:

> Travelers of the eighteenth century found the "cowpens" among the canebrakes and the peavine pastures of the South, and the

"cow drivers" took their droves to Charleston, Philadelphia, and New York. Travelers at the close of the War of 1812 met droves of more than a thousand cattle and swine from the interior of Ohio going to Pennsylvania to fatten for the Philadelphia market. The ranges of the Great Plains, with ranch and cowboy and nomadic life, are the things of yesterday and of today.[1]

Turner's generalization, which slighted the considerable Spanish contribution to the development of western American ranching, also obscured the substantial role played by untold throngs of anonymous frontiersmen, mostly small herdsmen and farmers, who from colonial times onward raised the vast majority of slaughter animals, including cattle, for the continuously expanding consumer market. From 1607 through 1983 the story of livestock raising in the United States has been the saga of diverse agrarian enterprises struggling against awesome obstacles to provide slaughter beasts economically yet profitably.

For almost three centuries herdsmen strived merely to gain control of the frontier. Colonial herdsmen proportionally no less than Great Plains ranchers suffered losses to Indian raids, to predators, and to capricious weather. As Turner observed, the frontier receded ever westward from the relentless pressure of pioneers, livestock raisers often leading the way, pasturing their cattle, swine, and sheep on the free grass of unclaimed land, until they were displaced by permanent settlers who acquired title to the acreage.

The story was repeated time and time again—along the Atlantic tidewater, in the foothills and valleys of the Appalachian Mountains, and in the rich Ohio Valley beyond. Inevitably itinerant herdsmen and mixed farmers were increasingly separated geographically from the butchers and meatpackers who processed their animals for consumers, necessitating, as early as the seventeenth century, relatively long trail drives and eventually the reluctant abandonment of busy roadways for more efficient albeit expensive forms of transportation. Transportation by water came first, then by rail. Commercial feedlots first appeared about 1690 near Boston and by 1840 were common throughout the upper midwestern corn

[1]Frederick Jackson Turner, "The significance of the frontier in American history," American Historical Association *Annual Report for 1893* (1894), p. 212.

belt, as entrepreneurs fattened cattle, swine, and sheep for assorted regional meat markets. By then ranchos dotted the southwestern borderlands from the Sabine River to San Diego Bay.

A subtle cycle was already oscillating throughout red meat's supply side well before the cattle ranch emerged as a significant agrarian endeavor. Profitable production depended primarily on cheap forage (either free grass along the vast unsettled frontier or inexpensive grain provided by bountiful harvests), save during aberrations of wartime, when average market quotations for slaughter animals invariably outclimbed those of other agrarian commodities. During the American Revolution, the War of 1812, and the Mexican War livestock prices soared only to fall precipitously once the shooting stopped. Similarly, the Civil War greatly affected livestock values, but for a variety of reasons after Appomattox prices did not tumble as quickly or as far as historical precedent might have suggested.

Both the wartime demand for foodstuffs and the unparalleled devastation wrought by war significantly reduced the re-United States' slaughter-animal count just as industrializing America, rapidly swelled by increased immigration, demanded more meat. Pork, until then the mainstay of the nation's masses as well as the principal raw material of meatpacking, was in unusually short supply at the moment that cheap Texas cattle became available in huge numbers to the interstate red-meat trade. About then several independent midwestern meatpackers began using practical methods of refrigerated transportation to undercut the prices of eastern slaughterhouses and butchers, which in time allowed them to gain control of the nation's lucrative fresh-beef trade. Vast fortunes were made, both in supplying live cattle and in processing the meat.

The cattle boom gave rise to the heroic age of ranching. After 1865 the big-pasture cattle ranch quickly spread northward from Texas to become by World War I the dominant agrarian enterprise on the Great Plains. Even as post–Civil War trail herds from Texas reached out to markets in Kansas and elsewhere, economic and political forces were combining to virtually exterminate the buffalo and to force the proud Plains Indians onto reservations. From the Rio Grande to the Canadian Rockies entrepreneurs took advantage of lax government policies toward the public domain to establish huge spreads and small, to capitalize on the beef bonanza.

Enticed by glowing popular accounts of fabulous profits awaiting anyone with a rope and a branding iron, foreign corporations
and dilettantes alike invested heavily in western American cattle
ranching. Inevitably the open range was overstocked, a fact made
abundantly clear during the middle 1880s, when drouths and blizzards battered the range-cattle industry to near-total destruction,
forcing out many of the newcomers. Some lost everything. Most
survivors adopted scientific range-management techniques. Only
those who held on as late as World War I saw live-cattle prices finally surpass the records set during the Civil War. Even so, with
their heirs facing hefty inheritance taxes on the appreciating value
of vast land tracts, many large ranchers liquidated, selling out to
smaller operators, in many instances directly to farmers. Nevertheless, by the time the era ended, cattle ranching was firmly fixed in
American lore, "the more colorful aspects [of] which have passed
from true narrative to the haze of fiction and legends."[2]

Meanwhile, millions of mostly anonymous small-scale livestock raisers, mixed farmers, and assorted animal feeders were producing the overwhelming majority of cattle, swine, and sheep that
supplied the red-meat chain of the United States. Price takers in an
essentially inelastic market, the small producers along with other
disenchanted elements throughout the agrarian sector following the
Civil War repeatedly demanded government intervention in the
marketplace. Eventually the public sector responded, putting an
end to the worst instances of land-grabbing by big-pasture ranchers,
creating the Interstate Commerce Commission to restrain railroads
that allegedly gouged helpless independent herdsmen, and codify-
ing corrupt business practices through assorted antitrust laws to control emerging industrial combines, such as the "beef trust," as the
principal meatpackers were popularly known.

Congress also lifted the Department of Agriculture—the first
of several advocacy agencies within the federal government—to full
cabinet rank to better assist the nation's struggling agrarian sector.
Before the turn of the century the USDA in turn had created the
Bureau of Animal Industry with which to help livestock raisers fight
costly infectious diseases in their herds and to disseminate animal-
husbandry techniques that translated directly into meatier, more

---

[2]Louis Pelzer, *The cattlemen's frontier* (1936), p. 15.

profitable beasts. By the time of World War I livestock producers in the United States, benefiting both from government assistance and from aberrant foreign demand for American red-meat products, enjoyed their most prosperous era in history.

Meanwhile, American meatpacking had developed from a myriad of wholly independent small businessmen into a relative handful of seemingly strictly regulated, publicly held multinational conglomerates. From colonial times to the Civil War, American meatpacking had changed slowly, almost imperceptibly, from a somewhat itinerant seasonal trade dominated by farmer-butchers to a more sedentary but still wintertime frontier endeavor whose preserved products (mostly pork) even then were marketed worldwide. After the post–Civil War completion of a transcontinental railroad system and the contemporary development of refrigeration technology, aggressive midwestern meatpackers seized control of the lucrative fresh-beef trade from local slaughterers and butchers, simultaneously integrating their businesses backward and forward to create complex, far-flung empires.

As early as 1866 entrepreneurs such as Philip Armour and Gustavus Swift—whose surnames are still synonymous with meat—conspired with selected competitors to divide markets among themselves and to fix prices, both those paid to livestock producers and those charged to consumers. Individually and collectively they crushed an incipient labor movement, and—as was eventually disclosed to the meat-eating public—routinely dispensed adulterated products. Consequently, early in the twentieth century the beef trust came under intense public scrutiny, leading to a degree of government supervision unprecedented in American history.

Between the two world wars both livestock raising and meatpacking suffered severe economic shocks. Following unequaled prosperity induced by an acquisitive public sector during World War I, livestock raisers reaped the consequences of overproduction—once the government stopped buying red meat. Cattlemen, swineherders, and sheepmen alike saw the prices of their animals plummet a full decade before the stock-market crash of 1929 signaled the onset of the Great Depression. Thereafter, buffeted by bad weather and afflicted by anemic market demand for slaughter beasts, stockmen of all sizes appealed for federal aid, which with the advent of the New Deal came in assorted guises, not all of which were wel-

comed by the recipients. Even with substantially greater public
props livestock prices did not recover fully until the second year of
World War II, when huge government outlays for red meat dramatically bid up commodity prices. Livestock raisers who had sold off
much of their breeding stock during the hard times of the 1920s and
1930s were unable to fill the enormous wartime demand, and the
shortage led to meat rationing throughout much of the conflict.

The meatpacking industry similarly faced difficult circum-
stances. Its traditional business tactics had been circumscribed since
the turn of the century by increased public regulation, and by World
War I interstate meatpacking was among the most controlled of
American enterprises. Moreover, in 1920, following further government investigation, the larger firms were ordered to divest themselves of many profitable sidelines. Some members of the beef trust,
shorn of moneymaking subsidiaries, consequently verged on bankruptcy. Reacting to what it believed was undue government meddling, the industry organized the American Meat Institute as a lobbying arm and even sought the cooperation of livestock raisers,
especially ranchers, who were similarly alarmed by an apparent decline in per capita red-meat consumption.

The AMI, along with individual meatpackers, also sponsored
independent academic research that eventually led to more efficient
disassembly methods as well as more succulent meats with longer
shelf lives. Despite such advances consumer demand for red meat
declined further during the Great Depression, causing many meatpackers to slash wages, a move that came simultaneously with the
advent of a new, aggressive labor movement, the CIO's Packinghouse Workers Organizing Committee. Management steadfastly refused to bargain with organized labor until forced to by the New
Deal's National Labor Relations Act (1935). Even so, concessions
were granted grudgingly.

Since World War II livestock raisers and meatpackers alike
have experienced marked attrition rates, albeit from decidedly different forces. Even though overall consumption of red meat between 1945 and 1983 in the generally affluent United States increased by a phenomenal one-fourth (most of that gain accruing to
beef), the number of livestock raisers steadily shrank, mixed farmers abandoning the trade far faster than did ranchers. A horrendous
cost-price squeeze that gripped agrarian America almost at the

onset of peace wrung much of the profitability from traditional livestock-raising methods simultaneously with the widespread appearance of large-scale feedlots and factory farms, which produced meat animals much more efficiently, thereby sharpening competition among producers.

Not even an unprecedented jump in wholesale commodity prices associated with the Vietnam War and the energy-related inflation of the 1970s, during which livestock quotations more than doubled, was sufficient to save many producers. The number of domestic enterprises regularly supplying slaughter beasts for the nation's red-meat trade consequently declined, and by 1983 there were fewer than half the 1945 total. Even so, the quantity of slaughter animals raised in the United States during the same period more than doubled, an amount still insufficient to fill domestic demand, leading to annually increasing levels of imports of red meat, especially beef.

The companion shake-out in meatpacking following World War II was the result of twin tremors that jolted the industry: a sudden geographical shift westward beginning in the late 1950s and a heightened level of competition which commenced soon afterward. The postwar development of huge feedlots and factory farms throughout the Great Plains and the Midwest allowed meatpackers to close antiquated urban plants far removed from a steady supply of slaughter animals and to replace them with large, labor-efficient, often computerized red-meat factories situated in the rural, usually union-free heartlands of the United States. Indeed, by 1970 the industry had so changed that the historic stockyards in Chicago were closed for lack of business.

New, aggressive firms that provided supermarkets, restaurants, and fast-food chains with meat precut virtually to consumer specifications all but eliminated the need for local butchers and consequently captured a large share of the interstate beef (and eventually pork) trade. They forced older, stodgier meatpackers (many of which after World War II had been bought out by acquisitive conglomerates) to modernize to survive. Obsolete plants were closed, labor requirements were further reduced, and unions were forced to submit to wage givebacks or suffer even more plant closings and job losses. One-third fewer meatpacking and processing facilities operated in 1983 than in 1945. Critics contended that, rather than being served by the drive toward efficiency, consumers were being gouged by a new breed of monopolists, who, as in days of old, sold inferior cuts of meat at inflated prices. Moreover, despite govern-ment assurances of wholesomeness, much red meat is reportedly dangerous to the consumer.

Thus the history of livestock raising and meatpacking in the United States from colonial times to the present is more than merely the romantic tale of big-pasture ranchers and a few giant meatpackers. It is also the story of small farmers and large, of big business and small, of continuous technological innovation, of changing consumer tastes and preferences, of labor's ongoing struggle with management, and of government assistance to private enterprise and, necessarily, government restraint as well.

2

Colonial Times to 1865

American livestock raising and meatpacking between the founding
of Jamestown and the end of the Civil War—the first long wave of
American economic growth and development—frequently were
disconnected business endeavors except along the continuously re-
ceding frontier, where they occasionally combined as primitive
farmer-butchers. In time more intensive use of the land pushed livestock raising westward. The industry was often dependent for its
profitability on free grazing far from consumers in towns and cities,
as well as from an emerging genre of more sedentary entrepreneurs.
Beginning as early as 1640, these packers processed pork for export
in a succession of seasonal meatpacking centers—Springfield, Massachusetts; New York City; Cincinnati; Louisville; and Chicago.
From colonial times onward drovers and herds of cattle, swine, and
sheep were commonplace sights on roads leading to fresh-meat markets in such places as Baltimore, Boston, Charleston, and Philadelphia. While the size and scope of this traffic expanded greatly
over the ensuing two and a half centuries, change—except for geographical shifts—was almost imperceptible until technology freed
the meatpacker from the bondage of winter processing.

In 1607, Jamestown-bound colonists included cattle, goats,
horses, poultry, sheep, and swine as live provisions aboard the *Susan
Constant*, but famine forced them to butcher all their beasts that
winter. Replacements that arrived in 1611 were protected by Governor Sir Thomas Dale, who ordered none slaughtered for three
years so that they might breed. In 1624, Edward Winslow imported
Devonshire red cattle to Plymouth, along with unknown strains of

hogs, sheep, goats, horses, and poultry. Supply ships from England regularly thereafter brought more livestock to the colonies, but the number of domesticated animals aboard small seventeenth-century vessels often was limited to a score or less; losses from rough seas, inadequate feed, and overcrowding frequently approached 50 percent and occasionally far more.

Everywhere in the colonies cattle, horses, and hogs were turned loose to forage in woods near the settlements, and, despite the omnipresent danger of wolves, snakes, and Indians, the beasts multiplied at an astonishing rate; only sheep, virtually helpless in any environment, required constant tending. In 1627 estimates placed 5,000 cattle in Virginia; twenty years later 20,000 cattle, 3,000 sheep, 5,000 goats, 200 horses, and 50 asses were counted in the colony. In those days enumerations ignored all classes of farm poultry and even swine, which were so numerous as to be considered pests by many settlers. In 1635 in Massachusetts livestock wandered unfettered about every village commons; many of Boston's streets literally originated as cow paths. Concord was settled that year primarily to provide ample grazing for domestic animals, and in 1636 William Pynchon led disenchanted Roxbury colonists who needed even more room for themselves and their livestock to found Springfield, which was then on the far-distant frontier.

About 1624 the Dutch introduced Flemish cattle to Manhattan Island and within a decade were selling surplus animals to the English in Massachusetts. The Dutch also sold breeding stock to the Swedes who settled along the Delaware River in 1638, because New Sweden did not directly import European animals in any significant numbers before 1643. In 1641, New Amsterdam governor William Kieft inaugurated annual fairs featuring cattle and hogs.

Colonial Maryland contained an indeterminate number of livestock. James Westfall Thompson wrote:

> Marylanders were indifferent both to agriculture and stock raising, and made little attempt to foster either beyond the bare necessity of livelihood. . . . in Maryland . . . there was no multitude of local regulations with respect to pasturage, marking, etc., such as prevailed in New England and the more northern colonies. . . . Long after New England towns had be-

gun to fence cattle in, the woods were still only pasturage in Maryland.[1]

The winter of 1694–95 killed an estimated 25,000 cattle and 60,000 hogs in Maryland and convinced farmers there of the wisdom of providing animals with food and shelter in winter.

Pennsylvanians were carefui herders. Very early they discovered red clover to be ideal fodder for cattle, and their dairy products reputedly were the sweetest in all the Americas. Governor William Penn supported annual livestock fairs all across his colony, and by the end of the seventeenth century Philadelphia, Chester, and New Castle contained thriving markets for farm animals. Exports of livestock and of packed meat from Philadelphia to the West Indies were common by 1700. Nowhere in colonial America did settlers take better care of livestock. Even on the Pennsylvania frontier it was unusual for the colonists' animals to be untended, turned loose to forage in the wild woods.

In the South animal husbandry conformed to the frontier tradition. In the Carolinas thick marsh grasses and a balmy climate combined to sustain rapid increases in the numbers of livestock, much to the displeasure of the colony's reactionary proprietors, who envisioned for themselves a fiefdom specializing in rice and indigo production. When they issued regulations seeking to prevent the importation of additional cattle from neighboring Virginia, independent-minded settlers abandoned the tidewater for the backwoods piedmont. There, in the foothills of the Appalachian Mountains, developed the first great cow country of American history.

Animals ran free, grazing on luxuriant river-bottom grasses and on tangles of peavines that choked hillsides. Cow-hunters captured wild cattle by chasing them on foot into the natural corral of a stream's fork. Once subdued, the animals were driven mostly by men afoot and shepherd dogs to "cowpens," forest clearings alongside which sprang up temporary frontier towns not much different from Dodge City two centuries later. Animals collected in the cowpens were eventually driven eastward in herds of several hundred

[1] James Westfall Thompson, *A history of livestock raising in the United States, 1607–1860* (1942), p. 45.

head to markets at Charleston, Baltimore, and even Philadelphia. With adequate pasturage a cowpen and its raw frontier village prospered for several seasons.

Inevitably, as historian Frederick Jackson Turner has described, herders were forced farther westward by settlers who cleared the land, broke it with the plow, and took away the free forage. Carolina herders looking for new pastures crossed the Blue Ridge Mountains about 1715 and encountered suitable grazing lands. Eventually they infiltrated the Shenandoah Valley, which briefly succeeded the Carolinas as the center for North American cattle raising, especially after "distemper" (probably pleuropneumonia) decimated herds in the Carolinas just before the Revolutionary War.

Cattle raising traditionally has received most attention from the historians, but sheep and swine production was also important in colonial America. Sheep were usually included among livestock provisions by early settlers, and very early in Virginia, Maryland, and the Carolinas, Leicestershire sheep were popular. Wolves, Indians, and climate combined to make sheepherding throughout the South a marginal endeavor at best. In 1624, Edward Winslow imported Wiltshire Downs and Romney Marshes to Plymouth, and Texels were common in New Amsterdam by the early 1630s. Estimates place 3,000 sheep in Massachusetts in 1633. Coastal islands such as Martha's Vineyard and Nantucket, isolated from predators, became veritable sheep runs; more than 15,000 animals were grazing on each island by the time of the Revolution.

While most colonials apparently harbored a "peculiar prejudice against mutton," William Pynchon, America's first meatpacker, as early as 1655 "was buying sheep for slaughter in Rhode Island and in 1656 at Sudbury, Massachusetts," Edward Norris Wentworth has observed. "By 1690 and for the century thereafter, from six to one thousand sheep were fattened [for slaughter] each winter in Hadley, Massachusetts."[2] While much American wool production was used domestically in homespun cloth, it nevertheless was singled out in the Navigation Acts of 1660 and 1699, the former enumerating the commodity as a controlled item and the latter banning it entirely from colonial export to England or even to another colony.

Swine receive no similar attention in histories of colonial

[2] Edward Wentworth, *America's sheep trails* (1948), p. 45.

America. Turned loose in virginal forests to root for acorns and nuts, hogs ran wild everywhere. They fought off wolves, scampered away from Indians, and reproduced at a relatively early age to become so numerous that they were classed as "vermin" in eighteenth-century Virginia. Throughout the southeastern colonies razorbacks damaged crops and were hunted with firearms. During the 1740s thousands were killed, cured, and packed in barrels in the Carolinas for export to the West Indies. In 1706, Hadley, Massachusetts, banned public pigs, and by the end of the century most New England communities required some sort of pen or sty for town-kept swine.

Hogs were probably more numerous than any other farm animals, but no uniform statistics of the period survive. Pork was the meat most commonly consumed in and exported from the colonies, and yet relatively little is known about swine production in America before 1800. Few historians have paid pigs much attention. Hog raising has never attracted much scholarly scrutiny, perhaps because, unlike cattle ranching, it was never considered glamorous or its practitioners heroic. Similarly, not much is known about early goat or poultry production, except that these animals were in colonial Virginia very early and elsewhere not long thereafter.

Agriculture prospered greatly during the Revolutionary War. Only in the immediate vicinity of battle was production disrupted, and then briefly. While foreign commerce suffered from British sea power—the West Indian cattle and meat trades, for example, were almost entirely suspended—the domestic sale of livestock and of processed meat expanded because of the inordinate demand of British armies in North America, which paid in pounds sterling. Moreover, the interruption of international trade temporarily attracted investment capital to agriculture, which was prospering. John Adams said, "The truth is that agriculture . . . [has] been so much increased by this war that it is much to be doubted whether they [the Americans] ever fed or clothed themselves more easily or more comfortably."[3]

Between the Revolution and the War of 1812 animal husbandry in America seemingly began to mature. In Massachusetts, where thin topsoils had been depleted by primitive farming tech-

[3]Quoted in Thompson, A *history of livestock raising*, p. 68.

niques, agricultural lands increasingly were given over to dairy farming and sheep raising. Wool production, heretofore almost wholly limited to domestic hand spinning, steadily expanded in importance after 1790, when the nation's first textile factory opened in Rhode Island. After 1800 commercial demand for finer fleece led stock raisers to import Merino rams for crossbreeding; Thomas Jefferson acquired some of these Spanish animals to improve the quality of his Virginia flock.

In 1791, in the first serious attempt at improving domestic beef cattle in New England, Charles and Benjamin Vaughan imported a Bakewell bull from England to the Kennebec Valley, in Maine. Indeed, underpopulated Maine might well have developed a frontier cattle industry similar to that of the Carolinas had its winters been less severe. By 1791 cattle raising along the Hudson River, in Westchester County, and on Long Island had propelled the port of New York beyond New London, Connecticut, then its regional rival, in total volume of exports. The Genesee Valley, in the central lake region of New York, first saw livestock production just before the turn of the century, its abundant supply of animals thereafter passing through the port of Manhattan.

Commercial butchering and meatpacking on Manhattan also increased markedly following the Revolution, as America reentered the West Indian trade in considerable volume; however, New York did not rival Philadelphia, where Quaker-German farmers continuously supplied meatpackers with quality slaughter animals. James Thompson says: "The counties around Philadelphia were the paradise of the American farmer. Buying lean cattle and fattening them was a profitable business. Stock farms abounded."[4] The Susquehanna and Wyoming valleys of Pennsylvania filled with stock farmers, who marketed their animals in Philadelphia. Only in sheep raising did the state lag; by 1800 there were more sheep on either Nantucket or Martha's Vineyard than in the whole of Pennsylvania. New Jersey and Maryland continued to be indifferent toward animal husbandry, the farmers there only intermittently providing winter fodder or shelter to farm animals.

Along Virginia's tidewater, many plantations lay in near ruin, the soil's yield significantly reduced because of the constant reliance

[4]Ibid., p. 73.

on tobacco as a cash crop. There were efforts to recover. Like his neighbor Thomas Jefferson, George Washington believed that improved breeds of sheep offered hope for the future, and likely he also would have upgraded his flocks if he had not been diverted to national service as president. Washington became the first breeder of mules in America when the king of Spain gave him two jacks in 1795. Matthew Patton, of Virginia, imported blooded English bulls in 1783, and Archibald Cary bought a shorthorn Durham sire, whose offspring thereafter populated the Shenandoah Valley. Appropriate to the times, the Society of Virginia for the Promotion of Agriculture was formed in 1811. The society advocated the importation of more European livestock to improve American strains. Along the Blue Ridge Mountains and in the Shenandoah Valley livestock abounded early in the nineteenth century. Hogs were so numerous that they continued to be nuisances and were often shot for sport. Cattle ran wild in the woods, much as before the Revolution, but increasingly they were branded or earmarked, an index of their enhanced value.

Farther south animal husbandry evolved from the free range to more sedentary stock farming. While wild cattle, hogs, and horses continued to roam the woods and glades along the frontier, animals were increasingly considered the chattel of the landowner on whose property they grazed. Footloose cow hunters who had once claimed any unmarked animals for themselves increasingly were hired by landowners to round up livestock and drive them to market at Charleston, Norfolk, Baltimore, and Philadelphia. Cowpens were replaced with permanent villages, some settled by Moravian Germans, who during the war had migrated down the Shenandoah Valley from Pennsylvania. They introduced diversified crops, dairy farming, and better techniques of animal husbandry. Other cowpens were uprooted by large landowners, who established huge plantations of thousands of acres by slash-and-burn methods that effectively drove out itinerant, landless herders of the peavine tradition. Some moved far west, along the leading edge of the frontier, eventually turning up in the Republic of Texas; others retreated to the pine hills and barrens, becoming the "poor whites" of American lore.

Scientific husbandry originated in America during this period. In 1749, Benjamin Franklin had called on colonial colleges to teach agriculture as a regular part of their curricula, and fifteen years later he participated in the founding of the Philadelphia Society for Promoting Agriculture. In 1792 the Massachusetts State Agricultural Society was formed. The next year Waltham, Massachusetts, sponsored an agricultural fair, and in the decades that followed, other communities throughout the northern and middle states organized similar groups and exhibitions. These promoted better agrarian techniques, such as the introduction of new breeds of cattle and sheep.

An agricultural press also appeared. The *Agricultural Museum*, published in Washington, D.C., in 1810, was the first of its genre. The *American Farmer*, one of the best and longest-lived agricultural publications, began in 1819. Between then and the outbreak of the Civil War more than 250 new agricultural periodicals appeared in the United States. Some, such as the *Rural New Yorker*, the *Genesee Farmer*, and the *Country Gentleman*, all issued in New York, had circulations in excess of 20,000 each and widely disseminated farm news. Articles touted improvement of livestock, the significance of various breeds, and weight and production records of prize stock.

Also before the Civil War the Ohio Valley became the center of the livestock industry in the United States. As during the colonial period, animal husbandry following the Revolution was practical and profitable only where land was cheap or forage was free. By 1784, Potomac River herders had driven their cattle across the Appalachians into present Kentucky in search of summer pasturage. Tom Shelby and Nathaniel Hart, early settlers at Boonesboro, began raising cattle about 1790, and bluegrass was introduced from Virginia not long thereafter. After the native Indian population was removed by the Treaty of Greenville (1795), the whole Ohio country was thrown open to white immigration. During the last five years of the eighteenth century 20,000 Americans crossed the mountains into the new West.

There they encountered rich soil and a growing season ideally suited to corn, a native crop already in surplus throughout the United States. Indeed, it was more profitable to feed the grain to livestock than to dump it on a glutted market. Paul C. Henlein says:

> Bluegrass pasture became one leg, and corn the other, upon
> which the cattle industry of central Kentucky stood. The corn

was shocked in the field following the Virginia custom, with about sixteen hills of corn making one shock. Some of the farmers learned to "riddle"; that is, they would cut only the corn that was ripe and build up the shocks gradually. The cattle-men built no barns. They wintered their two-year-olds out of doors on shocked corn, put them on bluegrass in the spring and summer, and then stuffed them with corn until February when the drive to market began.[5]

Pioneer stock raisers in Ohio's Scioto Valley, lying across Ross, Pick-away, and Franklin counties, used similar techniques.

Most Ohio Valley cattle were "scrubs," or mongrels. Ameri-cans who settled the region imported Devon reds, large yellow Danish cattle, black-and-white Flemish animals, West Indian cross-breeds, and Virginian and Carolinian beasts of mixed ancestry. These were crossed with Spanish cattle that had been introduced during the previous century from Florida and the Chickasaw Indian country, as well as small, dark cattle of uncertain ancestry from French Canada. Lewis Sanders, of Kentucky, learning of Matthew Patton's successful crossbreeding efforts in Virginia, imported eight "improved" shorthorn and four "improved" longhorn bulls from England in 1817. The offspring of these shorthorns soon grazed throughout the bluegrass country, but the longhorns disappeared. Between 1822 and 1860 shorthorns were imported from England in considerable numbers. In 1850, Shorthorn breeders counted 2,500 bulls scattered throughout the United States; ten years later the number stood at 3,300. Breeders also imported registered Devons and Herefords before the Civil War, but not in significant numbers.

The Ohio Valley cattle kingdom experience marked cyclical variations throughout the quarter century immediately preceding the Civil War. The 1830s were generally prosperous until a financial panic nationwide commenced in 1837 and a local drought forced livestock raisers to dump their animals on an already depressed mar-ket for whatever prices they would bring. Bumper corn crops in 1843 and from 1845 through 1849 induced farmers to raise more livestock, and a substantial increase in the supply of slaughter ani-mals suppressed prices. Livestock producers were caught in a curious paradox: when weather conditions forced them to dump animals,

[5] Paul Henlein, *Cattle kingdom in the Ohio Valley, 1783–1860* (1959), p. 6.

prices declined, and when weather allowed them to raise more, fatter beasts, prices also declined.

During the later 1850s the demand for grain by distilleries pulled up the price of corn to about forty cents a bushel, which all but priced the commodity out of the winter-feed market for livestock raisers. Scioto stock raisers then turned to "half feeding," whereby they provided hay and other fodder to cattle during the first half of the winter and expensive corn the last. The animals were turned out on grass in March and marketed between June and October. Such cost implications on the eve of the Civil War caused stock raisers to reduce their herds by one-sixth to one-third. Elsewhere in the Ohio Valley, especially in Illinois and Iowa, feedlots appeared as early as 1840. "Feeding corn to cattle and then using hogs to salvage the waste was a successful commercial agricultural pattern in central and northern Illinois and eastern Iowa," says James Whitaker. "By the time of the Civil War, cattle feeding operations of a similar type were well established. . . ."[6]

Excess Ohio Valley cattle very early were driven eastward across the mountains to assorted urban markets: reportedly 700 head in 1810, 1,500 in 1815, 7,000 in 1820, and 12,000 in 1831. Some farmers personally herded their animals, but most apparently relied on independent businessmen such as New Yorker Daniel Drew, who, for a fee, walked the animals to market for the owner or bought them, often on credit, for speculation in the East. In 1817 a man identified only as Drenning drove 200 head of Ohio cattle to Manhattan, the first western beasts known to reach that market. The New York *Press* reported: "They appear as fresh as if just taken off one of our Long Island farms. When it is recollected that they have been driven nearly one thousand miles, this fact will be considered a very remarkable one."[7]

The net profit on an 1805 drive from the Scioto River to Baltimore reportedly was thirty-two dollars a head. A few drovers like Drew became fabulously wealthy. Unscrupulous drovers sometimes swindled unwary backwoods farmers and then moved on to find new victims elsewhere. In 1842 one crook using worthless paper money issued by a defunct eastern bank cheated untold hundreds of

[6] James Whitaker, *Feedlot empire* (1975), pp. 18, 21.
[7] Quoted in Thompson, *A history of livestock raising*, p. 94.

Ohio Valley farmers out of their livestock. Most drovers, though, such as George Renick, of Ohio, were ethical businessmen who provided a necessary service. They collected from assorted cattle raisers herds ranging from one hundred to one thousand head and, with the assistance of one or two helpers and perhaps as many shepherd dogs, drove them eastward to market. Farmers along the way often earned extra income renting overnight pasture to trail herds for as much as five cents a head per night.

As the frontier moved westward, markets shifted, and methods of transportation changed. By the mid-1820s the Miami River valley, which had been settled about the time of the War of 1812, was reportedly supplying early Ohio meatpacking centers such as Chillicothe and Cincinnati with much of their beef cattle and most of their swine. After the war stock raisers along the Wabash River in Indiana found little immediate outlet for their surplus livestock save to ship them on flatboats down the Ohio and Mississippi rivers to New Orleans. When the National Road (Cumberland Road) reached Indianapolis and a canal connected the Wabash and Maumee rivers, linking the area to Lake Erie, the Indiana market expanded. By the 1830s the cattle kingdom had spread into the Sangamon Valley of Illinois, where prairie grasses provided summer forage and corn shocks winter feed.

Railroads appeared in the United States about then but did not immediately replace drovers. Early freight rates were considered outrageous by stockmen. In 1855 the Erie Railroad charged as much as $12.50 a head to ship live cattle from Columbus, Ohio, to New York, which was approximately one-third more than the cost of professional drovers, whose leisurely pace allowed animals to fatten en route. Moreover, cattle were sometimes overcrowded in boxcars, injured, and even killed in transit. Most area farmers consequently preferred to sell their animals to emerging meatpacking plants in Ohio, where prices invariably were lower than those along the East Coast, rather than pay high freight rates or trust unknown drovers with a whole year's production of animals.

Early midwestern meatpackers did not rely entirely upon area cattle raisers for raw material because hogs, which generally were driven fewer miles to market than were cattle, abounded throughout the Ohio Valley and in any case were the meat animal of choice among packers. Considered scavengers, swine ran wild in the woods

and were rounded up by farmers during the fall for the winter marketing. An abundance of cheap corn often allowed farmers to practice intensive feeding for a month to six weeks before driving the
animals to Cincinnati, Cleveland, Columbus, or Dayton, where
they were slaughtered and packed. Until railroad connections made
shipment eastward practical, most packed pork was floated westward on flatboats to markets in Memphis, Natchez, or New Orleans
and for export everywhere. Midwestern pork, however, was not
widely acclaimed for its flavor; area swine were often described as
"razorbacks"—"long and slim, long-legged and long snouted, slab-
sided, large-boned, gaunt bodied, flat eared, with arched back and
bristles erect from head to tail."[8]

About the turn of the century superior breeding stock was
imported into the United States by Timothy Pickering and John
Mackay, both of Massachusetts, and by Lewis F. and Richard L.
Allen, stock farmers near Buffalo. Bedfords, Suffolks, Hampshires,
and Berkshires were introduced from England and Poland Chinas
from the Orient and were crossed with assorted native strains to
produce new American types, such as Mackeys and Chesters, both
of which before the Civil War gained considerable attention east of
the Appalachians. The upper Midwest saw only gradual introduction of pedigreed pigs, most farmers instead allowing their razorbacks to run wild and breed indiscriminately, harvesting the increase each fall. Not until the manufacture of stout hog wire about
the turn of the twentieth century made penning practical did techniques markedly change. Meanwhile, outbreaks of hog cholera
throughout the region on the eve of the Civil War, especially among
animals fattened on distillery swill, reduced swine numbers appreciably; only in the remote Southwest, in Arkansas and Texas, did
hogs escape the epidemic.

The sheep industry similarly spread westward after the Revolutionary War as frontiersmen took flocks on their westward trek. As
during the colonial period, most animals were raised on the frontier
not for meat but for their wool, which was raw material for homespun clothing. By the end of the eighteenth century flocks were
common in western Pennsylvania, and entrepreneurs in Steuben-
ville, Ohio, established the first textile plant west of the Appala-

[8]Quoted in Paul Gates, *The farmer's age: agriculture, 1815–1860* (1960), p. 217.

chians. Sheep raising became quite profitable after 1807, when the Embargo Act prohibited the importation of foreign fleece, and wool prices jumped from fifty cents a pound to as much as four dollars a pound. Disruption of international trade patterns during the War of 1812 further exacerbated market conditions, and from Ohio eastward throughout New England farmers increased the size of their flocks and the quality of their animals. Estimates place 6 million sheep in the United States in 1810 and 10 million in 1812. Saxon and Spanish Merino and French Rambouillet breeds increasingly were crossed with assorted domestic animals, and improved flocks appeared throughout the Midwest. In 1813, George Rapp drove a flock of superior sheep from Economy, Pennsylvania, to New Harmony, Indiana, the utopian settlement. From there the beasts spread throughout Indiana and into Kentucky and Illinois.

A textile boom in the United States during the 1830s further encouraged the spread of flocks. Vermont, New York, and Pennsylvania led the nation in sheep raising until the Civil War, but throughout the Ohio Valley sheep also multiplied and migrated farther along the frontier, moving into Michigan, Wisconsin, Iowa, and Missouri by the end of the decade. The 1840 census reported 19 million animals scattered mostly throughout New England and northern and border states; six years later General Stephen Watts Kearny's army found large flocks of Spanish Merinos in New Mexico. By then sheep had been driven into Texas from Illinois, as well as from Mexico, and during the early 1850s an estimated 500,000 midwestern sheep were driven to California to capitalize on inordinately high gold-rush prices for meat.

By 1860 there were 22 million sheep in the United States. Still the prejudice against lamb and mutton remained, many observers before the Civil War dismissing the meat as dry, coarse, and flavorless. Merinos and Rambouillets imported after the Revolution to improve the quality of American fleece were never renowned for their succulence, and not until after the Civil War, when significant numbers of Leicester, Cotswold, South Down, Hampshire Down, and Shropshire Down rams were used for crossbreeding, did either the quality of meat or the demand for it appreciably increase.

South of the Mason-Dixon Line, where the first great cow country in the United States had developed before the American Revolution, animal husbandry lagged behind the Ohio Valley. Cash-crop economies—first tobacco and later rice, indigo, and cotton—continuously pushed landless, itinerant herders westward along the southern frontier, and even on small, marginal farms where diversification was a necessity, people resorted to slash-and-burn cultivation, which also displaced animals, however temporarily. Thompson observed:

> So lucrative was cotton that it shaped the whole southern economy. The large planters preferred to buy stock and feed in Ohio, Illinois, and Indiana, rather than compete in stock growing. The opening, about 1830, of a Southern market for the agricultural surplus and livestock of the Old Northwest was a godsend. . . .
>
> Here and there a planter might be found that had a flock of sheep, or who took pride in possessing a good-looking herd of cattle, but this was rare, except between Natchez and New Orleans on the west side of the river. The Opelousas country, an extensive and fertile prairie about 100 miles from New Orleans, was probably the best cattle country in all the Gulf region. Here great herds of cattle grazed for the New Orleans market, 12,000 head sometimes being sold in a single year.[9]

Otherwise, most of the Gulf Coast east of the Mississippi was not cattle country; the land was too marshy with too many insects, which pestered animals. The Texas Gulf Coast, on the other hand, eventually abounded with cattle, Texas Longhorns being trailed to Ohio markets as early as 1846.

Indeed, cattle, horses, oxen, sheep, and poultry—imported from New Spain as early as 1690 for dependent mission Indians—were widespread in Texas long before the leading edge of the American frontier splashed across the Sabine River. In 1786 the mission Espíritu Santo at La Bahía, inland from present Corpus Christi, counted 16,000 cattle. Contemporary San Antonio missions also contained numerous beasts: Valero (the Alamo), 1,200 cattle, 300 horses, and 2,300 sheep and goats; Concepción, 600 cattle and 300 horses; San Juan, 1,000 cattle, 500 horses, and a large but undetermined number of sheep and goats; San José, 1,500 yoke of oxen and 5,000 sheep and goats; and San Francisco, 2,200 cattle and 4,000

[9]Thompson, *A history of livestock raising*, p. 107.

sheep and goats. Other, more remote missions, presidios, and pueblos contained similar quantities of domestic livestock.

Early in the eighteenth century private holdings appeared, and by century's end the Spanish governor of Texas estimated forty-five ranchos in his province. Gil Ybarbo's 5,000-acre spread near present Nacogdoches, in east Texas, modest by contemporary standards in Mexico, where haciendas sometimes contained thousands of square miles, was huge by American standards and far more sophisticated in its diversification. Ybarbo raised grain, garden vegetables, horses, mules, cattle, oxen, sheep, goats, and poultry. Texas ranchos, many of which covered huge, treeless expanses, had their peons ride horseback to herd their cattle; they were called vaqueros, cowboys. Erasmo and Juan Seguin, father and son, who owned 2,000 acres near present Floresville, even experimented with cotton. Large operators, such as José Lorenzo de la Garza, who held a royal land grant of 53,000 acres in semitropical south Texas early in the nineteenth century, Ybarbo, Lorenzo, the Seguins, and the rest were members of a *mesta*, an association of landowners that formulated range rules, registered cattle brands, and represented group concerns to the Spanish government, especially concerning the Indians who frequently stole their livestock.

In 1519, Hernán Cortés had imported Spanish cattle to North America, and in 1541, Francisco Vásquez de Coronado trailed their progeny into the present United States. A Moorish strain related to the fierce fighting bulls of the arena, these Andalusian cattle first reached Texas 150 years later. Their gene pool being limited there, especially when they escaped into the wild, they mutated into Longhorns—skinny, blue-horned, mealy-nosed, motley brown beasts. Folklorist J. Frank Dobie wrote: "these cattle are more like deer than buffaloes—quick, uneasy, restless, constantly on the lookout for danger, snuffing the air, and moving with a light, elastic step. In their sense of smell they were fully the equal of deer. A wounded bull has been known to hunt his enemy by scent, trailing him on the ground like a bear." [10] By the time Stephen F. Austin's colonists reached Texas in 1822, wild Longhorns thrived in hundreds of small bands on the lush grasslands of the coastal plains, especially south of the Nueces River. Some settlers

[10] J. Frank Dobie, *The Longhorns* (1941), p. 23.

hunted them with rifles; others complained that marauding bulls raided their farms of cows and heifers.

During the Texas Revolution many rancheros fled to Mexico, abandoning their land and livestock. When the Republic of Texas declared these animals to be public domain, gangs of youths popularly called "cow boys" periodically rode south of the Nueces River into the heart of Longhorn country and chased the animals at a dead run until, winded, they were broken to the trail. Cow boys drove the skittish beasts on horseback, Spanish style, eastward for sale to settlers, often for no more than fifty cents a head. A few were driven on to New Orleans, where they sold for three dollars a head, tops. By the end of the Mexican War in 1848 the region south of the Nueces River had been so plundered by Texican hooligans and Mexican bandidos that the rancho there had all but ceased to exist.

Each of Stephen F. Austin's original three hundred families had received from the Mexican government a league (4,428.4 acres) for grazing and a labor (177.1 acres) for planting, which was infinitely more generous than practices in the contemporary United States, where the government auctioned off virgin tracts as small as 80 acres for minimum bid of $1.25 an acre, cash. While no subsequent wave of colonists, either under Mexico or under the Republic of Texas, enjoyed such largess, they found ample open range on which to graze livestock free of charge. Frontiersmen from the Ohio Valley tended to settle in northeastern Texas, whereas those steeped in the southern peavine tradition of livestock raising occupied the coast. Both brought with them common strains of livestock—horses, mules, cattle, oxen, sheep, and poultry—some of which they turned loose to forage, rounding them up twice a year, in spring and fall. Surplus cattle were increasingly mixed bloodlines of Anglo brindles and Spanish Longhorns, either "Texas-Mexicans"—tall, gaunt animals with enormous backward-curving horns—or "Long-haired Texans"—rounded, beefier beasts with hairy brown coats. Neither type had much local market value. Entrepreneur Gail Borden, later of dairy fame, while a Texas settler developed a cheap, dehydrated meat biscuit of Longhorn beef. He tried to sell it to the army, which was uninterested. Tougher than jerky, much of Borden's inventory was sold to forty-niners as staples for the trek westward to the gold coast.

Otherwise, in sparsely settled Texas there was little demand for Longhorns, except for their hides, which enjoyed some speculation because of booming New England shoe factories. Says historian Don Worcester:

> In the 1830s, Anglo cowmen drove small herds to New Orleans, and in the following decade they trailed cattle to Missouri, Ohio, and California. By 1842 many men drove herds across Indian Territory for sale to army contractors for supplied Forts Smith, Gibson, Scott, other military posts. These were fairly profitable years.
>
> By the early 1850s, Texans trailed to Arkansas, Illinois, Kansas, Nebraska, Missouri, and Iowa. Illinois feeders regularly fattened Texas cattle during the decade, and hundreds of Longhorn steers were sold to freighters and farmers to be worked as oxen. Kansas City became a market for Texas beef, and some Texas cattle were trailed on to Chicago.[11]

Early in the Civil War some Texans drove herds to market in New Orleans. Wrote Wayne Gard: "After that city fell to the federal forces of Captain David D. Farragut in the spring of 1862, some of the drovers still took herds to the Crescent City, exchanging them for United States gold. Confederate leaders protested against this dealing with the enemy, but it continued throughout the war. In June, 1864, Texas beeves brought forty to sixty dollars a head in New Orleans."[12]

By then the ranch, like much of Texas as a whole, had been anglicized. Indeed, the legendary King Ranch traces its origins to this era. In 1852 one-time Texas Ranger Gideon K. Lewis and riverboat captain Richard King, who had operated a cow camp south of the Nueces River for some time, purchased the abandoned 15,500-acre Rancho Rincón Santa Gertrudis, lying along the headwaters of Baffin Bay, for approximately two cents an acre; two years later they bought for eighteen hundred dollars the 53,000-acre de la Garza Rancho Santa Gertrudis on the west, which had been overrun and stripped bare of livestock by hooligan cow boys from the east. After Lewis was killed in a duel, King allowed Mifflin Kenedy, his partner

[11] Don Worcester, *The Chisholm trail* (1980), pp. 4–5.
[12] Wayne Gard, *The Chisholm trail* (1954), p. 38.

in riverboating on the Rio Grande and a sometime sheepherder, to buy into the ranch. During the Civil War, King and Kenedy laboriously cleared thousands of acres of mesquite scrub to plant cotton, a lucrative commodity when shipped through Mexico to Europe, and they invested their profits in more land, such as the Agua Dulce and Laureles ranchos near Corpus Christi.

By war's end King and Kenedy employed more than 100 vaqueros to ride herd on more than 33,000 Running W–branded Longhorns and almost twice as many sheep, goats, horses, and mules, which grazed on almost 500,000 acres of unfenced land. King Ranch chronicler Tom Lea wrote:

> Neither King nor Kenedy were ever exponents of the open range or free style of ranching. From their beginnings as stockmen, they believed that an efficient operation consisted in complete control of the water and grass on the land where their herds were pastured. The only way . . . to control was to enclose what was owned. A fenced range made a livestock breeding program possible by controlling the animals in the enclosures and by keeping out strays. In land where lawlessness was chronic, a fence was also legal notice to trespassers, thieves, and squatters.[13]

King and Kenedy, together until 1868 and separately thereafter, fenced huge tracts of land at a time before barbed wire, when such formal boundaries were beyond the resources of virtually all other southwestern cattle raisers. Without their thriving shipping business to subsidize their ranching venture, King and Kenedy would have found it impossible to keep cow boys at bay, so marginal was the state of ranching as an enterprise.

By the time of the Civil War, when American settlements in Texas had reached a line stretching from the Red River north of Fort Worth south to San Antonio, King and Kenedy's Santa Gertrudis Ranch near Corpus Christi and Milton Faver's spread in the remote, rugged Big Bend country along the Rio Grande, much farther west, were virtually lone outposts of permanent Anglo-American habitation. Almost unique among the newcomers, King, Kenedy, and Faver acquired title to the nucleus of the land they used. They were

[13] Tom Lea, *The King Ranch* (2 vols.; 1957), I, 254.

also the first to copy Spanish terminology and the technique of near-constant herding on horseback.

The owners of many other important cattle ranches that trace their origins to this era were not always as fastidious about valid land titles. Texas alone among the states retained its public lands when it entered the Union, and by 1860 the Republic and the state had given tens of millions of acres to settlers, war veterans, educational institutions, and assorted businesses to promote internal improvements. Millions more were sold to speculators either as specific land tracts or as unlocated land scrip. Land scrip, warrants, and certificates all circulated as money during the era of the Republic and later, the holder having the option of filing on unappropriated land or endorsing the paper, which circulated at about fifty cents an acre.

Land was thus cheap, far cheaper than land in the contemporary United States, and plentiful—so plentiful that few livestock raisers before the Civil War saw the need to "lay" their scrip for clear title. Abel Head ("Shanghai") Pierce, one of the more colorful cattlemen of the nineteenth century, ranched part-time on the Gulf Coast west of Houston by running his AP-branded beasts on open range. Samuel Maverick sought to solve the problem of open-range herding by placing his cattle on unclaimed Matagorda Island, off the Texas coast; inevitably some escaped to the mainland at low tide, giving rise to the allegation that every unbranded Longhorn was a "maverick." Barber Watkin Reynolds, whose desdendants became leaders in the Texas cattle industry after the Civil War, simply appropriated hundreds of thousands of acres along the Brazos River near Fort Griffin, in Comanche and Apache country. The Indians, as one of Reynolds's granddaughters later recalled, were "gradually being driven from their home and country, their hunting ground being taken without remuneration."[14]

After the Mexican War, John Chisum, who operated south of the Red River in partnership with New York financier S. K. Fowler, purchased several thousand acres of land west of Fort Worth, apparently with land scrip, but they ran their cattle over twice as much untitled rangeland. Their neighbor Daniel Waggoner owned 15,000 acres and, legend insists, grazed his herds on five times as much

[14] Sallie Reynolds Matthews, *Interwoven: a pioneer chronicle* (1936), pp. 39–40.

open range. In 1855, Oliver Loving moved his mixed-breed beasts from relatively settled Collin County, in northeast Texas, to Palo Pinto County, sixty miles west of Fort Worth—which was then on the very edge of the frontier. Rancher George Webb Slaughter arrived the following year, driven westward by sodbusters.

By 1861, Texas cattlemen were approaching the forbidding Great Plains, the very heart of Indian country. Everywhere, as military garrisons were abandoned and soldiers withdrawn for the Civil War in the East, emboldened Apaches, Comanches, and Kiowas reclaimed their hunting grounds. The frontier retrenched. Mabel Gilbert, who ran cattle and swine on state land near present Wichita Falls, fled to Fort Worth without his livestock. All along the frontier settlers similarly retreated, some counties losing more than half their population as the less resilient (or perhaps less foolhardy) relocated in safer environs. By the time of Appomattox the Texas frontier had receded almost sixty miles, to near where it had been in 1850. Abandoned cattle meanwhile proliferated at a fantastic rate.

North of the Red River ranchers suffered herd losses because of the Civil War, albeit to different raiders. Indeed, "The history of ranching in Indian Territory . . . serves as a corrective to the myth of an exclusive Caucasian range cattle industry," Oklahoma historian William W. Savage, Jr., has observed:

> The Five Civilized Tribes had practiced stockraising on their southeastern lands for decades before their removal to the West in the 1830s. . . . The prosperity of the tribes in Indian Territory was a flame that grew bright in the 1840s and 1850s, only to flicker and die during the Civil War. Inter- and intra-tribal strife during that conflict, together with the work of foraging parties from Missouri and Kansas, sharply reduced the numbers of Indian cattle.[15]

Throughout much of the rest of the Southwest the Texas experience was duplicated. In 1541, Coronado, while searching for the fabled Seven Cities of Gold, had driven 500 cattle, 1,000 horses, and 5,000 sheep into the upper Rio Grande Valley of New Mexico. Some of his animals were stolen by Indians, and others escaped to

[15] William Savage, Jr., "Indian ranchers," in Skaggs (ed.), *The ranch and range in Oklahoma* (1978), p. 34.

form wild herds. Virtually every Spanish expedition thereafter included some domestic livestock among its provisions, and many of these beasts also escaped and multiplied. By 1700, Pueblo Indians in the central cordilleras of New Mexico as well as missionaries of southern Arizona grazed Andalusian cattle. Also important were Merino sheep, whose wool soon found its way into fine Indian blankets. After 1821 additional strains of livestock were introduced to New Mexico by way of the Santa Fe Trail, a trade route between central New Mexico and western Missouri, on which occurred extensive interchange between the two areas throughout the first half of the nineteenth century. Surplus American oxen and occasionally even mules were sold at Santa Fe, but more frequently Missourians imported New Mexico asses for breeding. Sheep, the most important domestic animal in New Mexico, numbered perhaps 500,000 by the time of the Mexican War.

Animal husbandry began on the West Coast at eighteenth-century Spanish missions, which raised thousands of cattle, horses, sheep, and goats to sustain their neophyte Indian populations and the equally dependent nearby presidios and pueblos. About 1784 the governor of California gave retiring Spanish soldier Manuel Nieto 300,000 acres along the Santa Ana River, the first of numerous grants that ultimately created the great ranchos of the southern Pacific Coast. Reforms following the Mexican Revolution secularized the missions, stripping them of their land and herds and turning most of the acreage to selected elements of the Hispanic population, which soon became the landed aristocracy. Even so, livestock raising before the American occupation of California for the most part sustained merely a barter economy. Cowhides circulated as currency and were called "California bank notes" as far north as Alaska and as far south as Peru.

Cattle were butchered principally for their hides and tallow; both commodities were exported widely, as to New England traders who regularly called at San Diego and Los Angeles during the middle 1830s to supply Boston leather merchants and shoe manufacturers. In 1845–46, at the very apex of pre-American prosperity, southern California exported 80,000 cattle hides and 1.5 million pounds of tallow. A slaughter animal was typically worth four dollars a head, half of that being the hide alone. Some meat was dried and made into jerky; much more was wasted.

Then California's cattle industry experienced a boom-and-bust cycle that fully anticipated the experience on the Great Plains following the Civil War. The gold rush created a spectacular demand for slaughter animals that disrupted old trade patterns and distorted values. Argonauts after 1849 bid up the prices of all commodities in northern California, and southern rancho cattle suddenly brought $75 to $150 a head delivered in San Francisco. Countless herds of between one hundred and one thousand animals were driven northward along the coast or through the San Joaquin Valley. Cattle commanded such a premium that many southern ranchos virtually denuded themselves of livestock by selling off twice the number of livestock they could expect to recover annually through breeding. Windfall profits were conspicuously consumed, as on silver-inlaid saddles rather than on improved herds.

Even before the bubble burst in 1856, many southern California haciendas had already passed into different hands, in part because of the American land law of 1851 that forced verification of ancient Spanish land grants, some of which were not documentable, but also because of poor management. By then a steady stream of trail herds from the Midwest, Oregon, and Texas had clogged the San Francisco market, depressing the price for calves to as little as seven dollars a head. As early as 1852, 120,000 cattle and sheep were being driven through Nebraska bound for San Francisco, and similar numbers of Texas cattle that year followed the Gila Trail westward.

Stripped bare of breeder cattle during a bull market, southern ranchos had little choice but to restock with sheep; they were fortunate to find locally a relatively cheap supply. New Mexicans alone drove flocks totaling 100,000 head to the goldfields but, finding little market among lusty miners who craved beef, drifted southward on the grass. They sold bleating mobs for four dollars a head, twice what they would have brought in Chicago. In 1850 the government counted 20,000 sheep in California and in 1860, more than 1 million; during the Civil War, when southern cotton was lost to world textile markets, California wool enjoyed a brief boom.

On the far northwest Pacific Coast, in 1792 the Spaniards, in a futile attempt at holding the area against foreign encroachment, established a presidio on Neah Bay, in present Washington, and provisioned it with ten head of mixed cattle; an undetermined number of sheep, goats, and hogs; and all varieties of poultry. Some descendants of those animals, traded to infiltrating Britons and Americans, remained in the Northwest when the Spaniards withdrew after 1819. In 1811, Astoria, the commercial outpost of fur king John Jacob Astor at the mouth of the Columbia River, had also imported sixty hogs. The British brought two bulls and two heifers to the site when they occupied it during the War of 1812, and by 1817 small herds of cattle, hogs, and goats were grazing at Forts Boise, Hall, and Walla Walla, which were maintained by the Northwest (later Hudson's Bay) Company.

Oregon Trail pioneers (mostly New England Protestant missionaries) drove a variety of livestock in their trek across the Great Plains and Rocky Mountains in 1834. A decade later the migration westward to "the Oregon country," during which tens of thousands of cattle, horses, oxen, goats, sheep, and hogs were driven westward, became a veritable mass movement lasting until the Civil War. In 1837 some Pacific Northwest settlers purchased cattle from southern California ranchos and drove them northward along the coast and then over the mountains into the Willamette Valley. During the gold rush surplus Oregon cattle, hogs, and sheep were driven southward for sale at astronomical prices in San Francisco. When that market was glutted after 1856, Oregon livestock raisers turned to mining boomtowns in Nevada, Idaho, and British Columbia, which provided lucrative markets throughout the Civil War era.

Slaughtering and butchering in the United States also date to 1607, when Jamestown colonists, facing famine, ate all their livestock to survive the winter. Thereafter, as surplus swine, cattle, and sheep slowly accumulated, and, usually, just after the first freeze made meat preservation possible, frontiersmen and settlement dwellers alike slaughtered and butchered their excess livestock for personal and trade purposes. About 1640 some pork reportedly was "packed"—that is, cured, salted, and stuffed into barrels—by seasonal entrepreneurs for the bulk-meat trade. In 1635, Boston businessmen slaughtered livestock in the open and sold whole, half, and quarter carcasses to butchers and householders alike. As early as 1609 half a continent away Spanish settlers at Santa Fe similarly consumed their domestic livestock, although approximately in reverse order of preference. They never developed much of a retail butchering trade, however—not even later in California or Texas, where, for a time, rawhiders prospered. Some meat was jerked; much was wasted.

By 1641 the Dutch on Manhattan Island led colonial North America in the red-meat trade. "The slaughterhouses and cattle pens in New Amsterdam were almost as conspicuous on the landscape as windmills in Holland," historian James Thompson observed. "They straddled the ditch on the north side of the palisade, later Wall Street, the effluvia flowing down this streamlet through the Water Poort or Water Gate into the East River."[16] During the winter slaughtering season the small stream was called Bloody Run, and most towns had equivalent nuisances. After 1656, Manhattan officials required permits of anyone who wanted to slaughter or butcher animals on the island. Ten years later they ordered the killing grounds out of the community, beyond the stockade fence along Wall Street, and erected a public facility on present Pearl Street, between Wall and Pine. All slaughtering, including that for private consumption, was restricted to the public house, which was financed by users' fees. The obnoxious stench wafted across the settlement whenever the breeze came from the north. By the middle of the seventeenth century four thousand cattle and reportedly an even larger but indeterminate number of hogs, as well as some lambs, were slaughtered and butchered annually on Manhattan. About then island butchers organized in the fashion of a Dutch trade guild.

Commercial meatpacking in America began about 1660, the final year of the civil war in England, which had greatly disrupted trade and commerce throughout the British Empire. That winter in Springfield, Massachusetts, entrepreneur William Pynchon seized the opportunity to supply preserved meat on a sellers' market by packing pork in an empty warehouse. Previously he had raised livestock on the frontier and had even operated a primitive feedlot to fatten cattle on cornstalks for the Boston market. He also dealt in sheep, lambs, mutton, wool, and tallow, "but his chief business was pork packing," according to economist and industry authority Rudolf Clemen. "Between 1662 and 1683 he bought and packed great numbers of hogs, presumably in the main for the West Indian trade. Pynchon's records give some information as to the swine in colonial New England. Most of them were black or sandy in color and of no

---

[16]Thompson, A history of livestock raising, p. 39.

choice breed."[17] It cost the businessman between two and three pence per pound to pack pork; he sold it at Boston for seventy shillings per three-hundred-pound barrel.

Meat-preservation techniques, adaptations of frontier methods, were primitive. Hogs were killed—sometimes clubbed to death, other times stabbed, rarely shot—and hung to drain. Whole carcasses were usually dipped in vats of scalding-hot water to loosen hair, which was plucked out by the handfuls; sometimes carcasses were hung by nose rings and flayed in three-inch-wide strips, nose to rump. After either process they were gutted, the viscera being saved by some frontiersmen for sausage casings, chitterlings, and the like or—at least until the middle of the nineteenth century— thrown away as worthless by most commercial meatpackers.

Workers quartered carcasses and laboriously further divided them into fatback, tenderloin, hams, shoulders, sides, ribs, and so forth. They hand-rubbed freshly cut meat with generous quantities of assorted salt-based compounds, usually containing molasses and black gunpower, and crammed it into large barrels, called "hogsheads," of varying size. Rarely did seventeenth-century entrepreneurs such as Pynchon smoke their pork, and because beef did not preserve tastily or well, even as jerky, commercial cattle were slaughtered and butchered as needed, year round, for the fresh-meat trade. Similarly, lamb and mutton were rarely packed.

From Boston to Charleston, seasonal, somewhat itinerant, and mostly anonymous farmer-packers were common before the American Revolution and, as cities grew rapidly following the war, increasingly a nuisance. Wherever these businessmen located to ply their trade, however temporarily—usually in drafty, otherwise empty warehouses somewhere near a slaughterhouse—they offended their neighbors by clogging already crowded streets with herds of livestock, dumping offal wherever convenient with little or no regard for the consequences, and emitting an often overpowering, offensive odor.

When in 1763 the Common Council of New York attempted to regulate the malodorous red-meat trade, the butchers' guild conspired with Westchester County and Long Island farmers to withhold their product from the market and drive up the price of beef to

[17] Rudolf Clemen, *The American livestock and meat industry* (1932), pp. 23–24.

eight pence a pound, double the preboycott level. The lucrative market soon attracted distant Connecticut farmers, who drove their cattle to Manhattan, flooded the market, and ended the protest. Not until the Revolutionary War, when there was exaggerated demand for foodstuffs by opposing armies, did butchers again briefly defy municipal sanitation regulations. By the 1830s, New York City had banished slaughterhouses and their attendant meatpacking plants to beyond Forty-second Street, and by the time of the Civil War, to Eightieth Street and north.

In time, hounded businessmen abandoned eastern cities entirely, especially after improved water and rail transportation became available, and the industry slowly shifted westward as the frontier receded before it. The first known commercial meatpacker in the Ohio Valley was Elisha Mills, who established a pork plant in Cincinnati in 1818. Situated on a bend of the Ohio River, the community was ideally situated for the meat trade. The surrounding countryside on both sides of the river abounded with swine, and area farmers, some of whom reportedly were already corn-feeding their hogs, preferred to dispose of them locally even at a discount rather than to drive them eastward to Pittsburgh, Philadelphia, or some other distant market. The river also provided Mills and his eventual competitors with a practical, inexpensive transport for their huge barrels of packed pork. At first flatboats and later steamboats carted their products west and south for sale at St. Louis, Memphis, Natchez, and New Orleans, and Cincinnati-packed pork was exported to the West Indies as early as 1822. Few early statistics survive, but it is known that by 1833 Ohio businessmen were processing 85,000 hogs a year.

By 1844, twenty-six separate Cincinnati establishments processed $2.8 million worth of products, and during the winter of 1847–48 there were forty plants, some of which were very large. Bowen and Evans, for example, custom-packed 3 million tons of pork under contract for export to the principality of Westphalia. On the eve of the Civil War a newspaper reported:

> The farmers in the Eastern States can form no idea of the extent of pork trade of the West unless they personally inspect the slaughtering houses that are to be found in Cincinnati, and other large cities. Twenty thousand swine are very com-

monly slaughtered and packed for market in a single season by
one house; and the whole number slaughtered annually in these
establishments west of the Allegheny mountains averages
2,000,000 weighing each 200 lbs., of net pork, of which at least
one-fourth are slaughtered in Ohio. The number packed at
Cincinnati alone equalled 400,000 head in a single season.
During the month of December, the latter city is crowded almost to suffocation with droves of hogs and draymen employed
in delivering the barrelled pork on board of steamers. Some
1,500 laborers are employed in the business from six to eight
weeks [during the winter], and in many cases it is kept in full
operation both day and night, including Sundays, from the beginning to the completion of the season.[18]

By then Cincinnati-packed pork and lard were widely exported to
Cuba, Great Britain, France, and the German states, as well as to
eastern American cities.

Of this genre of midwestern pork packers economic historian
Margaret Walsh says:

> Little finance was needed to build an early meat-processing
> plant. As rivers were closed to navigation during the winter
> months, merchants had spare capacity in their warehouses, so
> they hastily and temporarily fitted them up with the simple
> tools of the trade, such as cutting instruments, tables, pickling
> vats, and lard kettles or tanks. If they had insufficient space to
> improvize hog pens and slaughter yards, or if nuisance ordi-
> nances prevented their presence within the city boundaries,
> packers could rent land nearby and transport carcasses to their
> converted warehouses or they could hire the services of the
> local butcher either for the benefit of retaining the offal or on
> commission.[19]

It is difficult to determine precisely the amounts of fixed and
working capital the typical backwoods entrepreneur needed. Government data for 1850, which Walsh considers incomplete, yield an
average investment of $19,000 with working-capital requirements
of about $60,000. Walsh's careful study found that plant require-

---

[18] Quoted in ibid., p. 97.
[19] Margaret Walsh, *The rise of the midwestern meat packing industry* (1982), p. 26.

ments ranged widely from place to place in the Midwest: Cincinnati, a low of $11,000 and a high of $75,000; Louisville, between $30,000 and $180,000; and St. Louis, between $20,000 and $107,000, the typical city pork packer spending between $100,000 and $125,000 a year to buy hogs and pay other operating expenses. Walsh continues:

> Few if any entrepreneurs in the pioneer Midwest had financial reserves of these dimensions. Yet contemporary sources boast of the proliferation of pork packers throughout the region. The apparent anomaly can be explained through the general activities of western merchants, through their ability to command credit both from local financial institutions and from distant wholesalers, and through the injection of capital by eastern or foreign venturers interested in acquiring western meats.[20]

Cincinnati packinghouses typically were situated on or near the Ohio River. Nearby were jumbles of private stock pens, where buyers and sellers met and traded. In 1850 a well-fattened four-hundred-pound boar brought eight dollars or less, the price sometimes including slaughtering. Techniques of area drovers and farmers varied: some preferred to drive hogs virtually to the packinghouse door before clubbing them to death and slitting their throats; others killed swine at the stockyards, dragging or hauling the carcasses a few hundred feet through dirt streets and offal-littered footpaths to plant entrances. More often the task was undertaken by separate slaughterhouses, such as those operated by Richard Coleman, who kept the entrails and bristles (valued at about fifty cents a hog) as his share of the endeavor. In some facilities, especially in more progressive Cincinnati establishments after 1851 that began integrating backward, slaughtering increasingly became an adjunct of meatpacking, a first, tentative step toward the division of labor that eventually transformed the industry into an efficient disassembly-line process.

In these modern plants squealing swine were herded into a stout pen beside the plant until no more could be crowded in, and workmen literally walked over their backs, striking each one a killing blow on the head with a two-pointed hammer especially de-

[20] Ibid., p. 28.

signed for the purpose. Dead and stunned animals alike were then hooked onto a dragline and hauled into a "sticking room," where throats were slashed and carcasses hung by the heels to drain, the blood running onto sawdust-covered floors that became coagulated bogs. A bled carcass was briefly dipped into a caldron of boiling water and deposited on a large wooden table for cleaning. As many workers as could crowd around the table set upon the dead beast independently, each with a specialized task. Some pulled off hairs and bristles by the handfuls, which had to be done while the carcass reeked of steam; others, working with sharp knives, scraped the skin more carefully. A half-dozen carefully coordinated workers could prepare as many as three carcasses a minute. The task was completed once the hind legs were stretched far apart with a stick called a "gambrel" and the remains were manually carried by three workers to the next station, to be hung on a hook for the "gutter," who stripped out the entrails. These dropped onto the sawdust floor and, along with other body fluids, collected until the mess became intolerable.

Once cleaned and gutted, the carcass was hauled to the cooling room, which was often little more than a well-ventilated section of the warehouse into which the freezing-cold winter wind penetrated. It remained there for twenty-four hours. When it was thoroughly chilled, a cutter severed the head with a cleaver; chopped off the feet, legs, and knee joints; split the carcass; and cut up the balance into hams, shoulders, and "middles." Some trimmed the pieces into proper shape and size for various markets. When lard prices were high, packers trimmed very closely, sometimes rendering whole shoulders into lard. A four-hundred-pound hog usually was reduced to two hundred pounds of pork and forty pounds of lard. Blood-soaked sawdust, entrails, and other unwanted body parts were swept up at the end of the day and dumped into the Ohio River.

Workers rubbed dry salt thoroughly into pork before it went into a huge vat filled with pickle (either brine or vinegar), which was sometimes spiced with saltpeter, said to give the meat a bright, healthy color. After it had soaked for twenty-four hours, or when the blood was sufficiently purged, the cut meat was transferred to fresh pickle not containing saltpeter but still strong enough with chemicals to float an egg. After another twenty-four hours the meat was moved to a finishing vat of pickle. Considerable care was necessary, especially for the finicky European market. Pork packed prematurely, before the salt sufficiently penetrated the meat, sometimes spoiled if the weather turned warm, making it virtually worthless. If the meat had not thoroughly cooled before it was placed in the first pickle vat, the vinegar fermented, which could cause the meat to develop deadly botulism. Eventually sanitation laws were imposed, but before the Civil War meat inspection was wholly voluntary.

Not all packers graded their meat, even though graded meat generally brought higher prices than unexamined products. The choicest, fattest animals were made into "Clear" and "Mess" pork, the distinction being that "Clear" did not include ribs while a hogshead of Mess contained ribs and two rumps per two-hundred-pound barrel. At that time "Prime" was a term for an inferior grade of meat taken from leaner animals. A barrel of Prime typically contained two shoulders, two jowls, and enough sides to fill out the contents. Most Clear pork was marketed in New England and in Europe, Mess pork found customers in the American merchant marine and the world's navies, and Prime was sold mostly in the slaveholding South as well as in the West Indies and to countless retail establishments throughout the Western world as an inexpensive food for the masses.

Clear meat, which commanded premium prices, received the most care. Typically workers "packed" fifty specially trimmed four-pound pieces of pork in stout wooden barrels manufactured by local coopers. The chunks of meat were alternated with generous layers of salt. At first the salt was inferior sodium chloride mined in the United States. After it was discovered that domestic salt contained impurities that affected the robust color of saltpeter-treated pork, turning it dingy yellow, coarse marine salt from either the Turks Islands, or in the Bahamas, or Setúbal (Saint Ubes), in Portugal, became popular with midwestern packers. Finally, 4 or 5 gallons of pure pickle was poured over the meat, and the barrel was sealed. Mess and Prime grades of pork along with some beef and much lard were similarly "packed," although rarely as fastidiously, in hogsheads, with capacities of 62.5 to 140 gallons.

Bulk pork made up of whole hams, shoulders, or sides was reserved either for the fresh-meat trade or for smoking, the far greater proportion going immediately to smokehouses to be cured and then packed in hogsheads weighing eight hundred to nine hundred pounds. Most of this product was shipped to New Orleans for further distribution worldwide. Most Cincinnati bacon went to iron-manufacturing districts in Pennsylvania, Kentucky, and Ohio; to East Coast fisheries; and to plantations along the lower Mississippi River. Cincinnati plants also custom-packed pork for area farmers, who supplied their own swine. They similarly sold bulk ham to small, independent enterprises which sugar-cured it for the retail market. Neither of these sidelines amounted to a substantial proportion of the meatpacking business, and by the Civil War very few large establishments carried on much specialty work.

Early Cincinnati slaughterhouses and meatpacking plants dumped hog offal, heads, viscera, blood, hair, and assorted trimmings into the Ohio River, which had enough flow to flush the unwanted waste downstream, where, presumably, it fed fish. Chicago packers, ejected from that city by local ordinances in 1849, tried a similar solution, dumping by-products into the South Branch of the Chicago River, but the flow was so sluggish that they soon had to pump water from the Chicago and Michigan Canal to purge the river of "the filth deposited by the slaughter house men, which had so corrupted the water as to make it stink unbearably at every turn of the paddle wheels of the numerous steam boats upon it."[21] When it became apparent that virtually every portion of a hog carcass could be melted down into crude lard, slaughterhouses and meatpacking plants alike installed and kept boiling large kettles into which scraps from trimmings and assorted by-products were tossed. At first this crude lard was sold to refiners.

Lard, the raw material of a number of valuable products, experienced a considerable boom before the Civil War. About 1842 it was found to be an economical substitute for whale oil, which was in increasingly short supply worldwide. Lard fueled lamps (until it was replaced by cheaper kerosene, about 1870), lubricated industrial machinery, and became a popular cooking oil throughout the Americas and, eventually, the Western world. It even enjoyed a lively market in the West Indies as a substitute for butter. Thirty independent refineries operated in Cincinnati in 1849, and they accounted for the bulk of the 5 million tons of lard processed in the United States that year. They fractured higher grades of crude lard

---

[21] Quoted in Clemen, *The American livestock and meat industry*, p. 120.

into its principal components (70 percent oil and 30 percent stearin) by mixing in alcohol and subjecting the compound to high temperatures. Stearin (a colorless, odorless, tasteless glycerol) was used as raw material for manufacturing candles and soap. Poorer grades of crude lard were processed into neat's-foot oil, valuable in tanning leather and as tallow for candles.

Potential profits from lard during the middle 1840s lured larger meatpackers into refining, and they installed more efficient rendering equipment, such as larger, enclosed boiler tanks into which pressurized steam was injected, thereby reducing from days to hours the time required to render scraps into crude. The new equipment was very dangerous, and explosions were common, but gradually the meatpackers (who were simultaneously absorbing the slaughtering business) took over lard refining. The last independent refiner in the United States, George Cleaver, of Chicago, went out of business in 1857.

Eventually meatpackers discovered that all by-products had value. Offal, hooves, horns, bones, dead swine, and spoiled pork were all transformed into glue by entrepreneurs, including one Chicago manufacturer who, it is said, "did not purchase their materials from the packers, but went out on the prairie and dug up the materials the packers had buried there during the day."[22] Meatpackers did not diversify into gluemaking until 1885, when Armour & Co. acquired the Wahl Brothers' glue factory. The residue from glue making and lard processing as well as offal, blood, and bones soon became commercial fertilizer, the demand for which increased markedly during the 1880s, when western bison-bone phosphates and Peruvian guano phosphates were in short supply. Hog bristles became brushes, and the hair stuffed mattresses.

Chemists alchemized hair, hooves, offal, and other wastes into ammonia, potash, glycerin, and gelatin; blood was used to tint paint. Cattle hides sold well throughout the period, tanned leather being in great demand by New England shoe manufacturers, but the commercial supply was meager and centered chiefly on western meatpacking centers, as at Alton, Illinois, which by then specialized in the beef trade. As already noted, much of the leather market

[22] Ibid., p. 132.

before the Civil War was supplied by the Spanish provinces that later became the states of Texas and California.

Most work in early slaughterhouses and meatpacking plants required unskilled labor, but according to Rudolf Clemen,

> Mechanical devices to lessen labor became more common year by year. In 1836 a steam engine, just introduced into one of the packinghouses for the purpose of grinding sausage meat, was considered a great curiosity. The pickle in which the meat was placed had to be changed several times during the process of curing. At first the pickle was carried in pails from tub to tub. An improvement on this was the pumping of the liquid by hand. The final introduction of rudimentary steam pumps for this purpose was heralded as a seven-day wonder.[23]

The work was hard and dangerous, and crippling on-the-job accidents—severed fingers, hernias, scaldings, and the like—were accepted by laborers as routine job hazards. Packinghouse workers did not attempt to organize or bargain collectively until well after the Civil War, when railroads and refrigeration allowed the industry to expand into a year-round endeavor.

The impact of technology on the meat industry was often subtle, as with the advent of railroads. In 1830, 23 miles of railroad track existed in the United States; in 1860, 30,626—almost all of which was east of the Mississippi River. While tracks linked the livestock-rich region that lay generally along the fortieth parallel to the slaughterhouses and meatpacking plants in Alton, Illinois; Buffalo, New York; Chicago; Cincinnati; Cleveland; and St. Louis, relatively little use was made of this integrated system before the Civil War. Livestock raisers and drovers east of the Mississippi usually shunned railroads because freight rates were universally high and because inexperienced early railroaders seldom cared adequately for animals in their charge. Livestock losses in transit were unacceptably high. Long journeys were rarely broken with feed and water stops, and when they were, stock cars were sometimes diverted onto sidings for days, whole shipments perishing from neglect. Sellers too often reached market with animals, dead

[23] Ibid., pp. 113–14.

or alive, fit only for glue factories. Moreover, most of the principal meatpackers were situated along major waterways, which before the Civil War provided an inexpensive alternative to rail shipment.

Even so, the meatpacking industry shifted westward as transportation became more readily available, and Missouri and Illinois eventually rivaled Ohio for leadership in the packing trade. After 1840 several slaughterhouses were erected in St. Louis to serve area farmers. As in Cincinnati, far-western packers in St. Louis and in upriver rival Alton apparently processed mostly pork, but no systematic data were kept until the census of manufactures of 1860. Alton reportedly had four plants in 1837, and meatpacking historian Rudolf Clemen estimates that their annual product was in the hundreds of thousands of dollars.

In Chicago in 1827, Archibald Clybourne, governor of the Potawatomis, built the first slaughterhouse to supply Indians and settlers, but he packed none of the mixed meats he butchered. George W. Dole, a local merchant, packed some beef in his warehouse during the winter of 1831–32, and the next year he put up 287 barrels of pork and 14 barrels of lard. By 1842 the total output of meat in the city was 16,209 barrels, about 5 percent of which was beef. All told it represented only about one-seventh of the state's production, most of the rest of which was in Alton. While Chicago's rise to prominence in the meat trade did not occur until the Civil War, its early entrepreneurs nevertheless were bold innovators. In the summer of 1857 two unidentified Chicago firms, experimenting in icehouses, packed 37,000 hogs, and the fresh summer product was snapped up at a premium price by local buyers. "Ice packing," as the technique quickly became known, was repeated profitably thereafter, anticipating the impact of mechanical refrigeration on the industry after the Civil War.

Chicago grew into a metropolis largely because of the meat trade. After 1825, Chicago, linked by the Great Lakes and the Erie Canal to East Coast markets, quickly became a center for agrarian commodities, such as livestock and meat. Harbor facilities soon appeared, and a canal to tap the Illinois River, and hence the Mississippi, was undertaken in 1836 and completed a dozen years later. It was virtually obsolete at the moment of completion, for by then a dozen railroads radiated from Chicago, directly linking the city's half-dozen meatpacking plants with the livestock-rich Middle West as well as the urban East. In 1848, to capitalize on the city's huge produce market, businessmen organized the Chicago Board of Trade for the open auction of commodity futures.

Chicago was in an ideal position to turn to good advantage the inordinate Union demand for foodstuffs during the Civil War. Entrepreneur Nelson Morris, who at age twenty-two had established a small Chicago pork plant, in 1866 seized the opportunity to ship live cattle by rail to the Army of the Potomac. He soon became the exclusive provisioner of Ulysses S. Grant's Army of the West, with a lucrative contract. Other Chicago businessmen followed suit, and by war's end the city had virtually supplanted Cincinnati as the livestock capital of the United States and was rapidly replacing it as the nation's pork-packing center.

Fundamental to that transition was the development of a centralized market, the Union Stock Yards. In 1861, Chicago contained six separate privately owned livestock pens scattered randomly about the city, and before the Civil War ended, two more had been built. The first large facility, the Bull Head Market, at Madison Street and Ashland Avenue, opened in 1848 and replaced several smaller yards belonging to individual slaughterhouses. It offered sellers and buyers a neutral site at which to hold livestock temporarily while sales were negotiated. During the next two decades competitive facilities sprang up alongside such railroads as the Michigan Southern; the Michigan Central; the Illinois Central; the Pittsburgh and Fort Wayne; the Chicago, Burlington and Quincy; and the Chicago and Northwestern. While some of the newer pens were large by the standards of the time (John B. Sherman's yards along the north lakeshore, for example, could hold 5,000 cattle and 30,000 hogs), none proved adequate to handle the voluminous wartime commerce.

Situated within the city and at considerable distance from each other, as well as from the several packing plants that had been ordered out of Chicago in 1849, separate yards "proved to be a source of great dissatisfaction to dealers, shippers, and packers." According to Clemen:

> [Stockyards] were in some instances two or three miles apart, and drovers were often obliged to drive their animals through the crowded streets of the city, from yard to yard, thereby under-

going the greatest inconvenience and, in many instances, actual loss, occasioned by the difficulty of driving and the rough
pavements, which lacerated and tore the hoofs of the animals,
producing pain and disease. The delay and the expense of this
method of traffic can be better estimated than told in figures.
Moreover, trade in cattle and hogs was quite often active in one
yard while at another it was extremely dull. The receipts at one
yard would sometimes equal the combined receipts of all the
others, thus rendering trade brisk at the latter and lifeless at the
former. The shippers found that the best way to get the strongest competition or the highest prices was to have their stock
where the buying strength was the strongest. Naturally the
buyers were more numerous at the terminals of the lines bringing in the largest number of cars of livestock, and as a necessary
result the shippers patronizing the smaller lines were placed at a
disadvantage, because they could not get buyers to look at their
stock . . . except when there was an insufficient number at the
larger stockyards to supply the demand. Commercial reporters
found the greatest difficulty in making up a summary of the
daily market, and consequently the figures upon which the
shippers would naturally rely proved unworthy of confidence.
Packers united with drovers and dealers in a demand for better
accommodations.[24]

Eventually even the railroads recognized the inefficiency of
disunity. In 1865 the Illinois legislature by special act incorporated
the Union Stock Yards and Transit Company. Nine cooperating
railroads subscribed 92.5 percent of its $1 million capitalization;
the balance was raised through private subscription. Construction
cost overruns forced investors to provide another $650,000 before
the facility was completed the next year. Situated on 345 acres of
swampy land just outside the city's southern boundary, it opened on
Christmas Day, 1865. Once they were fully developed the following
year, the Yards, containing hotels, restaurants, saloons, and offices,
were the largest such facility in the world. The interconnecting laby-
rinth of 2,300 separate livestock pens accommodated 200 horses,
21,000 cattle, 22,000 sheep, and 75,000 hogs. At first the Yards
pumped water some considerable distance from the Chicago River,
but this polluted supply was inadequate and was soon replaced by

[24] Ibid., pp. 85–86.

two artesian wells, each drilled to a depth of more than 1,000 feet. Participating railroads at first handled their separate freight in and out of the facility, but traffic snarled as each shipper selfishly looked to its own interest. Soon the facility absorbed the separate terminals and ran all the stockcars within its confines, bringing order to the enterprise.

The evolution of such a complex, centralized cash market—soon repeated in other meatpacking centers—was significantly enhanced by the contemporary appearance of livestock commission merchants, independent businessmen who brokered sales for buyers and sellers. Transactions had once been handled adequately by the people who herded the animals to market, but no itinerant drover could keep abreast of rapidly fluctuating livestock prices, especially in such a huge, geographically diffuse market as Chicago before the Civil War, and assure his client top dollar. Sellers therefore eventually turned to commission merchants, the first of whom reportedly began operating in Chicago in 1857. By the time the Union Stock Yards opened, a dozen firms—Solomon Sturges' Sons, Robert Stranhorn & Company, and J. L. Mitchiner and Company prominent among them—were vying for customers.

Joseph G. McCoy, who closely observed the nineteenth-century livestock trade both as buyer and as seller, wrote

> The business of live stock commission merchants is to take care of, feed, water, and render to the owner an account of such consignments of livestock, as he may be able to obtain either from his patrons direct or from such as may arrive with stock not consigned to any other house. It is a part of his duties to keep himself fully posted as to prices, not only in the market in which he sells, but of all distant markets, besides always keeping a sharp look out for live stock buyers for all grades, and in short, to keep and be a kind of general intelligence office concerning live stock men matters. . . . the rivalry [among firms] impels them to work for the highest prices, in order to please and hold their customers, and they usually know better than one who had just arrived, or is seldom on market, the true value of all grades of stock, besides they know the man, if any there be who desires any particular grade of stock.[25]

[25] Joseph McCoy, *Historic sketches of the cattle trade of the West and Southwest* (1874), pp. 281–82.

Livestock commission companies, a manifestation of the trend toward specialization that permeated the meat industry during the middle nineteenth century, began appearing wherever slaughter animals were bought and sold in large quantities. "Competition for the livestock trade was also fierce among the specialized livestock commission merchants who handled the growing meat trade," economic historian Mary Yeager has observed. "These shippers, who provided railroads with high volume meat flows, pressed for and received rebates from the railroads, often playing one road off against another."[26] Three major carriers, the New York Central, Erie, and Pennsylvania railroads, soon devised an "evener system" to avoid cutthroat rate wars. About 1875 they separately allied with Nelson Morris, Samuel Allerton, D. H. Sherman, and other major western shippers, who provided the roads with a steady, predictable flow of livestock in return for rebates of about 15 percent of the total freight bill. Two years later the principal eastern carriers organized the Eastern Trunkline Association, which pooled the livestock business of all cooperating shippers and thereby avoided ruinous price and rebate competition among the carriers. The system worked well until the introduction of the refrigerator car after the Civil War, which resulted in more efficient (and for railroads less profitable) commerce in fresh meat.

According to government statistics, by the time of the Civil War livestock slaughtering and meatpacking in the United States were rapidly expanding, prosperous business endeavors poised to expand. By 1860, 259 separate facilities existed in the thirty-three states, up from 185 at the time of the first census of manufactures ten years before. Their combined investment obviously had also grown, to $10.2 million from $3.5 million; so too had gross profits, to $5.8 million from $2.5 million. In 1860 the industry employed 5,058 persons an average of twelve hours a day for approximately fifteen weeks each winter season, paying them an average of $14.39 a week ($201.48 a year), for a total wages bill of $1 million. In 1850, 3,267 persons had labored in slaughtering and packing, earning an average of $26.85 a week ($375.93 a year), for a total wages bill of $1.2 million. Much of the savings in wages had come from

[26] Mary Yeager, *Competition and regulation: the development of oligopoly in the meat packing industry* (1981), p. 30.

the proclivity of profit-minded owners to invest in new technology, which had reduced the need for manpower even though output increased, but some undoubtedly was reverberation from the panic of 1857, which had resulted in much unemployment and wage cutting by employers in many industries nationwide. Indeed, Walsh says, "Progress might be gradual and piecemeal rather than swift and dramatic, but in the space of a generation, between the early 1840s and the mid-1870s, meat packing was transformed from its pioneer commercial status to the threshold of a genuine manufacturing activity."[27]

[27] Walsh, *The rise of the midwestern meat packing industry*, p. 7.

3

Age of Change, 1865–1920: The Ranch and the Farm

Between 1865 and 1920 livestock raising in the United States bifurcated into clearly distinctive agrarian endeavors—ranching and farming. Ranching entails the popular western drama of lore—the saga of self-reliant, tall-in-the-saddle westerners, Texans mostly, who tamed the forbidding Great Plains with their immense herds of Longhorn cattle and, incidentally, supplied the urban East with inexpensive beefsteak, thereby subsidizing industrialization. Mixed farming, the historically dominant supplier of America's red-meat animals, also expanded; indeed, throughout the whole period it continued to furnish the overwhelming majority of the nation's slaughter beasts, albeit anonymously.

In December, 1865, surveying the utter devastation of the Civil War, U.S. Agriculture Commissioner Isaac Newton said, "There has been a loss, to be sure, since 1860 by the waste of war in every thing but sheep."[1] From enumerations made in loyal states at the close of the conflict, he calculated that all classes of the nation's livestock had been decimated: horses by 10 percent, mules by 20 percent, and "neat cattle" (oxen, milch cows, and stocker, feeder, and all classes of slaughter beeves which were then usually lumped together as "other") by 7 percent. The heart of the eastern cattle kingdom had sustained stunning losses: Pennsylvania, 13.5 percent; Kentucky, 22.9 percent; Ohio, 18.4 percent; Indiana, 27 percent; and Illinois, 21 percent.

Substantial numbers of swine likewise had been slaughtered to

---

[1] U.S. Commissioner of Agriculture, *Report for the year 1865* (1866), p. 69.

feed contending armies and city dwellers alike. Maryland suffered the smallest decline of any loyal state (5.2 percent), Missouri the greatest (57.9 percent). Only Iowa and Minnesota among those reporting recorded gains in the numbers of hogs: 52.2 and 26.7 percent, respectively. In the North, swine numbers had declined by 21.7 percent. Sheep, raised principally for wool, had never been an important component of the nation's red-meat supply, a fact unaltered by war; their numbers consequently doubled, to 32.6 million, but their value varied little during the conflict, despite wartime inflation that otherwise doubled the general price level. By contrast, cattle prices more than tripled, to an average of $35.57 in December, 1865, and that of swine quadrupled, to $8.86 a head.

Enumerations the following year, which for the first time since secession included the South, overall depicted vastly greater ruin. The defeated Confederacy counted 4.8 million slaughter beeves, a 20 percent reduction in the total reported in 1860. Most states— Alabama, Arkansas, the Carolinas, Georgia, Louisiana, Mississippi, and Virginia—had sustained losses ranging from 15 to 55 percent. In all, Newton's census takers counted only 11.7 million beef cattle nationwide to satisfy the demands of 35 million increasingly urbanized Americans. Even so, the total of 1866 was 70 percent greater than that reported the year before in loyal states alone, which was the principal reason the average price of beef cattle slipped to $21.55 a head, a 39 percent drop. Still, the average price was more than 200 percent higher than before the war.

Southern swine growers had suffered too. Every state in the South, much as in the North, reported some decline. The 11 million southern hogs counted by enumerators in 1866 pushed up the nation's aggregate supply to 24.7 million head, one-fourth fewer than the 33.5 million counted before the war but almost double the 13.6 million counted the previous year in northern states and territories alone. The price of porkers consequently plummeted to an average of $5.43 nationwide, a 38 percent plunge.

By 1867 appreciable differences in livestock prices existed throughout the nation. In New York, where the number of cattle on farms had shrunk to 0.46 head per capita, the average price of slaughter beeves was calculated by the agriculture department at $39.46 a head. In Ohio, with a cattle-to-population ratio of 0.53, slaughter animals sold for $36.39 each, and in Massachusetts, with merely 0.15 head per capita, prices averaged $44.69. But in Texas, where enumerators guessed that there were 2.5 million slaughter beeves (3.6 per capita), prices reportedly hovered at about $5.59 a head. Edward Everett Dale asserted:

> As a matter of fact the figures given [by the USDA] are probably far too low. Men who have made a careful study of the subject usually agree that the number of cattle in Texas increased greatly during the war. Associations and live stock agencies of various kinds had been established during the years of warfare to ride the ranges, round up and brand calves and keep an account for absent parties. It seems probable that instead of a decrease of nearly twelve per cent the number of cattle in Texas actually increased greatly during the four years of war, particularly in some localities, and at its close numbered not less than five and probably eight head per capita of population.[2]

Dale thus placed between 5 and 6 million cattle in Texas at the conclusion of the conflict, and while the agriculture department estimated the average market price at above $5 a head, Dale said "Stocks of [Texas] cattle often were offered for sale upon the range at from one to two dollars a head, and that too without finding a purchaser."[3]

Astute entrepreneurs readily recognized the opportunity afforded by millions of wild, mostly unclaimed mavericks that roamed the southwest Texas countryside in small bands, from the Rio Grande to the Nueces River and beyond, even though the market for scrub cattle at war's end was ill defined. Anyone could acquire these animals. In the words of folklorist J. Frank Dobie, "all it took to make a cowman—an owner—was a rope, nerve to use it, and a branding iron."[4] The few Longhorns trailed into the Midwest by opportunists almost as soon as the Civil War ended fetched an unheard-of forty dollars a head. Word spread, and the cattle rush was on.

In 1866 Texans such as Oliver Loving, an experienced, middle-aged cattleman, and Charles Goodnight, a twenty-year-old novice,

[2] Edward Dale, *The range cattle industry* (1930), pp. 11–12.
[3] Ibid., p. 12.
[4] J. Frank Dobie, *The Longhorns* (1941), p. 51.

followed a trader's trace to Fort Sumner, an isolated garrison in the upper Pecos Valley of New Mexico Territory, and sold their gaunt beasts to government provisioners for an astronomical sixty dollars each. The path—ever afterward known as the Goodnight-Loving Trail, which skirted the northern rim of the treacherous Chihuahua desert (replete with quicksand at river crossings, water holes poisoned with alkali, and roving bands of fierce Indians)—was unquestionably the most dangerous of all the great cattle trails. Indeed, Loving and Goodnight lost one hundred head to Apaches on the trip in 1866, and the next year, while pushing another herd over the path, Loving was mortally wounded by Comanches. Most cattlemen preferred safer environs and easier trails.

The vast majority of the estimated 260,000 Longhorns trailed from Texas in 1866 set out for the Midwest, where a few drovers had found lucrative markets at war's end. Mindful that the Missouri Pacific Railroad had already laid track halfway to Kansas City, some intended to drive Longhorns to the railhead at Sedalia, Missouri, and ship them on to assorted urban markets. Others apparently gathered cattle with the more general intent of herding them northward over the Texas Road, or Shawnee (later Sedalia) Trail, for sale at the first opportunity. There was a plethora of problems—foul weather, rain-swollen streams, and a high desertion rate among youthful cowhands. Indians in the Territory occasionally stampeded herds to steal cattle or to ransom them, but more frequently the cattle bolted on their own when confronted with dark and, to prairie-bred beasts, forbidding woodlands of the Ozark Plateau.

Drovers also encountered open hostility along the way. Some of the rancor was the understandable enmity of borderlanders toward former Confederates, but most was simple outrage over the sudden appearance of "Texas fever" among native cattle soon after Longhorns were trailed by. Also called Spanish fever and, incorrectly, splenic fever (anthrax), it was actually piroplasmosis, a circulatory infection caused by the microbe *Babesia bovis* for which the cattle tick *Boophilus annulatus* served as intermediate host. Susceptible cattle easily contracted the malady, becoming lethargic or delirious within a week, cows giving less milk and bulls and steers often thrashing about and cracking their horns. Four out of five infected animals died, and the survivors were so emaciated that weeks' more feeding was necessary before marketing. The USDA eventually estimated that between 1865 and the turn of the century, when piroplasmosis was eradicated in America, 2.5 million cattle succumbed to it.

Made immune by centuries of exposure to the parasite, Longhorns never contracted the malady and, it was quickly noticed, ceased to be carriers once they were wintered in the North and had shed semitropical ticks (a few observers called the disease "tick fever"). During the 1850s, when Longhorns were first driven over the Shawnee Trail to midwestern stocker-and-feeder markets, farmers saw their cattle drop dead. Consequently, even before the Civil War several northern states and territories had circumscribed the importation of "diseased" Texas cattle, the state of Missouri authorizing local lawmen to shoot offending animals if necessary, but as commerce between the sections was reestablished following the war, these ordinances were unevenly enforced. The first trail herds of 1866 passed through with little difficulty, while latecomers sometimes encountered armed mobs.

Consequently, three-fourths of the Texans stayed home the following year. What was needed, in the words of Joseph McCoy, a twenty-nine-year-old Illinois cattle buyer, "was to establish at some accessible point a depot or market to which a Texan drover could bring his stock unmolested, and there, failing to find a buyer, he could go upon the public highways [railroads] to any market in the country he wished."[5] In 1867 entrepreneur McCoy created just such a market at Abilene, Kansas. He enticed the Kansas Pacific division of the Union Pacific Railroad to lay a siding to cattle pens he built at the remote hamlet as well as to give him a commission on every carload of cattle shipped. He also persuaded the governor of Kansas not to enforce that state's quarantine against transient Texas cattle and lobbied the Illinois legislature to amend its laws to admit Texas cattle shipped by rail from his pens. He advertised his facility with handbills and the first year attracted drovers with 35,000 head to his depot.

Situated near the geographic center of the Great Plains, Abilene lay at the heart of a sea of grass. Around the town in all directions was an unimaginably immense quarter-million-square-mile

[5] Joseph McCoy, *Historic sketches of the cattle trade of the West and Southwest* (1874), p. 40.

pampas, an almost trackless prairie virtually unbroken by the farmer's plow, grazed only by migratory buffalo—ample room upon which to hold huge herds of cattle awaiting sale or their turn at the railroad loading pens. Again word spread, and soon the Chisholm Trail became renowned in fact and fiction. Texans drove 75,000 cattle to McCoy's pens in 1868, 300,000 in 1869, 300,000 in 1870, and 600,000 in 1871. All told, before the cattleman's frontier passed it by, McCoy's facility at Abilene handled an estimated 1.5 million cattle, many of them shipped to markets in the urban East, principally Chicago.

The postwar "Long Drive," while similar to earlier episodes in American history dating to colonial times, contained far more traffic than ever before, and the West's horseback style of droving was fundamentally different from that of the East, where relatively tame, often hand-fed animals were herded afoot, usually with the assistance of shepherd dogs. Typically, foresighted Texans bought ranch cattle in the fall, when prices were lowest and, depending on the size of the herd, hired six to twelve men and boys to drive the animals to market. Others, especially opportunists not so well financed, simply gathered mavericks from the wild in early spring and after roundup and branding, set out for market, often in early March.

Most days on the trail were uneventful, even monotonous. After a predawn breakfast—usually consisting of sourdough biscuits, omnipresent beans perhaps containing boiled sowbelly, and scalding black coffee—the "waddies" slowly drove the cattle away from the "bedding grounds." The chuck wagon, with the cook at the reins, pushed ahead to find a suitable campsite and was trailed closely by the horse wrangler and his "remuda." Then came two or more riders on "point," two to six on flank, and two or more on "drag," riding herd on as many as three thousand.

During the first few days on the trail, as the cattle were being "road-broken," the hands kept beasts tightly bunched; later a herd might stretch out a mile or more, point to drag. A drive, leisurely paced to allow the animals to eat their way to market, halted at midday, the waddies in shifts partaking of chow, which varied little from breakfast or, for that matter, the evening meal. Drives stopped well before dark, usually near water, and the cattle were allowed to graze peacefully until evening, when they were "wound up" for night herding, a task divided into shifts among waddies. Lightning sometimes stampeded the notoriously skittish Longhorns, placing waddies in mortal danger, but the usual perils were prairie-dog holes, quicksand, treacherous stream crossings, vipers, predators, and occasionally Indians. Even so, trail bosses frequently forbade their crews to carry firearms, especially handguns that easily discharged and spooked steers.

All told, perhaps 30,000 different persons drove cattle over the Chisholm Trail and contemporary cow paths, and relatively few of them were the strapping Anglo-Saxon stereotypes of film and fiction. Recent research indicates that half or more were literally "cow boys," mostly poor southern youths, adolescents aged twelve to eighteen. Most of the adult men on trail drives were Mexicans, blacks, and Indians. Ability rather than racism prevailed along the frontier, where the labor pool was small, and capable people readily found employment on the trail as well as on the ranch. Vaqueros, of course, had originated with ranching in the Southwest; freed slaves, many from Texas and at home in the saddle, were also common; and even Indian cowpokes were not unusual, especially in the Territory, where native ranchers had prospered since before the war. Together these minorities made up as much as 40 percent of this specialized work force. The rest were white adult males uprooted by war, immigrant white men (especially Britons and Irish), some eastern youths attracted by popular accounts of adventure in the West (especially toward the end of the era), and even a few adventurous young women, some of whom were disguised as young boys.

Men, women, and children, black, Indian, and white, waddies earned $25 to $40 and "keep" monthly for laboring twelve to eighteen hours a day, seven days a week, for as long as three months at a stretch. Wranglers commanded as much as $50 a month, and cooks averaged $75. Trail bosses who had minimal losses usually received bonuses in addition to monthly salaries of $100 to $125. While capable teenagers and minorities alike frequently advanced to boss, recently freed blacks usually drew the most unpleasant duties. Little of the work was glamorous, and few drovers were the dashing heroes of the movies.

Kansas cattle towns (the mildly derisive term "cow town" was coined about 1885) have also been caricatured in popular culture. The image of Abilene, Ellsworth, Wichita, Dodge City, and Cald-

well as corrupt fleshpots—where, lining Main Street, gaudy saloons, bawdy bordellos, and riotous dancehalls featuring tinhorn
gamblers, comely *filles de joie*, and hurdy-gurdy dancers vied for
cowboys' money, and where daily gunfights added new residents to
boot hill—owes far more to Hollywood than to history.

Between 1867 and 1890, Kansas cattle towns indeed tolerated
considerable rowdiness by fuzzy-cheeked lads from Texas lest they
take their herds and go elsewhere. "Through the medium of the
range cattle trade," historian Robert Dykstra has written, "towns-
men sought the rare prize of city status."[6] Even so, only two towns,
Dodge City and Ellsworth, deserved their reputations for lawless-
ness, both earned before the advent of the cattle trade when buffalo
hunters, soldiers, and railroad construction crews cavorted there-
abouts. None of the cattle towns ever contained more than a dozen
saloons, many of them side-street holes-in-the-wall that dispensed
cheap, watered-down whiskey. Only two saloons, the Alamo in
Abilene and the Long Branch in Dodge City, were deluxe emporia,
containing bars for loungers, tables and chairs for sitters, and gam-
ing devices for the sporting crowd. Bordellos and prostitution were
mostly seasonal endeavors, and only Dodge City (the longest-lived
of the cattle towns) contained as many as two dancehalls during the
same season—one for whites, the other for blacks.

Nor were cattle towns as violent as legend insists—not nearly
as dangerous as many contemporary eastern cities. Each town enacted gun-control ordinances and, with revenues from special tax
assessments on the principal beneficiaries of the cattle trade, hired
police. Dykstra counted only forty-five homicides in all the towns
during their heyday; thirty-nine were killed by gunshot (sixteen by
the police), and only six died from handguns, none of them in the
legendary gunfight on Main Street. Frontier lawmen were seldom as
dashing as their celluloid versions; among the duties of Wichita city
policeman (he was never "marshal") Wyatt Earp were chimney inspection, street cleaning, and "fine" collection from prostitutes
such as his sisters-in-law Bessie and Sallie Earp. Each cattle town in
turn prospered briefly, and local farmers enjoyed extra cash from the
sale of chickens and eggs to feed the itinerants, but trails shifted,

---

[6]Robert Dykstra, *The cattle towns* (1970), p. 6.

along with the frontier, and none of the cattle towns, not even Wichita, became a metropolis because of the red-meat trade.

While the cattle towns thrived, ranching spread. Texans early on had wintered great herds of unsold Longhorns on the prairies surrounding Abilene and after fattening their skinny beasts on sweet spring grass, often sold them profitably the next summer, thereby demonstrating the carrying capacity of the northern plains. By the early 1870s cow camps dotted the Great Plains as far north as the Canadian border. During the same decade Harold Bugbee, Charles Goodnight, Jot Gunter, George Littlefield, and William Munson, among other pioneer ranchers, moved their operations from relatively settled regions to the pampas of Texas, the Panhandle-plains, alternately struggling to turn away giant bison herds to save the grass for their cattle and fighting off fierce Plains Indians.

Happily for cattlemen, the generally favorable weather conditions of the era coincided with the virtual extermination of the buffalo and the subjugation of the Indians, opening the whole Great Plains to herdsmen, who quickly occupied it. Government statisticians in 1860 counted 3.5 million cattle in Texas and in 1880, 4.9 million head, most of those gains on northwestern grasslands. New Mexico contained 90,000 cattle in 1860 and 170,000 in 1880; Indian Territory, 100,000 in 1860 and 500,000 in 1880; Kansas, 93,000 in 1860 and 1.5 million in 1880; Nebraska, 40,000 in 1860 and 760,000 in 1880; Colorado, an unknown number in 1860 and 350,000 in 1880; Dakota Territory, 2,000 in 1860 and 140,000 in 1880; and no cattle reported in either Montana or Wyoming in 1860 and 170,000 and 280,000 head, respectively, in 1880.

Its profitability often exaggerated, cattle ranching attracted the attention of popular writers and assorted investors. Joseph McCoy's *Historic sketches of the cattle trade of the West and Southwest* (1874), in which he told of fortunes made by Texans, and James Brisbin's widely read *Beef bonanza; or, how to get rich on the plains* (1881), a succinct if overexuberant prospectus for the whole industry, undoubtedly lured many into the business. Capital poured into cattle raising so rapidly that, in 1885, Walter, Baron von Richthofen, who was living in Denver, wrote: "Great cattle corporations—with means sufficient for all the wants of business, and operated by men of great ability, who have studied this industry, and can manage the same in a business-like manner—are rapidly filling up all untaken lands fit for good ranges, and will soon change this Western cattle-raising into a monopoly, as are railroads now in the East."[7]

Scottish journalist James MacDonald's *Food from the far West* (1878) was the first book to indicate that American ranching was ripe for foreign takeover. Cattle ranching was, of course, merely one aspect of contemporary British investments in Asia, Africa, Australia, and North and South America. The first Anglo-American cattle ranch was the Prairie Cattle Company, Ltd., of Edinburgh, Scotland, which in 1881 bought George Littlefield's half-million-acre LIT Ranch in the Texas Panhandle and, at the end of its first year's operation, paid investors a 28-percent dividend. This venture was followed in 1882 by that of the Matador Land and Cattle Company of Dundee, whose 1.5-million-acre holdings eventually stretched from Texas to Saskatchewan. A dozen other large, well-financed alien operations soon appeared in Texas and acquired the LX, Laureles, Rocking Chair, and Seven D ranches among others; by 1886 their investment in Texas alone totaled $15 million.

Before the turn of the century another thousand foreign and domestic cattle companies had incorporated under the laws of Colorado, Kansas, Montana, Nebraska, New Mexico, and Wyoming, their estimated investment aggregating $284.6 million. The most ambitious of these was the American Cattle Trust, which was organized in 1887 by such cattlemen as John Lytle and C. C. Slaughter to monopolize the beef trade as thoroughly as Standard Oil allegedly controlled petroleum. Capitalized at $10 million, American Cattle bought and leased 100,000 acres of northern rangeland, stocked them (as well as several Nebraska feedlots) with an incredible 250,000 head of cattle, and even purchased Nelson Morris's obsolete Chicago meatpacking plant. Lacking a distribution network for its product, American was unable to compete with Armour, Swift, and the rest of the "beef trust" and was forced to liquidate in 1890.

During its golden era ranching attracted unlikely participants. In 1884, Theodore Roosevelt, a twenty-six-year-old widower, bought part interest in a Dakota Territory spread. He was an eccentric even by eastern standards, and his speech was mimicked—"hasten for-

---

[7]Walter Baron von Richthofen, *Cattle-raising on the plains of north America* (1885), p. 99.

ward quickly there" for "hurry" becoming a favorite of cowboys. He returned to New York before the disastrous winter of 1886–87 and consequently made money in ranching. Equally quaint but less successful was textile heir Henry Mudge, of Boston, who bought thousands of acres west of Larned, Kansas, upon which to raise sheep in the age of cattle. He harbored the notion that notoriously dumb sheep might be assigned to pastures without tending and ordered his hands to summarily shoot those beasts that crossed a deadline. He did not do much better with the Durham cattle that he bought to replace his decimated sheep flock about 1884.

John and Charles Arbuckle, scions of a coffee magnate, and Horace Thurber, a shipping mogul, bought 50,000 acres of Union Pacific land north of Cheyenne and appropriated the intervening public lands, all 156 square miles of which they fenced and used to raise horses. With their socialite cronies in colorful riding habit they chased after terrorized coyotes shouting "Tallyho!" much to the amusement of PO Ranch cowboys. More laconic was William Finch, the seventh earl of Aylesford and companion of the prince of Wales (later Edward VII), who exiled himself on a ranch near Big Spring, Texas, to brood about his cuckold by George Blandford, the eighth duke of Marlborough, and his scandalous divorce.

A partial list of dilettante ranchers of the 1880s suggests the popularity of the nineteenth-century cattle ranch among investors. Union Pacific executives Oliver Ames, Sidney Dillon, and Thomas Durant ran cattle on railroad land along the North Platte in Nebraska, and New York Central principal William Vanderbilt owned a ranch in Colorado. Breakfast-food baron C. W. Post profitably operated a 250,000-acre ranch in Texas, which he eventually sold off to farmers. New York *Herald* publisher James Gordon Bennett, Jr., bought a Wyoming spread, and Chicago merchant Marshall Field invested in the Pratt-Farris Cattle Co., which operated in Nebraska, Wyoming, and the Dakotas. Isaac Ellwood, who made millions on barbed wire, acquired the 400,000-acre Spade Ranch in Texas, and meatpacker Nelson Morris bought a 250,000-acre Texas ranch he reportedly never visited. The least likely rancher of all was the Standard Oil Co. of Ohio, which ran 20,000 head of cattle in the Cherokee Outlet. Standard was in the process of enclosing 25 square miles of Indian land with barbed wire in 1885 when the Cleveland administration ordered all fences removed from Indian lands and the cattlemen out of the Territory.

Inevitably the range-cattle industry overexpanded, in the process heightening competition for the land. The story had been much the same since colonial times: livestock raisers cropped public forage until pushed farther west by the advancing farmer; however, during the heyday of the cattle ranch the free grass finally played out, forcing herdsmen to become landowners to survive. Conflicts between competing claimants pitted rancher against rancher, drover against shepherd, herdsman against farmer, and corporation against individual.

The open range closed first in Texas, where, upon entering the Union, the new state government had retained control of its public lands. By 1876 successive Spanish, Mexican, and Texas governments had sold or given away to settlers, speculators, and developers 70 million acres, leaving almost 100 million in the public domain. That year the state set aside about half the remainder to fund public education, offering this acreage for sale at $1.50 an acre or for lease at five cents a year. By then railroads were also claiming generous bounties that ultimately totaled 32.2 million acres for building track across the state. In one instance the state even gave land directly to a ranch—the 3,050,000-acre XIT—which was traded to investors in return for the construction of a new capitol in Austin. The largest cattle ranch in American history, the XIT was eventually surrounded by 6,000 miles of barbed-wire fence. Thus, as the land was being rapidly appropriated, erstwhile free-rangers such as Thomas Bugbee, Charles Goodnight, Jot Gunter, George Littlefield, and William Munson, who were moving onto the Texas plains, had no alternative but to acquire acreage. Sometimes they fenced far more land than they actually bought or leased.

Barbed wire, a fencing material uniquely suited to the treeless plains, became generally available during the mid-1870s, and competition between rival manufacturers drove its price down to $1.80 per 100 pounds in 1880, from $20 in 1874. In 1874, 10,000 pounds of the newfangled wire were sold in Texas, and in 1880, 40 tons. Most Texans who strung wire, such as widow Mabel Day, who enclosed her spread to thwart rustlers, owned or leased the acreage they fenced. Some did not. Charles Goodnight, for example, fenced indiscriminately; others blocked public roads and even enclosed farms they wished to absorb. By this means free-grazers were denied access to grass.

During the fall of 1883 night riders began cutting fences, at first improper fences and then any they encountered. Before order was restored the next year, an estimated $20 million in damages and three deaths had been attributed to the "fence-cutting war." Texas consequently made unauthorized fencing a misdemeanor, ordered illegal fences dismantled within six months, and required unlocked gates at three-mile intervals on the remaining legal ones. Fence cutting and malicious pasture burning were made felonies punishable by five years in prison.

In the rest of the West, where the land laws of the United States applied, the situation was more complex and at times far more violent. Numerous pioneer Great Plains ranchers, while running cattle on hundreds of thousands of acres of the public domain, acquired title under the Homestead Act (1862) to only the quarter section of land surrounding their headquarters, if possible containing a water hole. Sometimes they acquired land under preemption, which required only six months' residence. Many received another 160 acres under the Timber Culture Act (1873), an environment-modification experiment that required one-fourth (later one-tenth) of the acreage to be planted in trees. One Dakota cattle company filed on twenty-six quarter sections, all judiciously located along wooded streams.

More substantial thefts of the public domain were committed under the Desert Land Act (1887), which, according to historian Wallace Stegner, "could hardly have been better devised to help speculators and land-grabbers. . . . Fraud was [almost] never provable, but it was estimated 95 percent of final proof titles were fraudulent, nevertheless."[8] One celebrated case involved the Union Cattle Company of Cheyenne, which plowed a 35-mile-long furrow, called it an irrigation ditch, and through intermediaries acquired title to 33,000 acres under the law.

Many bought land from transcontinental railroads, often fencing in the alternating public sections as though they owned them. In northern Arizona the Aztec Land and Cattle Co. of New York

[8] Wallace Stegner, *Beyond the hundredth meridian* (1954), p. 222.

purchased 1.5 million acres from the Atchison, Topeka and Santa Fe, enclosed 3 million, and leased it all to the Hashknife Ranch of Texas, which was owned by a St. Louis syndicate. In Wyoming the Swan Land and Cattle Company, Ltd., of Edinburgh bought a half-million acres from the Union Pacific and fenced in a half-million more. Government investigations eventually disclosed that between 4.4 million and 7.3 million acres of the public domain were looted by livestock raisers, principally cattlemen.

"All told, it was the most unmistakable, wholesale, shameless instance of land grabbing that had yet been practiced in America," says historian Benjamin Hibbard. "Companies with headquarters in eastern cities, and even in England, fenced in as much as land as they wanted and some had the effrontery to claim in court that a man had a right to as much range as he could fence."[9] In 1887, Congress prohibited foreign enterprises or domestic firms more than 20 percent owned by aliens from acquiring additional land in the territories, a technicality easily evaded, as when the late-coming Scottish-American Mortgage Co. recorded its landholdings in the names of resident agents. Illinois, Minnesota, Nebraska, and Texas enacted similar restrictions, but none were vigorously enforced.

Individual cattleman sometimes battled one another for control of the range, as in the bloody Lincoln County War in which William ("Billy the Kid") Bonney came to infamy. Cattlemen also squared off over Texas fever. In 1882, Charles Goodnight and his neighbors imposed a "Winchester quarantine" against tick-laden south Texas cattle. Similar episodes followed all across the northern plains, culminating in 1885 with quarantine legislation in Arizona, Colorado, Kansas, Montana, Nebraska, New Mexico, Wyoming, and even Canada that effectively closed the cattle trails, thereby forcing south Texas cattlemen to rely solely on rail transportation. Texas fever was such a divisive issue that it prevented western American cattle ranchers, who otherwise held common interests, from organizing an effective trade association until after the turn of the century, when, as noted earlier, the USDA eradicated piroplasmosis.

Cowmen contested with shepherds, but their confrontation was not as universal as is generally believed. In Texas, for example, ranchers had run sheep with cattle before the Revolution, their re-

[9]Benjamin Hibbard, A history of the public land policies (1965), p. 477.

turn regularly being 20 percent greater than when one or the other was pastured alone. Elsewhere, though, cattlemen commonly were prejudiced against sheep. Folklore insisted that cattle, repelled by the scent, would not graze where sheep had trod, a fallacious but pervasive idea popular among ranchers who ran only cattle. It is nevertheless true that ovines cropped the grass close and, if left in place too long, could trample a pasture into dust, leaving nothing for bovines. Moreover, many early flockmasters were tramps who moved on whenever the grass played out, unmindful of or uncaring about the denudation they left behind.

After the Civil War, Pacific Coast sheep—mostly progeny of flocks driven to California during the gold rush—became an export commodity. In 1870 wethers worth $1.50 in San Francisco commanded $3.00 in Denver, and during the following quarter century about 2 million sheep followed trails eastward, mostly to midwestern feedlots in Kansas and Nebraska. "Adventure and adversity marked the way for the cowman pointing them north no more vividly than they met the flockmaster 'trailing them east,'" wrote historian Edward Wentworth. "To the perils of flooded rivers, stampedes, outlaws, and Indians, which spiced the routine of the cowboy, the flock driver added hazards of poisonous herbage, wolves, bobcats, coyotes, and eagles."[10]

Cowmen sometimes attacked flocks. In separate incidents in Arizona in 1884 cowboys trampled one bleating mob to death with a herd of frenzied wild horses and stampeded another into Little Colorado River quicksand. In Wyoming in 1889 a pasture was set afire, severely burning a shepherd's child and turning public opinion there against cattlemen. Even though many Great Plains ranchers restocked their pastures with sheep following the disastrous winter of 1886–87, and despite federal grazing regulations imposed on both herds and flocks by the U.S. Forest Service in 1905, ill will prevailed as late as World War I, when a licensed flock was attacked in Gunnison National Forest.

Many ranchers also remonstrated against "sodbusters," as farmers were contemptuously called by some cattlemen, but conflicts did not merely pit open-range operators against "nesters." Indeed, farm-

[10]Edward Wentworth, *America's sheep trails* (1948), p. 258.

ers often had preceded ranchers onto the plains. "At first," wrote historian Everett Dick, "the few scattered homesteaders who lived near the cattle trail were glad to have the cowboys 'bed down' for the night on their claims. . . . a herd of 2,500 cattle would leave the poverty stricken settler several hundred pounds of fuel at a time when cow chips were in demand."[11] Longhorns sometimes trampled crops and often spread Texas fever, about which farmers inevitably protested. In Kansas, to protect themselves, farmers repeatedly had their legislators impose quarantines, measures culminating in 1885 in a statewide ban on trail cattle.

As early as 1883 settlers also complained to the General Land Office about the hundreds of thousands of miles of barbed wire that were obstructing thoroughfares and closing off public lands. Interior secretary Henry Teller soon advised grazers, grangers, and travelers alike to cut offending wire. In 1885, Congress made unauthorized enclosure of the public domain a punishable offense, thereby theoretically granting everyone equal access to public grass, except in Indian Territory. There President Grover Cleveland ordered all whites out, for in some areas, as on the Cheyenne-Arapaho Reservation, cattlemen had all but evicted the Indians. This order forced an additional 200,000 head of cattle onto the already overcrowded, drouth-blighted ranges of Colorado, Kansas, New Mexico, and Texas at the same time the quarantines against trail cattle were imposed. The following fall and winter were blustery on the northern plains, and range cattle did not add much weight on natural forage. Overstocked, the ranchers saw prices for grass-fed beeves tumble to $2.40 a hundredweight in 1886 (about $8.00 to $10.00 a head), the lowest level since the panic of 1873. Hoping for better prices, many ranchers withheld their cattle from the market, only to suffer an unprecedented winter kill.

In November, 1886, a giant storm dumped so much snow on the plains from Canada to Texas that cattle had difficulty pawing through to the grass. Then, following a chinook in early January that provided a brief respite, a howling arctic blizzard battered the region with brutal cold, ranging from −42°F in Bismarck to −15°F in the Texas Panhandle. Cattle had once been able to survive such

[11] Everett Dick, *The sod-house frontier, 1854–1890* (1937), p. 145.

tempests by drifting on the wind, but now fences trapped them, and tens of thousands of heads piled up and froze to death. According to W. Turrentine Jackson:

> Some ranchers claimed to have lost 60 or 70 per cent of their herds. . . . Careful studies have now estimated the loss from frozen cattle on the northern range at slightly more than 15 per cent [about five times the usual winter kill], but the animals which did survive were so emaciated that tax assessors reduced the evaluations of cattle holdings in Wyoming by 30 percent. Some companies that had overestimated the size of their herds for years [to attract or keep investors] took advantage of the opportunity to reduce them to a realistic figure and blame everything on the weather.[12]

Generally, small ranchers who were able to hand-feed and -water their livestock fared better than large ranchers. Even so, from Texas to Canada, across the plains and into the Rockies, an estimated 900,000 head of western cattle were lost in the "big die-up." Pressed by their creditors for cash, many ranchers dumped livestock following roundup, prices for range stock consequently tumbling to $1.80 a hundredweight, the interwar-period low. The Dolores Land and Cattle Co. of Texas with assets of $2 million liquidated in the spring of 1887, citing the winter kill as cause; so too did the million-dollar Niobrara Land and Cattle Co. of Montana and Nebraska and the big Union Cattle Co. of Wyoming.

Others quickly adopted modern range-management techniques. Many western ranches that had run scrub cattle or perhaps "improved" cattle slowly restocked their ranges with purebred livestock. Indeed, as late as 1890 the USDA estimated that 81 percent of all cattle in America were "common" or "native"; fewer than 1 percent were purebreds, the balance being crosses of one variety or another. The majority of the blooded beasts were raised in the East, mostly on New England farms and the fewest in the ranching West.

America's "native" cattle were principally descended from infinite combinations of Spanish blacks, Devonshire reds, Dutch

---

[12] W. Turrentine Jackson, "British interests in the range cattle industry," in Frink et al., *When grass was king* (1956), pp. 259–260.

blacks and whites, and Danish yellows, subject to some limited infusion of pure-breds: Devons as early as 1623, Shorthorns in 1783, Herefords in 1817, and Brahmans (Zebus) in 1849. Longhorns entered the slaughter, feeder, and breeder markets during the 1850s, and "western cattle" (Texas beasts wintered in the North) were added to market nomenclature about 1868. Angus did not appear in the United States until 1873, when George Grant, a retired Scottish silk merchant living in Victoria, Kansas, imported a bull to cross with Longhorn cows; however, by the middle 1880s most western cattlemen preferred Hereford bulls to "improve" the bloodlines of their scrub cattle.

Experimentation increased following the great die-up. At the turn of the century Texas rancher Edward Lasater crossed Herefords, Shorthorns, and Zebus to concoct Beefmasters, a separate breed eventually recognized by the USDA. A decade later the King Ranch blended Zebus and Shorthorns to create Santa Gertrudis cattle, which were also formally recognized as a breed apart. Not all breeding occurred in the West. For example, about 1888, Ohio stock farmer W. S. Miller gathered some naturally polled Shorthorns and purposely replicated the phenomenon. About the turn of the century Iowa breeder Warren Gammon did likewise with polled Herefords. Both strains quickly became popular among ranchers who wished to eliminate the task of dehorning.

Ranch management also improved. The Scottish-owned Swan Land and Cattle Co. of Wyoming, facing bankruptcy after the big die-up, hired experienced cattleman John Clay, who restocked the 250,000-acre spread with both sheep and cattle, upgrading ranch herds with a larger proportion of purebred Herefords. To avoid another catastrophe, he laid in adequate supplies of strategically stored hay to see the livestock through bad weather. He also redeployed barbed wire as a ranch tool, to segregate herds for breeding purposes as well as to minimize drifting in winter, rather than merely as a boundary marker. By the turn of the century Swan was also improving its pastures by eliminating noxious plants such as locoweed and even reseeding some prairies with improved strains of grasses developed in USDA- and state-sponsored range experiment stations. Only the larger operations could afford costly "ecology programs," as the new science of range mangement was called. For example, the King Ranch alone among Texas spreads undertook the total elimination of mesquite brush from its pastures—an ongoing challenge.

While many western ranchers as late as World War I superciliously dismissed such newfangled techniques, climate caused change. Unfavorable weather commencing about 1895 again severely strained the carrying capacity of the Great Plains, bankrupting many marginal operators. Adverse conditions recurred after the turn of the century. "The drouth [of 1910] following the destructive winter of 1909–1910 forced cattlemen to adjust rapidly to the weather," says John Schlebecker. "To survive cattlemen had to rely even more on supplemental feeds. Ranch farming increasingly came to be usual, rather than exceptional. [Moreover], . . . laissez-faire cattle raising no longer worked on the range. In common with other Americans, cattlemen came to expect more help from their government."[13]

Other ranchers liquidated. Following the great die-up the giant XIT Ranch of Texas had restocked with 100,000 head of Angus, Herefords, and Shorthorns, which it scientifically scattered among its seven divisions and ninety-four fenced pastures. Even so, it consistently lost money throughout the balance of the century. In 1888 it also established a demonstration farm to attract grangers to whom it wished to sell its 3 million acres piece by piece at maximum prices, but, in competition with the Homestead Act and other federal largess of the era, it attracted little interest until after the turn of the century. In 1901 the XIT sold its Yellow House (or Southern) Division (225,858 acres at two dollars an acre) to pioneer cattleman George Littlefield and soon thereafter curtailed its livestock operations, ceasing cattle raising altogether in 1912. During the next two decades it disposed of the balance of its vast holdings to latecoming homeseekers for as much as thirty dollars an acre.

Between 1900 and 1920 at least seventy other prominent western cattle ranches—including Littlefield's LFD (née Yellow House), C. W. Post's Curry Comb, and C. C. Slaughter's Running Water—were sold off to farmers. Indeed, as historian David Gracy has observed:

[13]John Schlebecker, *Cattle raising on the plains, 1900–1961* (1963), pp. 41, 44.

The principal land owner in the cattle regions—the cattle-man—has all too often been depicted as the mortal enemy of the settler, as a man bent upon eradicating the pesky sodbuster. This notion, as applied to the Panhandle-Plains [of Texas] at least, is difficult to substantiate, as precious little animosity and violence is apparent between the entrenched rancher and the advancing settler. . . . Available evidence points unmistakably to the conclusion that the rancher, once abandoning his initial opposition to the *thought* of settlers on the range, actively fostered settlement through purchase of the farmer's produce, through patronage of businesses in the new, nearby towns, through sale of his acreage to the agriculturalist, and thorough monetary assistance to the struggling purchaser of his ranch land.[14]

The big breeders and feeders who remained in the trade increasingly looked for more profitable beasts, which led to a renewed interest in livestock fairs. Under scattered shade trees in Fort Worth in 1896, north Texas cattlemen commenced showing off "fat stock" to each other and to prospective buyers from the packers. The event attracted so many persons that the city of Fort Worth soon undertook sponsorship of the annual Southwestern Exposition and Fat Stock Show, furnishing grounds and eventually building a coliseum for the show's use. About then the International Livestock Exposition commenced in Chicago, and it was followed by the initiation of other important shows in Denver, Houston, Kansas City, and San Francisco. Through such events information about breeds and techniques of husbandry spread among large-scale operators, in the long run resulting in the production of higher-quality slaughter animals.

Even so, it is eminently arguable that the historical cattle ranch in America has received undue attention, then and now. When its star glittered the brightest during the 1880s, large-scale ranching all told accounted for merely 14.4 percent of slaughter-beef production in the United States. In 1880 livestock raisers (small, mostly anonymous diversified farmers) all told owned 51.4

[14]David Gracy II, "A preliminary survey of land colonization in the panhandle-plains of Texas," *The Museum Journal*, Vol. 11 (1969), pp. 60–61.

million cattle, 47.7 million swine, and 35.2 million sheep. Indeed, in that year western ranchers raised many more sheep (7 million) and almost as many swine (2.1 million) as beef cattle (3.8 million). Even in Texas, the very cradle of the ranch-cattle industry, there were four times as many cattle on farms (3.9 million) as on ranches (1 million). Moreover, Texas ranchers owned twice as many sheep (2.1 million) as Longhorns (900,000); however, unlike their contemporaries elsewhere in the West, few Lone Star cattlemen could bring themselves to raise hogs, merely 11,000 of the state's 2.5 million head in 1880 being recorded as "range swine."[15]

Although ranch-cattle production figures are inconsistently broken out of USDA statistics following the turn of the century, it is evident that big operators remained a minority. In 1910 the whole output of the ranching kingdom (Texas, Kansas, Nebraska, Oklahoma, South Dakota, Colorado, New Mexico, Montana, North Dakota, Wyoming, and Idaho, in order of production) amounted to merely 30 percent of American beef-cattle production, down from 39.4 percent in 1900, the largest share ever recorded.

Some of those ranching states and territories (especially Texas and Oklahoma) also contained substantial farm-beef production; moreover, Iowa (the center of the cattle feedlot business since the 1840s) throughout the whole period held as many beef cattle as any ranching state except Texas, and Florida's output consistently surpassed that of the northern mountain states—Idaho, Montana, North Dakota, Wyoming—much of its production coming from tropical grasslands reminiscent of the King Ranch of south Texas. The cattle ranch as a business endeavor was thus significant not for the magnitude of its livestock production but for its control of the land, an appreciating asset. Cattle ranching nevertheless attracted aggressive entrepreneurs and dilettantes, just as it has ever since held historians and popularizers spellbound.

The American farm meanwhile evolved from a subsistence frontier endeavor to an important component in a complex, integrated national economy. Sustained industrial growth between the Civil War and World War I transformed the United States from a sleepy, rural country to a bustling, urbanized nation dependent on an efficient agrarian base to provide foodstuffs inexpensively. In 1860

[15] U.S. Bureau of the Census, *Live stock on rang* (1891), p. 6.

only one American in five lived in a city; in 1900 four of ten were urbanites; and in 1920 slightly more than half lived in urban places.

In 1850 farm output was almost precisely divided between agronomy (50.5 percent) and animal husbandry (49.5 percent). Typical of America's 1.4 million agrarian enterprises was a 202-acre farm yielding an annual income of $549. At the turn of the century, when four times as many farmers produced slightly more than four times the gross agricultural output, the average American farm totaled merely 136.5 acres and yet yielded virtually the same gross annual income ($545 per household) as half a century before, measured in dollars that had appreciated in value by 300 percent during the same period. In 1920 the typical farm contained 147 acres and produced for its owner-operator $1,939 in annual income, as measured in dollars that had depreciated by one-half since the turn of the century. Overall, even with a fluctuating dollar, agriculturalists in 1920 earned 237 percent more than had their counterparts before the Civil War—even though, as measured by parity (an index of prices received and paid by farmers: 1910–14 = 100), net agrarian income had slipped by 11 percent since the end of World War I.

Much of this increased agrarian productivity was due to mechanization—better plows, harrows, reapers, even combustion-powered tractors—but some also accrued with a slight but perceptible shift toward animal husbandry (52.3 percent) and cash crops (47.7 percent). Contributing to larger agrarian revenues was a tilt toward beef-cattle production. In 1850 a typical mix of red-meat animals on American farms amounted to 23 percent neat (domestic) cattle, 48 percent swine, and 29 percent sheep. In 1900 the blend was 38 percent neat cattle, 32 percent swine, and 30 percent sheep; moreover, beef cattle's share of net cattle had increased to 68.2 percent, up from 54.5 percent in 1850. In 1920 the combination was 26.1 percent neat cattle (about half of which was beef cattle), 34.8 percent swine, and 19.1 percent sheep, which reflected an aberrant demand for American pork worldwide that was exacerbated by World War I.

Despite markets that sometimes oscillated wildly in the short run—cattle prices, for example, tumbling 40 percent in one day's frantic trading during the panic of 1873—livestock values during the last half of the nineteenth century remained remarkably stable. In 1850 fat steers brought on average $25 each in New York and, fifty years later, $26.50 in Chicago; in 1850 swine brought $4.80 a head in Cincinnati and in 1900, $5.36 in Chicago; and in 1850 slaughter lambs sold for $2.00 each in Rhode Island and in 1900, $2.97 in Chicago. Values soared early in the twentieth century. In 1910 the USDA calculated the average cow's worth at $24.54, and in 1920, $52.64; swine in 1910, $9.05, and in 1920, $20.00; and in 1910 sheep, $4.06, and in 1920, $10.59.

The boom in beef cattle soon after the Civil War led many midwestern farmers to feed scrub western cattle for the slaughter market. According to historian James W. Whitaker, Illinois farmer John Alexander

> received shipments of Texas cattle numbering from 109 to 600 head every week from May 31 to July 26, 1868. Most came from Cairo, but some were from Abilene, Kans., via Chicago. Alexander paid $35 a head for over 4,000 Texas cattle the next year and after six to nine months of grass and some corn expected to sell them for $70 a head. That he expected a profit of at least $100,000 indicated why many men wanted to process Texas cattle.[16]

Despite initially excellent returns, outbreaks of Texas fever among native cattle soon soured feeders on Longhorns unless they had been wintered on the northern plains and, thus tick-free, posed no danger to domestic livestock. Too, weight gains were not spectacular among either Texas or western cattle, and about 1870, Alexander and other feeders shifted back primarily to native cattle, buying mostly two-year-olds to fatten for as long as two years on grass or grain, whichever offered the greatest return on investment.

As westerners increasingly crossed their livestock with Angus, Hereford, and Shorthorn bulls during the 1880s, a ranch-farm symbiosis evolved. Midwestern feeders bought two-year-old improved range stock (as well as comparable native cattle), which they grain-fed for at least a year. As beef-cattle production was thus homogenized by midwestern feeders, average prices for all slaughter cattle began to slide downward: from $6.25 a hundredweight for 1,200-to-1,500-pound steers in Chicago in 1882 to $5.90 in 1884, to

[16] James Whitaker, *Feedlot empire: beef cattle feeding in Illinois and Iowa, 1840–1900* (1975), p. 58.

$4.70 in 1888, and finally to $3.90 in 1889. Cattle prices did not rebound to above $5.00 until the turn of the century, and they did not surpass record 1865 levels until World War I.

Having remained remarkably constant since the end of the Civil War, cattle prices more than doubled between 1910 and 1920. In 1865 the USDA estimated the average Union cow to be worth $35.57, a price not exceeded until 1914, the first year of World War I in Europe, when quotations reached an average of $38.97. Indeed, for most of the intervening four decades the average price did not even top the more modest 1866 figure of $21.55 a head, which reflected the impact of cheap Texas cattle on the market, save for temporary aberrations between 1869 and 1872, 1883 and 1886, and 1898 and 1901. Prices for the period bottomed at $16.41 in 1891.

Even though few cattle and relatively little fresh beef were exported during World War I—for the domestic livestock industry was hard-pressed to satisfy even domestic demand (the United States being a net importer of beef, most European imports by then originating in Argentina)—live-cattle prices in the United States climbed an unprecedented 71.3 percent, to crest in 1919 at an average of $54.65 a head ($9.97 a hundredweight). Cattlemen received a record 190 percent of parity, closing out the era in 1920 at 170 percent.

Cattle prices were often affected by swine production because beef and pork meet the same needs. Indeed, as the USDA reported in 1889, "a considerable influence [was] exerted upon the demand for beef by the quantity and price of pork products. In other words when the production of pork is abundant and the price low there will be less beef consumed than when these conditions are reversed."[17] Thus American farmers often competed with one another in a red-meat market that was essentially inelastic in the short run, and because mixed farmers frequently raised both beef cattle and swine, ironically they figuratively cut their own throats. Success with one virtually assured the typical farmer of declining revenues with the other.

Like many other activities of the nation's agriculture, swine production was caught up in the great westward movement. During

[17]"The beef supply in the United States and the leading conditions governing the price of cattle," in USDA, *First report of the Secretary of Agriculture* (1889), p. 67.

the late nineteenth century the center for hog raising shifted from the upper Ohio Valley to the grain-belt states of Illinois, Iowa, Kansas, Missouri, and Nebraska. Ohio, Tennessee, Kentucky, Virginia, and the Carolinas—historical centers of hog raising, where animals once had been turned loose to forage in the woods—all declined in swine production, the increase in human population crowding out unpenned porkers. Historian Fred Shannon has observed:

> The Midwest's strong leadership in hogs resulted from its predominance in corn growing. It was more profitable for the farmer to feed his corn and sell the swine. Cattle feeders also learned to keep one hog to fatten on corn that each four cattle wasted. The resulting pork was almost clear profit. Also, it had long been noted that a bushel of corn would put ten or twelve pounds on a pig, so it became a rule that if hogs were selling at five dollars a hundred pounds the grower could afford to feed them fifty-cent corn, or ten-dollar hogs on dollar corn.[18]

According to one report by the USDA's Bureau of Animal Industry, by 1890 pork prices were primarily a function of the corn crop. Empirical data collected over eighteen years showed that "the price of hogs increased with the price of corn without regard to the amount of hog product placed upon the market. After an advance in prices of corn and hogs for a series of years the price of corn dropped one year before the decline came in the price of hogs."[19]

Overall hog prices rose by 550 percent between 1865 and 1920, most of the gain coming in one giant leap during World War I; otherwise prices varied greatly, the American farmer as frequently as not the victim of his own overproduction. To catch a rising market, pig producers often substantially increased their output in a relatively short time by withholding gilts from the slaughter market and breeding them, each sow giving birth to an average litter of eight to twelve sucklings in less than four months and each pig in turn being ready for slaughter or breeding in another six months.

At the end of the Civil War swine prices had crested at $8.86 a head, a figure not bettered until 1910, when auction averages

---

[18]Fred Shannon, *The centennial years* (1967), p. 193.
[19]"Conditions affecting the price of hogs," in USDA, *Report of the Secretary of Agriculture* (1890), p. 101.

reached $9.05 on brisk urban and foreign demand; otherwise, for most of those intervening four decades pig prices had ranged from $4.00 to $6.00 a head, only twice in all those years (in 1903 and 1907) exceeding $7.00. Like cattlemen, hog farmers had suffered the ill effects of the national business cycle. In 1873 slaughter-hog prices dipped 10 percent on the heels of the stock-market panic, and in 1893 prices dropped 5 percent; both declines were the products of economic uncertainty.

Export of American pork and pork-fat products, following a trichinosis scare in the late nineteenth century, climbed to an impressive 1 billion pounds a year by 1914, up from about 600 million at the turn of the century. When European swine herds were decimated by battle and the exigencies of wartime demand, the Allies substantially increased their procurement of American pork, raising the total export to 1.5 billion pounds in 1916. The increased export reduced the size of the swine herd in the United States by 8 percent, to about 60.2 million animals, and bid up wholesale prices by 40 percent, to $11.82, in the process. By the time America entered the war, pork was unquestionably a strategic commodity. Hog prices soon skyrocketed on aberrant demand, average prices vaulting to $10.51 in 1914, $11.82 in 1917, $19.69 in 1919, and, finally, $22.18 in 1920, a record not to be surpassed until the second year of U.S. participation in World War II.

Throughout the whole interwar period sheep, raised mostly for wool, which was in great demand for the booming American textile industry, competed very little with cattle and swine in the red-meat trade, as historically had been the case. In 1899, the first year for which comprehensive government data on civilian food consumption are available, Americans ate 150.7 pounds of red meat per capita (48.1 percent beef, 47.6 percent pork, and 4.3 percent lamb and mutton); in 1910 they consumed 146.4 pounds per capita (53 percent beef, 42.6 percent pork, and 4.4 percent mutton); and in 1920 they ate 136 pounds per capita (49.3 percent beef, 46.7 percent pork, and 4 percent mutton). Indeed, had shepherds not contested cowmen for grass in the West, sheep might well be ignored altogether in this study.

Sheep raisers—either eastern farmers who typically held flocks of fewer than two hundred head or western ranch or range operators with bands of a thousand or more—possessed dual-purpose animals, sometimes selling half or more of their spring lamb crops on the slaughter or feeder markets. Moreover, because the production cycle for sheep (five months of gestation and ten months of feeding for the slaughter market, or eighteen months to sexual maturity) is somewhat shorter than that for cattle but longer than that for swine, sheep raisers less frequently than either cattlemen or pig farmers depressed their inelastic market with substantial overproduction. Sheep prices consequently remained remarkably constant following the Civil War, hovering at about $2.00 a head until the turn of the century, when the demand for wool drove up average prices to around $5.00, slaughter lambs going for $6.00. Prices for both crested on wartime demand in 1918, sheep selling for an average of $10.75 and lambs for $13.96—both records destined to stand until World War II.

Poultry and fish, relatively cheap substitutes for red meat, increasingly competed for the urban consumer's protein dollar. Before the broiler industry emerged during the 1930s, poultry production in the United States was mostly a farm sideline, usually under the supervision of the farmer's wife. Sales consisted of both chickens and eggs, which were collected at assorted rural points and transported to urban poultry houses for distribution.

Refrigerator railroad cars, first available during the 1870s, quickly expanded the poultry and egg business nationally, and it soon became a subsidiary trade of the giant meatpackers. In 1909, the first year for which data are available, America's farms produced 498.1 million chickens (worth forty-four cents each wholesale) and 25.3 billion eggs (for which farmers received an average of twenty cents a dozen). In 1920 farmers raised 514.3 million chickens (worth a record ninety-seven cents each wholesale) and hand-collected 29.7 billion eggs (worth forty-three and a half cents a dozen wholesale, also a record). The fish catch for the entire period is unknown, but between 1880 and 1914 the total commercial yield from the nation's lakes, streams, and coastal waters consistently surpassed 1.4 billion pounds annually, climbing above 2 billion pounds during World War I.

Overall, by 1920, 6.5 million American farmers and ranchers operated on 955.9 million acres in private holdings (402 million in cropland, 328 in pastureland, and the balance in woodlands or other lands for specialized uses). All told, 11.4 million men, women, and children labored in the agrarian work force: 6.5 million owner-operators, 2.3 million wage earners, and 2.6 million unpaid family workers. In 1920 the average farmhand earned $830 a year, which was about 60 percent of the $1,424 average compensation in the United States for all full-time workers in major industries, such as mining (average $1,700), manufacturing ($1,497), construction ($1,924), transportation ($1,721), trade ($1,418), finance ($1,623), service ($1,081), and government ($1,375).

Between 1865 and 1920 livestock raising for the American red-meat trade shrank as a percentage of the nation's gross national product, while meatpacking's share steadily expanded. Toward the end of the 1860s the value of meat-animal production aggregated $1.4 billion and constituted 20.9 percent of the GNP, estimated at $6.7 billion. Counting the then minuscule value added by slaughtering and meatpacking, the entire meat chain's share of the American economy amounted to 22 percent, substantially larger than the share of any other single industry in the United States. By the turn of the century the value of red-meat animal production had doubled, but the entire meat chain's contribution to the GNP (estimated by the government at about $16.8 billion) had decreased to 16.6 percent—livestock, 11.9, and meatpacking, 4.7 percent. In 1920 livestock raising for the meat trade accounted for approximately 8 percent of America's $17.6 billion GNP; meanwhile, meatpacking had continued to increase its relative share, to 10.9 percent of total output, making it larger than any other food-product industry, any individual consumer semidurable good (such as clothing or personal furnishings), or, for that matter, any consumer durable good, including automobiles. Indeed, the American meatpacking industry had grown so huge and powerful that by 1920 it was the principal target of government regulation in the United States.

While the meatpacking industry became increasingly concentrated, a few companies accounting for the vast majority of output, livestock raising became increasingly competitive, in part because federal aid to agriculture throughout the period encouraged greater meat-animal production. First and foremost was the liberalization of land laws. Beginning in 1785 the federal government had steadily made acreage more easily available to settlers, reducing both the price and the size of the cash outlay needed to acquire land directly from the public domain. Even so, the government did not actually

give land away until the Homestead Act (1862), which required
five years' residence, improvements, and a $10.00 filing fee for title
to 160 acres. The law also allowed any settler after six months to
commute his land through preemption by paying $1.25 to $2.50 an
acre for final title. Comparatively few public-domain entries were
filed under the Homestead Act during the Civil War, but immediately thereafter tens of thousands of new acres in the middle-
border region of Iowa, Kansas, Minnesota, and Nebraska quickly
came into production.

Thereafter "free land" lay principally on the forbidding Great
Plains or in the rugged Rocky Mountains, and most settlers were
unprepared for agriculture in the semiarid West. Dryland farming,
punctuated by periodic drouths, proved unreliable: crops often
withered under a blazing sun, and even on the grassy Great Plains
livestock were sometimes forced to walk great distances for grass
merely to survive. In 1880 the government estimated that during
favorable weather periods in the West "one livestock unit" (where,
for grazing-measurement purposes, five sheep equal one cow) required an average of 24.7 acres of land in Texas and 145.7 in Arizona, other plains and mountain states and territories averaging
somewhere in between. Given the constraints of pasturage, a homesteader holding merely 160 acres could run no more than a dozen
cattle or sixty sheep in the unlikely event that he devoted his whole
operation to stock farming. As public land authority Benjamin
Hibbard has noted: "The great weakness of the Homestead Act was,
and is, its utter inadaptability to the parts of the country for which
it was not designed. The idea of the farm small in acres within the
semi-arid regions was tenacious, but untenable. It was even vicious
in its operation." [20]

All told, between 1865 and 1900 homesteaders claimed more
than 180 million acres, most of it in the semiarid West, title to
merely 80 million acres eventually being conveyed to successful
settlers. Between 1865 and 1880 only 4 percent of all filings were
commuted under preemption, but from 1881 to 1904 approximately
22 million acres (about 23 percent of all homesteads) were thus obtained. In North Dakota more public land passed into private hands
through preemption than through final-proof homestead proce-

[20] Hibbard, A history of the public land policies, p. 409.

dures. Acreage was also acquired through the Timber Culture Act (1873), which gave away another 160 acres to each homesteader, provided one-fourth (later one-tenth) was planted in trees. Even though cattle ranchers fraudulently acquired tens of thousands of acres under the law, most of the 11 million acres distributed went to mixed farmers, 70 percent of these filings lying in the Great Plains states of Kansas, Nebraska, and the Dakotas. In Kansas and Nebraska as early as the 1870s, during years of bountiful harvests and low grain prices, primitive commercial feedlots fattened livestock for the national slaughter market. Most feeders were mixed farmers, some of whom bought cheap western cattle and lambs and often hired others to feed the animals. Too, most mixed Great Plains farmers also raised swine, which was fed on assorted farm refuse.

Other federal largess included the Kinkaid Act (1904), applying only to the western panhandle of Nebraska (a desolate land long rejected by homesteaders and preemptors), which gave away whole sections of 640 acres. Within ten years all but a quarter million of the original 7 million available acres had been settled. This success prompted Congress in 1909 to enact the Enlarged Homestead Act, which made it possible for a homesteader to file on 320 acres in nine semiarid western states and territories. By 1912 three more states had been added, making an estimated 193 million acres suitable for disposition under a law that required residence, cultivation of one-fourth of the land, and certification that all of the acreage was unirrigable. In the same year Congress also reduced the residency requirements of all the laws to three years.

Because the preponderance of American farmers practiced mixed agriculture, these giveaways encouraged livestock production as well as crop cultivation. Not so with the Grazing Homestead Act (1916), which was designed specifically to promote animal husbandry. Differing from the Enlarged Homestead Act in that the acreage need not be cultivated, it conveyed to individual stock raisers 640 acres of public land certified by the secretary of the interior as "good only for forage or grazing." Theoretically, timber and mineral lands were excluded from filing, as were water holes and established trails; commutations were forbidden. By 1923, 31.4 million acres of public domain in virtually all the western states and territories excluding Texas had been filed on by livestock raisers under the Grazing Homestead Act.

The government in Washington found other ways to assist various components of the agrarian economy, as in the creation of the Department of Agriculture in 1862. "The newcomer to the administrative scene was unique in more than one respect," public administration authority Leonard White has written. "It was the first client-oriented department; it was firmly based on science; it had a strong sense of mission; and it represented a new set of relations between federal and state governments."[21] Isaac Newton, the first commissioner of agriculture, owed his appointment by Abraham Lincoln to political cronyism and was roundly criticized by the press for flagrant nepotism. Nevertheless, he established the precedent of appointing outstanding scientists to key posts.

Erratic leadership followed Newton's death in 1867. Horace Capron, who served Andrew Johnson, was able but was soon replaced by Ulysses S. Grant's appointee, Frederick Watts, a senile retired judge who personally supervised the tying of seed packets to guarantee that no string was wasted. Rutherford B. Hayes's commissioner, William G. LeDuc, while maintaining the USDA's scientific orientation through superior appointments, feuded continuously on both sides of the aisle in Congress, making few friends for the fledgling department. His successor, George B. Loring, a noted physician-turned-politician who had served two terms in the U.S. House of Representatives, mended most of the ties that LeDuc had severed, and Norman J. Colman, an agricultural journalist who helped write the Hatch Act (1887), which authorized funds for the establishment and partial support of state agricultural experiment stations, succeeded Loring as commissioner and, in the waning days of Grover Cleveland's first term, became the first secretary when the department was finally elevated to cabinet status. Jeremiah Rusk, appointed by Benjamin Harrison, served as secretary of agriculture until his death in 1893. By then the USDA's principal thrusts toward the advancement of agriculture, especially on behalf of the nation's animal industry, were well established.

Beginning in 1865, the USDA issued annual bulletins that included the latest information concerning animal husbandry: breeding information on cattle and swine, rationales for raising sheep for

[21]Leonard White, *The republican era: a study in administrative management* (1958), p. 232.

the mutton market, data on poultry production, and even suggestions for commercial fish farming, along with the latest techniques in agronomy. Also helpful to early livestock raisers in the United States was the USDA's continuous barrage of warnings about a plethora of animal ailments endemic to America. In addition to sporodic articles that began appearing in 1875, the whole *USDA Report* for 1880 was given over to diagnoses, etiologies, and prophylaxes—such as existed—of more than a dozen diseases that each year decimated domestic herds and flocks, including pleuropneumonia (or "lung plague"), Texas (or tick) fever, foot (or hoof)-and-mouth disease, and bronchitis in cattle; cholera, plague, and trichinosis in swine; and cholera in fowls.

Pleuropneumonia, a contagious lung disease that first appeared along the eastern seaboard during the early 1870s, appeared in a shipload of live cattle exported to Great Britain in 1878. Responding to English threats to embargo American livestock, U.S. treasury officials asked exporters to submit to voluntary inspection to secure health certificates for their cattle. Not satisfied, the British government in 1879 ordered all American cattle butchered at the port of debarkation within ten days of arrival, which stifled the English market for American stocker and breeder cattle. In 1881, pressed by cattlemen who feared the loss of substantial overseas markets, Congress appropriated $15,000 with which the treasury secretary was "to procure information concerning and to make inspection of neat cattle shipped from any port in the United States to any foreign ports, so as to enable him to cause to be issued to the shippers of such cattle certificates showing in proper cases that such cattle are free from the disease known as pleuro-pneumonia."[22]

The action was wholly inadequate, even though augmented during succeeding sessions of Congress by larger appropriations (reaching $50,000 annually) and by the creation of a Treasury Cattle Commission, which was charged with inspecting exports and gathering information on the disease. In 1882 the commission asked Congress to broaden its powers to allow it to regulate the interstate transportation of cattle, which it believed would be a more effective method of controlling pleuropneumonia than relying wholly on export regulations. Cattle raisers were of a similar mind. Having found

[22]Quoted in Ernest Osgood, *The day of the cattleman* (1929), p. 167.

that state and local governments either were reluctant to impose effective livestock sanitary regulations on their own breeders or tended to appoint local veterinarians who enforced regulations by whim, in 1883 western ranchers—the most powerful of all livestock raisers—then organizing in Chicago as the National Cattle Growers' Association, responded affirmatively when Commissioner of Agriculture George Loring asked their wishes regarding federal action. Overwhelmingly they favored Washington's involvement in the fight against both pleuropneumonia and Texas fever, and they appointed a legislative committee to consult with both the Treasury Cattle Commission and the USDA to secure from Congress appropriate legislation to control contagious diseases.

Vehemently opposed were south Texans, commission merchants, stockyard companies, and meatpackers, who, according to historian Ernest Staples Osgood, "were of no mind to see the competition between the northern and southern cattle destroyed by an embargo on the latter [because of Texas fever]. Such an eventuality, they feared, would place them at the mercy of the northern stock growers."[23] Voluminous petitions from Chicago, by then the center of American meatpacking, opposed any federal action as an unwelcome intrusion into states' rights. In 1884 the Forty-seventh Congress nevertheless authorized the creation of Bureau of Animal Industry and attached it to the Department of the Treasury; subsequent modifications soon transferred the bureau to the USDA, permitted it to formulate rules and regulations designed to suppress livestock diseases, allowed it to expand funds only in those states and territories that cooperated with its control efforts, and authorized the commissioner of agriculture to ban diseased livestock from interstate commerce. The effectiveness of the measure was significantly diluted when, through the combined efforts of Texans and Chicago lobbyists, "the so-called splenic or Texas fever" was specifically excluded from coverage under the law as a contagious or communicable disease.

Although thwarted, the Bureau of Animal Industry quickly achieved remarkable success under the direction of Dr. D. Elmer Salmon. In 1886 the bureau was authorized to purchase and destroy diseased animals, and Salmon eagerly cooperated with state and

---

[23] Ibid., p. 171.

territorial agencies to locate the focal points of pleuropneumonia, principally east of the Appalachian Mountains. Between 1886 and 1892 the bureau spent $1.5 million buying and destroying sick animals, cremating the remains to prevent sale of the carcasses to "pudding butchers," who sometimes used contaminated meat to make spicy, poisonous sausage. In 1892, Salmon reported that pleuropneumonia had been eradicated in the United States.

By then the legal definition of Texas fever had also been changed, allowing Secretary Rusk in 1889 to quarantine all or parts of fifteen southern states. Bureau scientist Theobald Smith within a year had isolated *Babesia bovis*, the microscopic parasite to which the cattle tick played intermediate host, and two years later USDA veterinarian Victor A. Norgaard showed ranchers gathered in convention in Fort Worth that the ticks died whenever cattle were dipped in a pesticide.

The bureau paid scant attention to trichinosis in swine until 1890, when it was ordered by law to investigate. Widespread crop failures in Europe twenty years before had led to a marked increase in the export of American farm commodities; the value of this international agrarian trade (principally in grain, beef, and pork products) rose to $459 million in 1880, from $233 million in 1874, a sizable increase that had substantially ameliorated the depressed agricultural market in the United States associated with the panic of 1873. By 1880 pork (600 million tons worth $80 million) constituted 10 percent of America's foreign trade, 89 percent of which went to Europe. The market for American pork waned, however, after a University of Vienna professor of anatomy, Richard Heschl, claimed to have found *Trichinella spiralis*, the parasitic nematode worm that causes trichinosis, in 20 percent of the imported hams he randomly inspected. Although Heschl later withdrew his findings as exaggerated, his original report was widely circulated in the European press.

In 1879, after his government verified the presence of *T. spiralis* in some American pork, King Humbert I banned its importation into Italy, an action copied before year's end by royal governments in Greece and Portugal. The Hayes administration vigorously objected, contending that American swine were no more subject to trichinae than were those of any other nation and that actions of Mediterranean monarchs amounted to little more than disguised protectionism. Despite protests and even threats of retaliatory trade restrictions by five successive U.S. presidents by 1891, Austria-Hungary, Denmark, France, Germany, Rumania, Spain, and Turkey had also banned in whole or in part the importation of American pork.

The obvious solution, "a rigid system of inspection of all meat products for foreign export," was called for as early as 1883 by the National Cattle Growers' Association; however, meatpackers objected to federal intrusion into their operations, and in 1890, Bureau of Animal Industry head Salmon publicly doubted that "the people of this country are quite ready to have sanitary laws applied to the eradication of swine disease."[24] Nevertheless, to avoid a trade war with western Europe, the White House pushed through Congress a meat-inspection bill which President Benjamin Harrison signed into law on August 30, 1890. It directed the bureau to conduct microscopic inspection of pork intended for export, authorized the president to ban any contaminated product from international trade, and empowered him to embargo any goods of any foreign nation "which by unjust discrimination" prohibited the importation of American pork. Imperial Germany protested that American inspection was inadequate, for it certified only the final packed product, which was difficult to analyze thoroughly. Congress amended the law the following spring, requiring the bureau to inspect swine at the time of slaughtering, providing the product was intended for export. Satisfied, boycotting Europeans soon dismantled their trade barriers.

Interestingly, pork destined for the domestic market was wholly excluded from coverage under the federal meat-inspection acts of 1890 and 1891. After 1890 the bureau scrutinized both animals and meat products intended for export, commencing slaughterhouse certifications at the Eastman & Co. plant in New York City in the spring of 1891. By year's end the principal meatpackers in Chicago, Kansas City, Milwaukee, Omaha, and Jersey City had also opened their export products to the bureau's scrutiny. Even so, federal meat inspection was inadequate, as the "embalmed beef scandal" of 1898 demonstrated.

[24]Quoted in John Gignilliant, "Pigs, politics, and protection: the European boycott of American pork, 1879–1891," in *Agricultural History*, Vol. 35 (1961), p. 11.

In addition to eradicating pleuropneumonia, controlling Texas fever, and holding its own against trichinosis, the Bureau of Animal Industry investigated numerous other animal ailments. Its scientists experimented with vaccines for tuberculosis and blackleg in cattle and developed a serum for hog cholera which, though imperfect, saved an estimated three-fourths of the swine treated. The effective use of quarantines against pleuropneumonia and Texas fever led the bureau to impose similar regulations regarding other livestock diseases, such as cholera in swine and scabies in sheep. Sheep scab was all but eradicated toward the end of the century, but because of careless handling by herders, it broke out once more during World War I.

Washington's assistance to the livestock industry also came obliquely, as through the Morrill acts (1862 and 1890) and the Hatch Act (1887). The first Morrill act promoted agricultural education by apportioning among the states 30,000 acres of public land for every senator and representative each state had in Congress, proceeds from the sale of which (about $10 million) would endow "agricultural and mechanical colleges" throughout the land. Populous northern states received disproportionately larger shares than rural agrarian states of the South and West. The federal land-grant endowments were also use-restricted (for buildings and equipment), forcing each of the states to shoulder most of the operating costs of vocational education, and, according to agriculture historian Fred Shannon, the first Morrill act "left the way open for an amount of federal meddling far out of proportion to the support granted."[25]

The law nevertheless widely disseminated scientific technology across the land. Before its enactment only Maryland, Michigan, and Pennsylvania had agricultural colleges; by 1900, sixty-four colleges and universities (or branches) in forty-five states and three territories had received land grants with which to promote agriculture. Seventeen states, mostly eastern states such as New York, turned over their shares of the funds to existing state universities, one of which (West Virginia) divided its endowment between two schools, one white and one black. By 1898 thirty-one other states and territories had created new colleges, southern states generally following the West Virginia model of duplicate but hardly equal facilities.

[25] Fred Shannon, *The farmer's last frontier: agriculture, 1860–1897* (1945), p. 274.

As a rule "cow colleges," as they became derisively known, established departments of general agriculture, animal industry, dairy husbandry, and horticulture, as well as experiment stations or farms and extension divisions. The second Morrill act (1890) gave $15,000 (later $25,000) a year to each state to be used exclusively for instruction "in agriculture, the mechanical arts, and the industries of life"; these monies—as much as some rural states had heretofore had received all told from Washington to promote agriculture—addressed some of the inequities of the first act and inspired a proliferation of vocational curricula in American public education.

Moreover, in recognition of the USDA's inability to deal effectively with all varities of agrarian problems, the Hatch Act gave each state and territory $15,000 for the creation of state experiment stations. Typically these agricultural laboratories were created in conjunction with land-grant schools, as at the Agricultural and Mechanical College of Texas, which in 1888 launched research projects into every aspect of the state's varied crops and livestock, the results of which were published regularly.

Large and small livestock raisers alike also asked their government for help with the railroads—as did most other agriculturalists of the era. They believed that they were gouged by common carriers and overwhelmingly advocated passage of the Interstate Commerce Act (1886), which in time allowed regulators to fix freight rates. Ranchers and farmers also complained that the railroads often crowded animals into cattle cars and to maintain schedules or for a variety of other reasons often failed to care adequately for the beasts in their charge. Losses in transit during the last half of the century, which came out of the shipper's pocket, averaged 15 percent. Congress responded in 1873 with legislation theoretically requiring humane handling of livestock in interstate commerce, but the law was so ineffectual that in 1906 Congress enacted the "twenty-eight-hour law" (the limit that interstate livestock shipments could be denied feed or water), which cut losses by two-thirds.

Unintended federal assistance to the livestock raiser could be immediate in its impact and ultimately quite damaging. During World War I, the Food Administration—headed by Herbert Hoover and charged by Congress with increasing the production of strategic commodities (such as pork), restraining domestic consumption so that more products might be diverted to the war effort, and, insofar as possible, stabilizing prices—used a variety of ploys to affect the red-meat supply. Appealing to patriotism, the agency urged Americans to observe "meatless Tuesdays, wheatless Wednesdays," and the like. Civilian consumption of red meat declined by about 4 percent (from 140.1 pounds per capita in 1916 to 135.3 in 1917), most of that forgone pork, the consumption of which decreased by an impressive 20 percent. Thus prices were somewhat constrained. Although the agency was powerless to fix retail prices, it did suspend trading in some commodity futures, such as red meat, for the duration of the war to prevent speculation. Moreover, granted substantial latitude by wartime legislation in dealing with the principal interstate meatpackers, the Food Administration limited processors' markups to 9 percent of operating costs (or about 2.5 percent of sales), which, as federal investigations later disclosed, afforded the big packers a respectable 5.6 percent return on capital investment.

Even so, wholesale and retail meat prices doubled during the war, in no small part because of price guarantees to farmers by the Food Administration. Well aware that little could be done quickly to increase the size of the nation's cattle herd, the agency concentrated instead on swine, with their one-year production cycle. Offering farmers at least $15.50 a hundredweight (or a minimum price equal to a ratio of 13 to 1 on the average price of feed corn) for their entire hog output in 1918, the Food Administration induced an orgy in the barnyard. The national swine herd swelled to 64.3 million head by 1919, despite a simultaneous 15 percent increase in the slaughter rate in 1918 (65.1 million head) to accommodate foreign demand, which by then had doubled to 2.9 billion pounds of pork and pork-fat products. The boom busted abruptly at war's end, and exports shrank to fewer than 800 million pounds in 1921. The price of pigs, having crested at $16.69 a hundredweight in 1920, plummeted to $7.63 in 1921, when federal price guarantees were withdrawn.

Government involvement in the marketplace often brought countervailing consequences. While assistance to agriculture was intended to raise farmers' and stock raisers' income, larger yields inevitably depressed commodity prices, reducing agrarian revenues in the process. New farmlands brought into production through the Homestead Act and other largess resulted in widespread overproduction, which, along with an imperfect market in agriculture, contributed to declines in farm prices between 1870 and 1900: wheat by 40 percent, corn by 25 percent, cotton by 60 percent, and livestock by 35 percent. Moreover, the value of money had appreciated enormously since the Civil War, the purchasing power of the 1900 dollar being three times that of 1865. For the debtor, such as an American farmer who regularly was forced to borrow to buy land, implements, seed, and livestock, "the unreasonable high interest rates usually exacted . . . [meant that the farmer] was paying what would have amounted to about a twenty or twenty-five per cent rate of interest on a non-appreciating dollar." [26]

Farmers were victims of a dynamic economy. Between 1865 and 1920 the American red-meat chain was thoroughly integrated nationally by the simultaneous development of interconnecting transportation systems (first the railroads, then trucking) and giant meatpacking companies. Spectacular railroad expansion in the United States (30,626 miles of track in 1860 and 193,346 in 1900) homogenized the market for livestock nationally, allowing for the creation of ten principal livestock markets (Chicago, established in 1865; Kansas City, 1871; St. Louis, 1872; Omaha, 1884; Denver, 1886; Sioux City, 1887; St. Joseph, 1893; Wichita, 1893; and Fort Worth, 1902). These proved to be constriction points affording advantage to relatively few buyers, as a government investigation eventually showed. Inevitably sellers (literally millions of farmers and ranchers) became price takers in a classic example of an oligopsonistic market, that is, a market in which a handful of buyers (in this instance fewer than a thousand packers nationwide), in collusion or not, set prices.

Large and small livestock raisers alike blamed meatpackers for most of their economic ills, real and imagined. Federal investigations eventually disclosed that either grain or livestock could be shipped cheaper from Chicago to Liverpool, England, than from Iowa farms to processing points in Minneapolis or Chicago. Grain elevators and stockyards, which constituted local or regional monopolies, also allegedly exploited the farmer by fixing prices. Following World War I the Federal Trade Commission charged that since the middle 1880s the "beef trust" had systematically conspired

[26] John Hicks, *The populist revolt: a history of the Farmers' Alliance and the People's Party* (1931), pp. 89–90.

to "manipulate livestock markets; restrict interstate and international supplies of food; control the prices of dress meats and other foods; defraud both the producers of food and consumers; crush effective competition; secure special privileges from railroads, stockyard companies, and municipalities; and profiteer."[27]

Livestock raisers had long been convinced that they were victims of the beef trust. In 1883 the big-rancher-dominated National Cattle Growers' Association advocated federal control of the meatpackers, and, according to the FTC, much of the original impetus for antitrust legislation in Congress originated with the cattlemen's discontent with being price takers in the marketplace. Contemporary mixed farmers, who produced most of America's red-meat animals, just as readily had gravitated toward the People's (Populist) party, which openly advocated solutions far more radical than mere antitrust legislation to solve the monopoly problem in the United States.

[27]U.S. Federal Trade Commission, *Report on the meat-packing industry: summary and part I* (1919), pp. 32–33.

4

Age of Change, 1865–1920: Meatpacking

Between the Civil War and World War I, that period historians are fond of calling the "age of enterprise," the United States metamorphosed from a backward rural country into the globe's leading industrial giant, and meatpacking underwent stupendous change. Technology transformed it from the localized, seasonal endeavor of a couple hundred small businessmen into a year-round, fast-paced, nationally integrated commodity supply system dominated by five giant companies commonly called the "beef trust." The growth and development of American meatpacking in little more than half a century was nothing short of phenomenal. In 1850, 185 establishments nationwide prepared $12 million worth of red meat; in 1919, 1,304 plants produced $4.2 billion worth, measured in dollars that had appreciated in value by one-third. By then American meatpacking was among the nation's largest contributors to the gross national product, only recently having been surpassed by the automobile industry as America's largest employer.

From the Civil War to 1879, as the demand for beefsteak increased in America's cities, western meatpackers searched for a practical refrigerator car with which to tap that lucrative market. Using the refrigerator car between 1879 and 1886, a half-dozen firms developed intricate distribution systems stretching from midwestern packing plants to most eastern cities, and between 1886 and 1920 they came to dominate the whole red-meat trade, a controversial position that inevitably led to government regulation.

Meatpacking remained a mostly seasonal endeavor until well after the Civil War, as it had been since the days of William Pynchon in the middle of the seventeenth century. Nature continued to be the packer's icebox, meat (especially pork) being cured in assorted western cities (Cincinnati, Chicago, and St. Louis) during the winter and shipped eastward during the cold months to prevent spoilage. As late as 1880 most slaughter cattle were disbursed in relatively small lots to wholesale butchers nationwide for the fresh-beef trade.

Rapid postwar railroad expansion and complementary developments in refrigeration technology prompted change. In 1865 the United States contained approximately 35,000 miles of railroad track. By 1880, 93,000 miles of track connected rural western livestock supplies with assorted markets, including both the fast-growing eastern fresh-beef trade and midwestern pork packers. As the pace of rail laying accelerated—to 193,000 miles of track by 1900 and 254,000 miles by World War I, thereby effectively tying the nation together—practical refrigerator car designs became increasingly available, allowing midwestern meatpackers to enter the lucrative East Coast fresh-beef trade.

Primitive refrigerator cars, merely ordinary boxcars insulated with sawdust and packed with block ice, had first appeared in New York in 1851 to carry dairy products. In 1861 a similar "sweat box" hauled fresh meat between Chicago and New York. "Certainly the temperature could not have been very low," observed industry authority Rudolf Clemen, "and no circulation of air was provided."[1] The meat was placed directly on the ice, which discolored it, and much of the product was putrid upon arrival. The first American refrigerator-car patent was awarded in 1867, but the design was inefficient because the vehicle could be iced only when it was empty, and it provided no internal air circulation. Better models followed, culminating in 1879 with the Swift-Chase car, which featured externally accessible ice bunkers and a forced-air circulation system.

Even before the refrigerator car was perfected, several entrepreneurs tested the market for fresh western beef on the East Coast. Notable among these was Detroit meatpacker George H. Hammond, who in 1869 successfully hauled dressed beef in primitive refrigerator cars to Boston wholesale-meat merchants. Encouraged by the results, Hammond bought several cars and began seasonal shipments to New England jobbers, sometimes delivering

[1] Rudolf Clemen, *The American livestock and meat industry* (1923), p. 215.

spoiled meat even during the winter months. In 1871 he built a second packing plant in Indiana, just across the state line from Chicago's Union Stock Yards, near an ample supply of slaughter beeves, and beside an ice-harvesting plant. Several independent wholesalers from Boston to Hartford were soon distributing Hammond's dressed beef, a novelty as late as 1874 which sold at a premium of two cents a pound over locally butchered meat. The business expanded, and in 1875, the sales of the George H. Hammond Co. totaled $2 million, up from $1 million two years before.

Hammond's success attracted competition. In 1872, Thomas Rankin tried to organize the Refrigerator Cars Quick Transit Meat Company to ship dressed beef from a proposed north Texas meatpacking plant to New York City, but he failed to attract investors. In 1874, Chicago pork packer and livestock dealer Nelson Morris commenced winter shipments of frozen beef in ordinary boxcars, and in the fall of 1875, Nofsinger & Company of Kansas City dispatched two carloads of western beef to Philadelphia and Boston but priced their product too high to generate much demand.

More successful was New York meat wholesaler T. C. Eastman. He secured patent rights to the Bates refrigeration process (an airtight chamber with a steam-powered blower), installed it on a North Atlantic freighter, and in 1875 successfully shipped dressed beef to England. Within two years he had equipped three steamship lines (Anchor, White Star, and Williams & Gueton) with cold-storage units; organized Eastman's Ltd. of London to distribute the meat to retail butchers throughout England, Ireland, and Scotland; and was shipping four thousand carcasses a week. According to economic historian Mary Yeager, "The savings as well as profits were enormous. A live steer cost £8 10s. to send from New York City to London in 1878, as opposed to 30s. dressed. It cost Eastman about $26 per head for preparation, freight, and cost of transit, including commissions to agents on the other side. The average price realized was about $90, netting him roughly $64 a head!"[2]

Such profit potentials lured others into a dressed-beef trade. During the winter of 1875–76, hoping to eliminate "the waste of shipping the whole animal east instead of shipping only the parts

[2] Mary Yeager, *Competition and regulation: the development of oligopoly in the meat industry* (1981), p. 54.

which were needed there,"[3] Boston meat merchant Gustavus Swift purchased several carloads of dressed-beef carcasses from George Hammond's Detroit plant and transported them over Canada's Grand Trunk Railroad to his brother Edwin's butcher shop in Clinton, Massachusetts, and to his own wholesale facility, Hathaway & Swift, in Boston. Their returns were so good that in 1877 the Swift brothers opened their own packing plant in Chicago—already the locus of the American livestock market and quickly becoming a center of pork packing as well—rented the few available common-carrier refrigerator cars, and began regular shipments eastward. In 1878, Gustavus Swift hired Boston engineer Andrew Chase to improve on existing refrigerator-car design, and the following year they patented the Swift-Chase car, which set the standard for refrigerator-car efficiency.

Lacking sufficient resources to manufacture the cars, Swift tried without success to interest several railroads. Carriers were concentrating on general-service fleets (boxcars, flatcars, gondolas, and the like) and left exotic rolling stock to private-car lines. Moreover, since the Civil War, members of the Eastern Trunkline Association, a "pool" among key railroads, had invested substantially in livestock cars as part of their "evener system" that shared the ever-increasing volume of slaughter beeves supplied by western ranchers and farmers to eastern urban markets. None saw logic in investing in expensive refrigerator cars that might undercut their receipts from livestock traffic. Indeed, for a time William Vanderbilt, of the New York Central Railroad, which handled Hammond's cars, refused to couple onto any other private cars.

Gustavus Swift consequently mortgaged all his personal property and had ten cars custom-built by the Michigan Car Co. He also persuaded Canada's Grand Trunk Railroad, which carried very little livestock, to haul his cars around Vanderbilt to customers in New England and signed contracts with ice harvesters all along the Great Lakes to ensure adequate supplies in transit. Although Swift was later sued by George Hammond for alleged patent infringements (a case Swift eventually won) and even though he appeared to be forestalled by Vanderbilt's boycott from more general distribution, he

---

[3] Louis Swift and Arthur Van Vlissingen, Jr., *The Yankee of the yards: the biography of Gustavus Franklin Swift* (1927), pp. 8, 130.

nevertheless quickly expanded to become the nation's largest domestic supplier of dressed beef. Swift Refrigerator Transportation Co. was operating year round.

By slaughtering in Chicago, Swift avoided shipping the 60 percent of a steer that was either waste or inedible by-product. Because he could ship three dressed carcasses for what it cost to ship one live steer, he undercut eastern slaughterhouses by as much as seventy-five cents a hundredweight. According to Rudolf Clemen, Gustavus Swift and his brothers "spent much time visiting local slaughterhouses and butchers throughout the East, urging them to give western dressed beef a trial. At the same time G. F. Swift's policy was not combative, but co-operative. He still shipped live cattle, even sending to those who also handled some of his dressed beef."[4] Swift often formed partnerships with local meat dealers, thereby providing himself with eastern outlets with minimal conflict. When local cooperation "was not forthcoming, Swift hired a salaried manager to distribute meats directly from the railroad car," Yeager says. "If necessary, he applied stronger pressure by lowering prices and forcing the wholesaler to capitulate."[5] In Fitchburg, Massachusetts, Swift crushed Lowe and Sons, hired the elder Lowe to distribute his meat in Massachusetts, and employed the sons to work in his Chicago packing plant. By 1883, Swift had thus gained direct access to urban markets from Boston to Washington, D.C.

As the dressed-beef trade expanded, it quickly outgrew the distribution capacity of independent wholesale grocers, and branch-house systems and refrigerator-car routes soon evolved. Armour & Co., a Chicago pork packer that had entered the dressed-beef business in 1882, was already using branch houses to distribute processed meats, and it adapted the concept to fresh beef by building large cold-storage facilities at key locales. This proved to be an efficient manner of organizing national sales and distribution systems, and by 1889 the five largest American meatpackers operated 544 branch houses nationwide, and by 1916, about 1,000.

While branch houses adequately served densely populated urban places, they were impractical for most small cities and towns or for remote rural areas. Again, Armour & Co. led the way. In the

---

[4] Clemen, *The American livestock and meat industry*, p. 235.
[5] Yeager, *Competition and regulation*, p. 60.

middle 1880s it had dispatched a salesman with a carload of hams and lard, which he peddled to rural grocers at each whistle-stop. "Peddler-car" service for dressed beef followed but was sporadic until 1887, when Armour established two regular car routes through rural Indiana, Minnesota, and Wisconsin. Other packers soon recognized the peddler cars as a practical method of expanding their markets, and by World War I an estimated 16,000 small American towns and cities in a dozen states were regularly served by refrigerator-car routes. Not until the end of World War I did trucks emerge as versatile alternatives to the railroads. In 1919, Detroit's Sullivan Packing Co. hauled fresh meat to Toledo in six hours instead of two and a half days by rail. Crude ice-refrigerated long-haul trucks soon appeared.

Many interests opposed such innovations in the red-meat trade. The Eastern Trunkline Association, for example, had readily understood the challenge to profits represented by the rapidly expanding dressed-beef industry, and in 1881, to protect cooperating railroads' mutually high fixed-cost investment in livestock cars and stockyards, as well as the differential in earnings between hauling more weight on the hoof than on the hook, it "attempted to fix the [freight] rate for dressed beef at a certain percentage above that of livestock, basing the percentage on the cost advantages of dressed beef."[6] The agreement soon disintegrated because noncooperating railroads, such as the Grand Trunk of Canada—and even some Eastern Trunkline pool members, such as Vanderbilt's New York Central—sometimes secretly gave preferential rates or rebates to Swift and Hammond, as well as to newcomers Armour and Morris, on the theory that some revenues from these shippers were better than none.

The National Cattle Growers' Association and the National Butcher Protective Association, both of which had vested interests in the broadest possible continuation of livestock shipments, lobbied for solutions more radical than discriminatory freight rates against the fresh-beef shippers. At the behest of affected citizens nineteen states and territories even considered banning the importation of dressed beef altogether. Four states—Colorado, Indiana, Minnesota, and New Mexico—actually enacted such restrictions.

[6]Ibid., p. 92.

In 1886 the U.S. Supreme Court struck down the Minnesota law as an unconstitutional infringement on federal interstate commerce powers, thereby granting the "Big Four" (as Armour, Hammond, Morris, and Swift were already known) unrestricted access to local markets.

The interests of the packers were also furthered by passage of the Interstate Commerce Act (1887), which established the Interstate Commerce Commission and outlawed pooling agreements, such as the Eastern Trunkline Association's evener system, as well as the payment (though not the receipt) of rebates. "By outlawing railroad pools and prescribing rules for the railroads without placing any constraint on shippers," wrote Mary Yeager, the ICC "exacerbated competition among the railroads and made them even more vulnerable to demands of large shippers, especially those like Armour and Swift who also owned their own cars."[7]

In 1886 the "large shippers" were the Big Four. Swift & Co., the largest (with 31 percent of Chicago's entire output, or about 3 percent of all American fresh-beef production), had grown steadily since the Swift brothers had entered the dressed-beef trade in 1875. By then their thrice-expanded Chicago plant processed three thousand carcasses a week; the meat was sold and distributed principally through two dozen branch houses, mostly along the eastern seaboard. The branches were regularly supplied by four hundred company refrigerator cars. By then the brothers had also installed expensive refrigeration equipment on twenty North Atlantic freighters to follow Eastman into the export trade. In 1883, debt-ridden to finance rapid expansion, as well as a substantial inventory of perishable product, the Swifts incorporated to secure the protection of limited liability. Gustavus became president and chief executive and operating officer. At first the company's wholesale beef prices were determined by supply and demand, but as its structure became more complex, it calculated average costs and priced its products accordingly, a technique copied by the other big meatpackers and made practical, the government eventually charged, by conspiracy among them.

Philip and Simeon Armour, who had followed the Swifts into the business in 1882, were the most aggressive of the new beef provi-

[7] Ibid., p. 104.

sioners. They incorporated in 1884 to expedite the consolidation of their separate holdings. By 1886, Armour & Co. accounted for 24 percent of the Chicago output, or about 1.5 percent of the national total. Building on experiences in pork—in which the need to control the whole process had already caused packers to absorb independent slaughterhouses and by-product producers—the firm led the industry in vertical integration. As mentioned earlier, Armour pioneered the development of branch houses and peddler cars, which greatly expanded sales and distribution. By 1886 the company maintained six branches in New York and operated a fleet of three hundred refrigerator cars nationwide. Armour also bought the Wahl Brothers' glue factory in Albany, New York, and hired a chemist to devise economical means of reclaiming value from assorted packinghouse wastes. Thus evolved soap works, fertilizer works, and other profitable subsidiaries designed to turn animal remains into everything from "acid phosphate to . . . violin strings. . . ."[8]

Armour was also the first dressed-beef firm to expand out of Chicago, erecting a facility beside its Kansas City pork plant in 1884 to capitalize on an abundant supply of cheap western beeves. Moreover, Armour could ship three carcasses to the East Coast for the cost of transporting one live steer to Chicago. Swift arrived in 1888, Schwarschild & Sulzberger (S&S, later Wilson & Co., Inc.) in 1893, Morris and Cudahy Brothers Co. in 1900, and National Packing Co. in 1903. Similar scenes unfolded throughout the livestock-rich Midwest and Great Plains, beginning with Cudahy in Omaha in 1887, Swift in St. Louis and Cudahy in Sioux City in 1892, Morris in St. Joseph and Swift in St. Paul in 1897, Cudahy in Wichita in 1900, Swift in Fort Worth in 1902, and National in Denver in 1903. As often as not they were lured west by civic boosters who gave the packers free shares in local stockyards and tax abatements.

Livestock dealer and pork packer Nelson Morris had followed Swift and Armour into the dressed-beef trade in 1884 and within two years was Chicago's third largest fresh-beef producer, with 17 percent of the city's output. Once an "evener" for Daniel Drew's Erie Railroad, Morris became perhaps the red-meat trade's most diversified participant ever. Not only did he acquire transport and

[8]FTC, *Report on the meat-packing industry: summary and part I*, pp. 96–102.

peddler cars, establish branch houses, and render by-products, but he ranched in Texas, operated a stock farm in Nebraska, and finish-fed both cattle and swine on distillery mash in Illinois.

The George H. Hammond Co. of Indiana, whose shipments of western beef to Boston in 1869 had created the dressed-beef trade, by 1886 was merely the fourth-largest beef processor in the Chicago market, with 14 percent of the metropolitan output. Like its com-petitors Hammond integrated its operations both backward toward supply and forward toward the consumer, but after founder George Hammond died, the company was acquired by foreign interests that directed it to concentrate on the export market. In 1901, Armour & Co. acquired the whole Hammond operation.

Market entry was difficult for newcomers. In 1884 the Span-iard Antonio de Vallombrosa, the Marquis de Morés, who ranched in the Dakotas, organized the Northern Pacific Refrigerator Co. to process beef even closer to supply to cut transportation costs fur-ther. The firm's facility in Medora, Dakota Territory, with a daily capacity of seven hundred cattle, was the largest plant west of Chi-cago, but the supply of slaughter beeves proved unreliable for year-round operation. Moreover, Vallombrosa failed to establish a net-work of independent retailers to handle his product, leaving him at the mercy of the Big Four, who froze him out of the marketplace. As already mentioned, the American Beef Trust Co., a coalition of western ranchers, also tried to enter the dressed-beef trade, but its lack of an effective distribution system rendered it helpless in com-petition with the "beef trust." Market entry was not impossible for well-financed interests that understood the red-meat trade. In the late 1880s two midwestern pork packers, Cudahy Packing Co. and Schwarschild & Sulzberger, added dressed-beef departments, and during the 1890s their market shares grew appreciably.

By World War I only one of America's twelve largest meatpack-ing centers, New York, ranked fifth by volume, lay east of the Ap-palachian Mountains. Chicago, the nation's largest producer of red meat, was followed closely by Kansas City and Omaha in total beef output and was surpassed by them in pork production. All the cen-ters—Chicago, Kansas City, Omaha, St. Louis, New York City, St. Joseph, Fort Worth, St. Paul, Sioux City, Oklahoma City, Denver, and Wichita, in order of size—were dominated by the now Big Five meatpackers (Swift, Armour, Morris, Cudahy, and S&S), ranging from a low of 50 percent of pork packing in Wichita to 100 percent of beef, pork, and lamb in numerous other cities. While the United States counted more than a thousand meatpackers nationwide, the Big Five (the beef trust) dominated the industry, aggregating two-thirds of its fresh-beef output and about half of all its total red-meat production. In New York City, for example, they controlled 97.7 percent of fresh-beef distribution.

One contemporary federal investigation of the American red-meat trade noted that since 1886 there had been

> an agreement between the then leading packers, namely Armour & Co., Swift & Co., Nelson Morris & Co., [and] Hammond & Co., to refrain from competition, . . . that there was collusion with regard to the fixing of prices and the division of territory and business. The conditions revealed by [the *Vest Report*, a detailed congressional] investigation of [the enterprise, including the alleged beef trust], it may be remarked, were in part responsible for the passage of the Sherman Antitrust Act on July 2, 1890.[9]

Even so the new law—an expression of Populist antimonopoly sentiment that made illegal "every contract, combination in the form of a trust or otherwise, or conspiracy in restraint of trade"—for a time had virtually no impact on the collusion in the red-meat trade.

In 1886, along with Chicago pork packer Samuel Allerton, Armour, Hammond, Morris, and Swift had apportioned among themselves the whole northeastern United States, where each had extensive marketing outlets—and where the market had "filled up" first. They devised crude formulas for uniform profit margins, used common price lists to bid for cattle, and oftentimes applied their collective might to compel retailers to accept their products in lieu of those of rivals that were not part of the "Allerton Pool." In 1892, when most southeastern and midwestern markets were also saturated by branch houses and through peddler cars, cooperating packers extended the agreement to all southern and border states east of the Mississippi River. Then, on the eve of the panic of 1893, Cudahy entered the market aggressively, triggering a price war. Burdened with a hefty debt to finance rapid expansion, Swift almost

[9] Ibid., p. 46.

folded. To survive, it slashed wages 10 percent, engendering much labor ire.

A new pool, expanded to include Cudahy, commenced in May, 1893. Government investigations eventually disclosed that representatives of the Big Five

> met regularly [in Chicago] in a suite of rooms leased in the name of Henry Veeder [an attorney and the son of Swift executive Albert Veeder], who acted as secretary and statistician of these meetings. . . . rent for these rooms and other expenses connected with these meetings were apportioned among the packers in proportion to their shipments of dressed beef. At these meetings the territory was divided and the volume of business to be done by each packer was apportioned upon the basis of statistics compiled by Veeder, penalties being levied when one of them exceeded his allotment in any territory.[10]

While the pool discontinued formal meetings in 1896, Veeder continued to act as agent of the Big Five, which expanded to Six in 1898, when S&S was added to the conspiracy, and shrank to Five once more when Armour & Co. acquired Hammond in 1901. This clandestine association seemingly disintegrated in 1902, when the U.S. Department of Justice filed sweeping charges of conspiracy and restraint of trade against members of the "Veeder Pool." When the allegations were not specifically controverted by the packers, the U.S. Supreme Court issued a permanent injunction against the pool on May 26, 1903.

About then Armour, Morris, and Swift jointly created the National Packing Co., which was intended as a step beyond the Veeder Pool. At the outset National's holdings were considerable, with an estimated $15 million in assets transferred to it by its cooperating owners (Fowler Packing interests, Friedman Manufacturing, G. H. Hammond operations, Anglo-American Provision, United Dressed Beef, Ruddy Brothers, St. Louis Dressed Beef & Provision, Sturtevant & Haley, Continental Packing, Omaha Packing, and Stock Yards Warehouse). On its own National soon acquired large and small food-related firms: in 1904, *Provision Dealers Dispatch*, Atlantic Dairy Express, German-American Provision Co., National Car

---

[10] Ibid., pp. 46–47.

Lines Co. of New Jersey, and Anglo-American Refrigerator Car Co. of Illinois; in 1905, Milwaukee Stockyards Co., North American Provision Co., Hamilton (Ontario) Stockyards Co., Ltd., Planking-ton Packing Co. (Milwaukee), and Denver Union Stockyards Co., and 60 percent interests in Colorado Packing & Provision Co. and Western Packing Co.; in 1906, 90 percent of Smith Brothers, the remaining 40 percent of Colorado Packing & Provision, 75 per-cent of Union Rendering, and all of Northwestern Glue; in 1907, through secret purchases by Frederick Joseph of S&S, the partial ac-quisition of New York Butchers Dressed Meat Co. ("a concern orga-nized by the butchers of that city to protect them[selves] against the [beef trust] combination"[11]); in 1909, the remaining 40 percent of Western Packing, all of La Blanca (a Buenos Aires, Argentina, slaughterhouse); in 1910, Northern Reduction Co.; and in 1911 Record Stockman Publishing Co. of Denver. In an *Everybody's Magazine* series entitled "The Greatest Trust in the World," pub-lished in 1905 (and compiled the following year into a best-selling book under that title), muckraker Charles Edward Russell pointed to National Packing Co. as proof that the big meatpackers were combining in a way "that promises greater fortunes and greater power than ten Standard Oil Companies. Reaching out, absorbing industry after industry, augmenting and building, by great brute strength and by insidious, intricate, hardly discoverable windings and turnings, day and night this monstrous thing grows and strength-ens until its grip is at the nation's throat."[12]

In the waning days of the Theodore Roosevelt administration the U.S. Department of Justice launched an investigation of meat-packing. Criminal indictments against National and ten of its sub-sidiaries were handed down on March 21, 1909, under provisions of the Sherman Antitrust Act; however, Federal Judge Kennesaw Mountain Landis quashed the indictment because the statute of limitations protected packers up to 1905 and because much of the government's case thereafter rested on inferences drawn from prior evidence. The Department of Justice consequently contemplated filing civil proceedings to seek National's dissolution, but largely be-cause of the lingering notoriety from Russell's allegations and from

[11] Ibid., pp. 246–47.
[12] Charles Russell, *The greatest trust in the world* (1905), p. 5.

the virtually simultaneous publication of Upton Sinclair's sensational book *The Jungle* (1906), the government instead strengthened its evidence and refiled criminal charges, this time against Louis Swift, J. Ogden Armour, Edward Morris, their National Packing Co., and its many subsidiaries.

The government alleged that National Packing was little different from the Veeder Pool, which the court had ordered dissolved in 1903, and that Louis Swift and the others, through National, engaged in collusion by refusing to bid against one another in wholesale livestock markets and thereby fixing market prices, by maintaining cartellike quotas for market division among participating firms, and by fixing wholesale prices for all classes of fresh meat. At about the same time as the beef-trust case the Supreme Court had applied the "rule of reason" in antitrust proceedings against Standard Oil, deciding that the petroleum monopoly was indeed an "unreasonable restraint of trade" within the meaning of the Sherman Act. That doctrine was injected into *Louis Swift et al.* v. *U.S.* Barred by Judge Landis's ruling from introducing evidence of the packers' misconduct before 1905 and held to the rule of reason as a test of "good trust, or bad," the prosecution failed to persuade a jury, which acquitted the defendants of all charges on March 26, 1912.

Before that decision, however, Armour, Morris, and Swift had jointly approached Attorney General G. W. Wickersham about dissolving National Packing Co. to avoid further litigation. Soon after it lost *Louis Swift et al.* v. *U.S.*, the Department of Justice agreed to voluntary division of National among the Armour, Morris, and Swift companies according to equity interests. Wrote Eliot Jones in 1921: "Notwithstanding the claim of the Department of Justice that the dissolution of National Packing Company accomplished a substantial restoration of competitive conditions, the outcome of a large number of suits and the facts brought to light in later investigations, notably those of the Federal Trade Commission, made it clear that the activity of the government had availed comparatively little."[13]

Indeed, federal investigations eventually disclosed that by World War I two or more of the Big Five held joint interests in 117 corporations: 8 livestock loan companies scattered about the na-

---

[13] Eliot Jones, *The trust problem in the United States* (1921), p. 486.

tion; 7 market publications specializing in livestock or meat news; 5 terminal railroads at major stockyards; 2 other railroads; 18 stockyards stretching from Brighton, Massachusetts, to San Francisco; 22 banks with total resources of $979 million; 6 domestic and 2 foreign packing plants; 5 packing-machinery supply firms; 2 cottonseed-oil companies; 3 cold-storage warehouses; 1 foreign and 12 domestic rendering plants; 9 land-development companies; 8 public utilities; 6 miscellaneous businesses ranging from an auditing firm to a sand-and-gravel company; and 1 creamery-butter and cheese factory.

Individual Big Five firms separately held controlling interests in 564 domestic and foreign enterprises: cattle ranches, stockyards, packing and rendering plants, railroads, private-car lines, cold-storage warehouses, and other food-related enterprises such as poultry and egg operations, creameries and dairies, fish canneries, oleo-margarine plants, and pineapple plantations, as well as unrelated banks, publishing companies, sporting-goods manufacturers, and a plumbing shop. The Big Five also separately or collectively held substantial minority interests in another 145 businesses (banks, stockyards, railroads, packing and rendering plants, and the like), totaling an estimated $5 billion in assets.

Even so, a "beef trust" existed in the United States only in the broadest sense of the term. A trust, actually an intermediary holding device originally employed by the Standard Oil Co. in the 1880s to circumvent Ohio laws that forbade its chartered companies from owing or being owned by alien (out-of-state) corporations, the term in America came to mean an industrial monopoly. According to economist Eliot Jones, "A trust (industrial monopoly) may be said to exist when a person, corporation, or combination owns or controls enough of the plants producing a certain article to be able for all practical purposes to fix its price." [14] The Federal Trade Commission reported that "in 1916 the Big Five's percentage of interstate slaughter, including subsidiary and affiliated companies, was as follows: cattle 82.2, calves 76.6, hogs 61.2, [and] sheep and lambs 86.4." [15] The Big Five's combined position was indeed adequate for control, which, the government repeatedly contended, they exercised.

[14] Ibid., p. 1.
[15] FTC, *Report on the meat-packing industry*, p. 33.

Unlike Standard Oil, the big meatpackers—Armour, Hammond, Morris, Swift, and later Cudahy and S&S—for the most part retained their separate corporate identities, limiting their cooperation principally to pooling agreements such as the several accords reached between 1886 and 1901. Between 1902 and 1912 they came closest to outright merger in the manner of Standard Oil and other contemporary trusts when Armour, Morris, and Swift operated National Packing Co., into which they had transferred some wholly owned subsidiaries, but it does not appear that they seriously considered making National the holding-company apparatus for all their combined interests in the way that Standard Oil Company of New Jersey for a time consolidated the Rockefeller interests.

Clearly, as economic historian Mary Yeager has written, the industry constituted an oligopoly, that is, a marketplace of many buyers (in this instance millions of consumers) dominated by a few sellers (five principal meatpackers), and the oligopoly (in this instance the beef trust) could and did fix prices. Indeed, Yeager added, "Prices came to be set or 'administered,' as a function of costs rather than merely of market forces, so that whether cooperation was achieved through explicit agreement, tacit understanding, or simply custom, the results were similar: the achievement of relatively stable market shares and prices. . . ."[16]

Although doubtless accurate, Yeager's analysis is incomplete, for the beef trust was also an oligopsony, that is, a marketplace of many sellers (in this instance millions of livestock producers) dominated by a few buyers (the beef trust), which similarly affected price control. In a 1940 study conducted at the behest of Congress, economist Clair Wilcox declared:

> Market sharing, either by agreement or by convention, has existed in the meat industry for many years. Between 1885 and 1902, price and production agreements ruled the trade. The packers acted together to depress the price of livestock by offering high prices until they attracted large shipments to the stockyards, then withdrawing from the market until shippers, in desperation, were ready to sell at any figure they could get, and finally returning to the market one at a time, while the others

[16] Yeager, *Competition and regulation*, p. xxii.

stood aside, to buy their supplies at whatever price they chose to pay.[17]

Meatpackers held a position analogous to that of the refineries of the Standard Oil trust: both were funnels through which raw materials from millions of independent producers must pass to reach millions of consumers—ideal constriction points at which to exert market control.

Indeed, on January 29, 1913, even as National was being dismembered, Arthur Meeker for Armour & Co., Louis F. Swift for Swift & Co., and Thomas E. Wilson for Morris & Co. met with representatives of Cudahy Packing Co. and Sulzberger & Sons (successors to S&S) "on percentages of livestock to be purchased by each . . . [and] on joint percentages to be used in general legislative and litigation matters." The next year an "international meat pool [was] formed. Armour, Swift, Morris, and Sulzberger interests in conjunction with certain British and South American firms [sought] to control shipment of meat to the United States and Europe."[18] By then the United States was a net importer of beef, with Armour, Swift, and Wilson (successor in 1916 to Sulzberger & Sons) operating plants in Argentina, Brazil, and Uruguay that exported meat to both large international markets, Europe and North America.

Although he had campaigned for election in 1912 on a platform of vigorous trust-busting, President Woodrow Wilson did not order the Federal Trade Commission to investigate interstate meatpacking until 1917. While that inquiry was in progress, the United States entered World War I. On August 10, 1917, by executive order the Food Administration was authorized to oversee voluntary and, later, mandatory compliance with production requirements of assorted foodstuffs, including red meat. The Big Five meatpackers were limited by wartime regulation to profits of 2.5 percent on sales, not to exceed 9 percent on average capital investment.

On July 3, 1918, the FTC reported that

five great packing concerns of the country—Swift, Armour, Morris, Cudahy, and Wilson—have obtained such a dominant

---

[17] Clair Wilcox, *Competition and monopoly in American industry* (1940), p. 182.
[18] Ibid., pp. 251–52.

position that they control at will the market in which they buy their supplies, the market in which they sell their products, and hold the fortunes of their competition in their hands.

Not only is the business of gathering, preparing, and selling meat products in their control, but an almost countless number of by-product industries are similarly dominated; and not content . . . they have invaded allied industries and even unrelated ones. [19]

Citing the packers' ownership of specialized transportation facilities as "the instruments of control," FTC commissioners William B. Colver, John Franklin Fort, and Victor Murdock urged Populist solutions: public ownership through the wartime Railroad Administration of all railroad livestock cars, all privately owned refrigerator railroad cars, the nation's principal stockyards, and "such branch houses, cold-storage plants, and warehouses as are necessary to provide facilities for the competitive marketing and storage of food products in the principal centers of distribution and consumption." [20]

This was far too radical a solution for Congress to contemplate. Instead in 1919 the Department of Justice announced that it was preparing evidence for a federal grand jury in New York to indict the Big Five on multiple antitrust violations. Those proceedings were suspended in 1920 when Armour, Cudahy, Morris, Swift, and Wilson submitted to a consent decree enjoining them from entering into any contract, combination, or conspiracy in restraint of interstate trade or from attempting to monopolize or actually monopolizing any part thereof. Specifically, the major meatpackers were required

to dispose of their holdings in public stockyards; to dispose of their interest in stockyard railroads and terminals; to dispose of their interest in market newspapers; to dispose of their interest in public cold storage warehouses, except when necessary for their own meat products; to disassociate themselves from the retail meat business; to discontinue using their facilities in any manner for the purchase, sale, handling, transporting, distributing, or otherwise dealing in certain commodities commonly referred to as unrelated to the meat industry [including

[19] FTC, *Report on the meatpacking industry*, p. 24.
[20] Ibid., p. 26.

fish, vegetables, fruits, confectionary, soft drinks, preservations of all kinds, spices and relishes, coffee, tea, chocolate, cocoa, nuts, flour, sugar, rice, bread and crackers, cereals, grain, grape juice, and miscellaneous wholesale grocery lines] . . . ; [and] to disassociate themselves from manufacturing, selling, jobbing, distributing, or otherwise dealing in such unrelated commodities, and from ownership of any capital stock in corporations engaged in manufacturing, selling, distributing, or otherwise dealing in such unrelated commodities. Individual defendants are enjoined from owning, severally or collectively, voting stock aggregating 50 percent or more in any corporation, or a half interest in any form or association engaged in manufacturing, jobbing, selling, transporting, distributing, or otherwise dealing in certain unrelated commodities enumerated in said decree.[21]

The sweeping consent decree thus sought to restore competitive market conditions by dismantling the complex vertical business structures developed by the large packers to assure themselves of steady supplies of raw materials and reliable marketing outlets.

According to some critics, the edict was the product of exaggerations by a "youthful and over-zealous FTC." Economists Robert Aduddell and Louis Cain argue:

> If the FTC's charges of collusion at all levels of the meat business were correct, one would expect some clear manifestations of success. First, there should have been a trend toward higher profits for the major packers, but that did not occur. As the FTC admitted, the evidence was that the other [independent] packers typically had higher profit rates than the majors. . . . Second, the margin between wholesale meat prices and livestock prices should have increased, but the FTC found no convincing evidence that this was the case. In fact, the FTC collected no price data at all, and what exists is suspect given the major packers' ownership of a portion of the livestock news media. . . . Third, new entry should have been blocked, with perhaps, a decline in the number of meat packers and independent wholesalers. Again there was no evidence to support this point. The number of firms increased, as did the total slaughter. While no firm entered at the national level, this should not be

[21] *Packer consent decree*, Document No. 219 (68th Cong., 2d Ses., 1924–1925), Serial 8413, pp. 2–3.

expected since local-regional, independent packers had the higher rates of return. [22]

In any case, the Consent Decree of 1920 purportedly dissolved the "beef trust."

Organized labor was not convinced. Before the Civil War, when meatpacking was a seasonal endeavor, a substantial proportion of its work force had been composed of area farmers who supplemented their incomes in slaughterhouses and packing plants during otherwise idle winter months. Skilled butchers for the most part found regular year-round employment in the retail fresh-meat trade, working their way up from apprentices to journeymen to master owners. After the Civil War, as the dressed-beef trade came to be dominated by a few packers and as refrigeration technology transformed the red-meat industry into a year-round business, seasonal employees were replaced with full-time, mostly unskilled workers. Simultaneously, because more fresh meat was cut up at central packing plants and at branch houses, the demand for skilled butchers steadily declined.

Employment in meatpacking expanded dramatically after the Civil War. According to government data, in 1870 8,366 persons (including 202 women and 258 children under sixteen years of age) earned $2.6 million, or an average of $305 each a year, an almost meaningless generalization considering the enormous variation in hourly compensation. Industrialization more than tripled the industry's employment—particularly in Chicago, St. Louis, and Kansas City—to an average of 27,300 in 1880 earning $410.5 million, or $385 per worker a year, a seemingly impressive increase of 26 percent that was made more meaningful by a simultaneously deflationary gain of 33 percent; however, the 1880 work force toiled year round, unlike its earlier counterpart that had labored about three months a year during the winter. In 1880 children, who performed simple, menial, repetitive tasks such as running and fetching and gathering up scraps, constituted 4 percent of the industry's labor force, up from 3.5 the decade before. The number of women workers in 1880 is unknown because statisticians ignored them.

[22] Robert M. Aduddell and Louis P. Cain, "Public policy toward 'The greatest trust in the world'," *Business History Review* LV (1981), pp. 218, 235.

In 1890 approximately 44,000 laborers (about 42,400 men, 900 women, and 700 children under sixteen years of age) worked in meatpacking, collectively earning $24.3 million, or an average of $552.70 each, a huge gain in earnings made a third more valuable by the ongoing deflationary trend. By then large plants had opened in Denver, Omaha, Sioux City, St. Paul, and Wichita. Following an industrial depression from 1893 to 1897 employment levels surged again at the turn of the century, with approximately 68,500 workers (about 63,800 men, 3,000 women, and 1,700 children) employed by meatpackers, some of this gain coming in such places as Fort Worth, Los Angeles, Oklahoma City, and St. Joseph. While the number of workers increased by 55.5 percent, their aggregate earnings rose by only 37.4 percent, to $33.4 million, which represented an average decline of $64.41 in individual annual earnings, to $488.29 each.

Unskilled positions in meatpacking increasingly came to be filled by immigrants, especially Eastern Europeans, and by women. By 1910 almost half of the work force was composed of Bohemians, Slovaks, and Poles. Women, who routinely were paid less than men for comparable work, by then constituted almost 10 percent of the total. In 1920 about 60,000 persons (undifferentiated statistically by age, gender, or national origin) worked in meatpacking, earning an average annual wage of $403.85 each. Meanwhile, the general price level—having declined steadily between 1865 and 1895 so that a dollar bought three times as much at the end as at the beginning of the period—had climbed steadily in the new century, mostly during World War I, leaving labor with a mere 4.7 percent gain for the whole period. As Louis Swift said of his father, "He did not hold his men by paying excessive wages and salaries."[23]

Disassembly lines that had first evolved in Cincinnati pork-packing plants were refined in Chicago and adapted to beef, and an increasingly sophisticated division of labor steadily improved the output per worker. Laborsaving devices—friction hoists, overhead conveyors, chutes, and moving benches—steadily reduced the need for manual labor. During the middle 1880s five "splitters" halved 80 carcasses an hour; ten years later four workers handled 120 an hour. Even so, much of the "marvelous speed and dexterity so admired by

[23] Swift and van Vlissingen, *The Yankee of the yards*, p. 112.

visitors" to packing plants, socialist A. M. Simmons asserted at the turn of the century, "is simply inhumanly hard work."[24] Mechanization in meatpacking, as labor economist John R. Commons succinctly observed, prevented "the slowest man from regulating the speed of the gang."[25] Mechanization also substantially reduced labor costs to about "42 cents per carcass, whereas, under the primitive system of country slaughter houses, the labor-cost was probably $3 per carcass."[26]

According to labor historian David Brody, speedups, coupled with hourly wage rates that varied between fifteen and fifty cents, provided the packers a way of

> scheduling work to maximize economy. The bulk of livestock shipments normally arrived in the early part of the week. . . . There was therefore very intense work during the first two or three days, but almost invariably short time at the end of the week. The arrangement, while concentrating the work and saving feeding and storage charges, gave the workmen an irregular and uncertain schedule. During the peak fall and winter months, the work week was usually close to fifty hours; in the slack season it often fell to thirty. The regular employees of the beef department in one plant averaged about two thirds of full time from 1886 to 1904.[27]

Assorted visitors and government investigators alike remarked on appalling working conditions throughout the meatpacking industry. Contaminated water frequently leaked from upper-floor refrigerator rooms onto the heads of workers below, the stagnant, foul-smelling effluent sometimes collecting several inches deep on lower floors. People routinely worked in poorly lit, unventilated chill rooms. Rheumatism, pneumonia, and tuberculosis were widespread, and job accidents commonplace. "Thirteen men died in the Swift plant in Chicago from June 1907 to December 1910," Brody says. "No safety programs existed in the early period, nor any plant hos-

[24] A. M. Simmons, Packingtown (1899), p. 24.

[25] John Commons, "Labor conditions in slaughtering and meat packing," Quarterly Journal of Economics, Vol. 19 (1904), p. 3.

[26] John Commons et al., A history of labour in the United States (4 vols.; 1918, 1935), III, xxvi.

[27] David Brody, The butcher workmen (1964), pp. 5–6.

pital in Chicago yards until Swift & Co. opened its medical department in 1900."[28]

Cafeterias did not exist, and laborers ate at their workbenches or squandered meager earnings at saloons, such as Whiskey Point, near Chicago's stockyards. Toilets were primitive, and changing rooms nonexistent. Packers viewed such frills as needless extravagances that contributed nothing to productivity, and corporate benevolence rarely extended beyond the largess of Armour & Co.'s gift of a Christmas turkey to each employee in 1901 or of S&S's arrangement for a Kansas City bank to remain open late to cash employees' pay vouchers instead of having them discounted by local saloons, or of Gustavus Swift's gratuitous advice to his workers to buy stock in the company.

Low wages and abysmal working conditions naturally caused clamor among workers for collective bargaining. Organizing efforts early in the 1880s, just as the industry was shifting to year-round operations, were almost offhandedly crushed by the packers, but in February, 1886, the Knights of Labor (then representing about three-fourths of organized labor in the United States) targeted meatpacking, soliciting members first in the Chicago stockyards. Labor historian Theodore Purcell writes: "At that time the Federation of Organized Trades and Labor Unions, the incipient AFL, was beginning a nationwide campaign for the eight-hour day. The Swift Knight-Butchers sympathized, and threatened a strike under John T. Joyce of the cattle-butchers. With suprising speed, the eight-hour day was granted and more packinghouse workers at once joined the Knights."[29]

Following the Haymarket Riot in Chicago in the spring of 1886, during which a bomb allegedly discharged by anarchists seriously prejudiced public opinion against all unions, Philip Armour organized the National Independent Meatpackers Association, which announced a return to the ten-hour day. Armour and other members of the Allerton Pool also fired known Knights, and the organization retaliated with a strike. Ironically, workers were ordered back to work by the Knights' head, Terence Powderly, who, "resentful that the eight-hour day came from his rival Federation, . . .

[28] Ibid., p. 7.
[29] Theodore Purcell, *The worker speaks his mind on company and union* (1953), p. 43.

broke the strike. After that the Knight-Butchers declined to almost nothing. For fifteen years no man would dare to organize in the open again for fear of his job."[30]

Meatpacking workers remained quiescent until 1894, when the tiny (sixteen-hundred-member) independent Chicago Stockyards Butchers' Union, organized during the early 1890s, answered the American Railway Union's call for a general strike in its battle with the Pullman Company. Asserting that their action also protested a recent industrywide pay cut, CSBU members urged others to join them in a walkout. Thousands throughout Packingtown responded, only to be readily replaced from the teeming mass of unemployed—mostly immigrants and blacks, who were denounced by labor as scabs. Violence was widespread. The black strikebreakers were often targets. Several were beaten, and a few were hanged in effigy from utility poles. A Morris & Co. warehouse was put to the torch; ammonia tanks exploded in the fire, scattering chunks of meat about the yards while destitute women scurried around gathering up the windfall.

The strike dragged on in Chicago and spread. According to business historian Clarence Bonnett, "In July, 1894, the meat packers of South Omaha were struck by the butchers for an increase of 5 c[ents] an hour in pay (also partly in sympathy with striking Chicago butchers). The packers obtained plenty of nonunion men, and when the strikers assaulted the strikebreakers, deputies were sworn in, and when those proved unequal to the task the state militia was called out."[31] The strike in Chicago was similarly crushed when President Grover Cleveland ordered federal troops into Chicago's rail yards "to protect the mail." By late summer plants throughout Packingtown were operating at full capacity once more. The Chicago Stockyard Butchers' Union disintegrated.

Throughout the 1890s strikes—mostly spontaneous walkouts—reflected labor's continuing dissatisfaction with working conditions and with unilaterally slashed wages, as during the panic of 1893, when Swift & Co. cut its pay rates across the board by 10 percent. During the middle of the decade workers walked off the job

[30] Ibid., pp. 43–44.
[31] Clarence Bonnett, *History of employers associations in the United States* (1965), p. 395.

in Kansas City, East St. Louis, and Hammond, Indiana, to protest both wage reductions and increasing mechanization in meatpacking, which replaced skilled butchers with semiskilled hackers. Fearing for their jobs, Chicago sheep butchers unsuccessfully struck in 1894 to prevent the introduction of the "ring system," a division of labor originally devised for the efficient disassembly of swine and later adapted to cattle butchering. Two years later Chicago hog butchers walked off the job when the "winter rate," customarily an additional dollar per day in compensation for the heightened seasonal pace in slaughtering, was cut to seventy-five cents citywide; they returned to work on company terms or were replaced.

By 1896 the AFL carried on its rolls five packinghouse locals in Kansas City (two of which were extinct), two in New York, one in Hammond, and one in Fort Worth, and five retail butchers' locals nationwide. Vertical integration of meatpacking had rendered local unionism ineffectual. The Big Five operated multiple facilities in scattered locations, and in the event of a localized strike key workers could be shifted from one place to another, as happened in Chicago in 1894, or production in one plant could be expanded to take up slack elsewhere, as with Hammond & Co. in 1893, when its principal Indiana facility was idled. AFL head Samuel Gompers invited the associated locals to send delegates to the Federation's 1896 convention in Cincinnati to organize the red-meat workers nationally. Only four representatives appeared, but they founded the Amalgamated Meat Cutters and Butcher Workmen of North America, which recognized that it was impossible to draw jurisdictional lines between wholesale and retail branches of the business or between butchers and hackers. The union's creation marked the real beginning of organized labor in meatpacking, even though it was impotent at first. George Byer, its first president, was fired from his job as a sheep butcher in Armour's Kansas City plant and blacklisted. He soon resigned his position with the union and became a policeman. The AFL then boycotted Armour's Kansas City operation and, later, its Chicago plant, without noticeable effect. At Gompers's insistence the boycott was lifted in 1898, Armour announcing in return that it would not discriminate against union members in future hiring.

During its first three years of existence Amalgamated created a body of constituent locals and by 1900 counted two dozen chapters

and 4,000 dues-paying members (equally divided among packinghouse and retail workers), but none of them was in Chicago, the
center of the red-meat trade with more than 25,000 of the industry's
68,000 employees. Packers there, openly repressive since the strikes
of 1886 and 1894, offhandedly crushed Amalgamated's one local in
1897 and summarily discharged and blacklisted its 35 members.
Without significant union presence in Chicago, where wage and
working standards were set for the whole nation, Amalgamated was
destined to remain an ineffectual band of scattered locals.

In 1900, Michael Donnelly, a butcher from South Omaha who
succeeded Byer as Amalgamated's president, moved to Chicago to
organize Packingtown. He met with some success. Following a spate
of initial dismissals of union men, the companies began to tolerate
some union activity, especially among key skilled craftsmen. Widespread prosperity generated brisk sales for fresh meat, and packers
easily passed along to retailers the higher labor costs. Moreover, by
then the industry was led by the less combative scions of its found-
ers: J. Ogden Armour replaced Philip at Armour; Gustavus, Jr., succeeded his father at Swift; and Edward Morris replaced Nelson
at Morris. All of the younger men were, in Brody's words, "more
amenable to a new approach to labor relations." [32] Donnelly worked
diligently to maintain discipline among the rank-and-file, and
he convinced management that the most economical way to avoid
production disruptions was to deal with Amalgamated, which by
mid-1901 represented many cattle, hog, and sheep butchers; beef
carriers; boners; casing workers; and sausage makers in the Chicago-
Hammond area.

While they never officially recognized Amalgamated, Armour,
Cudahy, Morris, S&S, and Swift effected a truce with the union.
Only Swift among the Big Five ever publicly admitted that it carried on formal discussions with organized labor. Most companies,
such as Armour, reached understandings with union representatives
but steadfastly refused to put anything in writing. Small packers,
forced to compete with the nationally integrated, more efficient,
conspiratorial Big Five, offered far more resistance. Jacob Dold
Packing Co. of Buffalo and Wichita and the Kingan, Morrell Co. of
Ottumwa, Iowa, for example, totally rejected any semblance of col-

---

[32] Brody, *The butcher workmen*, p. 36.

lective bargaining, yet in 1904, Amalgamated forced the Louisville Packing Co. of Kentucky to come to terms. Slaughterhouses in Baltimore, Cincinnati, Evansville, New York City, and Wheeling were also organized, but the vast majority of independents held firm against the union.

Essentially an industrial organization, Amalgamated was unusual among early AFL affiliates, most of which were craft-oriented. Amalgamated actively recruited semiskilled (processing and byproducts) workers as well as blacks, who were frequently employed by meatpackers as strikebreakers. In 1902, Donnelly even chartered a women's local—over vehement protests by numerous members who believed that women workers undercut men's wage rates. Following a bitter wildcat strike by Chicago sausage makers in 1903, during which large numbers of immigrant women replaced picketing men, Amalgamated in general convention narrowly defeated a proposal to expel women, replacing it instead with a demand for "equal pay for equal work," which the packers ignored.

While seemingly broadly based on the theory that the union should embrace all those "who were a branch of the craft," it primarily benefited highly skilled workers, who made up about one-fourth of all employees. In 1903, Amalgamated negotiated industrywide pacts for cattle and sheep butchers that raised their wages 15 percent and increased the size of their work gangs by about one-third, thereby offsetting common production-line speedups. The agreement constituted the zenith of early union bargaining with management.

Spotty though its success might have been, workers flocked to Amalgamated, swelling its membership by the time of its fifth convention in 1904 to 56,000 persons, in a labor force estimated at 74,000. The rank-and-file, invariably more impatient than their leader, demanded significant wage improvements ranging from "equalization" of skilled rates nationwide (based on Chicago's scale) to an increase of eighteen and a half to twenty cents an hour for virtually all classes of unskilled workers—livestock handlers, canners, sausage makers, oleomargarine workers, fertilizer laborers, and so on. Mindful that the economic recession which gripped the nation that year (labeled the "Rich Man's Panic" by the press) had already doubled urban unemployment, Donnelly counseled restraint; nevertheless, in June he presented his membership's demands to representatives of the Big Seven—Armour; Cudahy; Morris; National; S&S; Swift; and Libby, McNeill & Libby.

Though willing to discuss equalization of skilled rates, the packers rejected out of hand pay raises for the unskilled, offering instead a two-cent cut to sixteen and a half cents an hour. Amalgamated consequently struck nationwide, and 50,000 workers walked out. With three weeks' supply in their coolers as cushion, the Big Seven continued operations, drawing on an abundant supply of blacks and immigrants, using supervisory personnel in key skilled positions, and forgoing almost all by-product output. It was soon evident that the big packers could produce at substantial levels without the strikers, and with small packers eager to help meet demands, no shortages resulted. There was no public outcry. By summer's end production nationwide was near normal.

There was sporadic violence. Black strikebreakers were beaten and threatened with lynching. Riots erupted in Chicago, Kansas City, and Omaha. The governor of Iowa dispatched several companies of militia to Sioux City to maintain order. Chicago public officials, retail butchers' associations, livestock raisers' groups, and even Secretary George Cortelyou of Theodore Roosevelt's new Department of Commerce and Labor publicly appealed to both sides for restraint and for the packers to show compassion. Donnelly, his strike funds gone by late August and his membership deserting, going back to work on company terms, asked to meet with management without prior conditions; the packers refused. Finally a delegation of concerned citizens, led by social reformer Jane Addams, secured an audience with J. Ogden Armour and, in the name of humanity, urged him to end the strike to avert further bloodshed and much suffering among the strikers. Armour agreed to rehire strikers as needed, giving former workers preference but at lower wage rates than before the strike. He would not commit to bargain ever again with Amalgamated.

The strike of 1904 devastated Amalgamated. During the decade that followed, membership shrank to fewer than 6,000 from a high of 56,000. Severely criticized by those who stayed in the union, Donnelly resigned in 1907 and was reduced to a series of menial jobs, ending up as a camp cook in Texas, where he vanished from history. His rank-and-file fared far better. Many of the concessions Donnelly won for them, such as the introduction of regular, full-time work schedules after 1903, remained in effect, as did the improved rate for skilled beef and mutton butchers. Compensation for unskilled workers declined in 1905, but soon wages overall began to rise as prosperity returned and the unemployment rate nationwide dipped. The unskilled base was raised to seventeen and a half cents an hour, where it remained until World War I. Meanwhile, some enlightened labor policies had evolved, as at Swift & Co. where an employees' benefit association was organized in 1907 under corporate aegis, "followed by a series of real improvements in working conditions, cafeterias, restrooms, compensations and accident insurance, safety programs, and so on."[33]

Such largess mollified workers only temporarily. Its output having more than doubled between 1904 and 1917, Swift & Co.'s profits climbed to $9 million from $4 million, its dividends to $5 million from $2 million. While wholesale meat prices rose by 13 percent, wages remained at or near 1904 levels. In 1917, undoubtedly made nervous by the increasingly successful organizing efforts of socialist (later communist) labor leader William Z. Foster among unskilled stockyard workers in Chicago, the Big Five raised the minimum wage to twenty-seven and a half cents and hour. The ten-cent increase was granted virtually overnight in order to buy labor peace so that the packers could meet wartime quotas set by the Food Administration. Productivity rose. Fringe benefits were introduced: Swift and Wilson created pension funds; Swift increased its guaranteed work week to forty-five hours, up from forty hours; Armour erected a gymnasium for its workers; and the American Meat Packers Association began to coordinate an approach to employee welfare, especially at the Chicago stockyards. By year's end Amalgamated's rolls had swelled to 30,000 persons.

Faced with the invigorated union's demand to reinstate collective bargaining, the packers refused. Swift & Co. dismissed several union leaders at its newly acquired Libby, McNeill & Libby subsidiary. Threatened with the disruption of a wartime strike, the Wilson administration quickly imposed binding arbitration through its Mediation Commission. In March, 1918, after hearing both sides, Federal Judge Samuel Alschuler found for Amalgamated and decreed an industrywide reduction in hours to eight per day, from an average

[33] Purcell, *The worker speaks his mind on company and union*, p. 47.

of ten; wage increases of four and a half cents an hour for those earning thirty cents or less an hour; four cents an hour for those earning between thirty and forty cents; and three and a half cents an hour for those earning more than forty cents an hour (whereas the union had called for across-the-board dollar-a-day increases); and time-and-a-quarter rates for the first two hours of overtime, with time-and-a-half thereafter.

While the Alschuler order did not require meatpackers to recognize Amalgamated, workers inferred as much. By 1919 the union's membership had swelled to 100,000 of the 161,000 workers nationwide. The packers consequently stepped up their hiring of blacks, who were less likely to be union members. "By 1919, Swift was one of the largest employers of Negroes in the Chicago area," Theodore Purcell observes, "with over 3,200 Negroes, or 26 per cent of the . . . Chicago [meatpacking] work force. The situation was greatly aggravated by the race riot of July, 1919, which set back unity and cooperation in the Yards at least ten years."[34] Nevertheless, as the era came to a close, organized labor in the meatpacking industry appeared resurgent.

It was the plight of the packinghouse worker, specifically in the context of the 1904 strike in Chicago, to which Upton Sinclair's novel The Jungle (1906) had tried to call attention. Sinclair mused years later, "I aimed at the public's heart, and by accident I hit it in the stomach."[35] Socialist Sinclair was only one of the many social critics of his age, including Lincoln Steffens, who railed against municipal graft and corruption; Ida Tarbell, who flayed the Standard Oil trust; Ray Stannard Baker, whose exposé revealed railroad machinations; Thomas W. Lawton, who ferreted out financial fraud; and Charles Edward Russell, who claimed that there was a "beef trust." In the fall of 1904, Sinclair

> set out for Chicago, and for several weeks lived among the wage slaves of the Beef Trust. . . . I went about, white-faced and thin, partly from undernourishment, partly from horror.
>
> I sat at night in the homes of the workers, foreign-born and native, and they told me their stories, one after one, and I made notes of everything. In the daytime I would wander about

[34] Ibid., p. 36.
[35] Upton Sinclair, The autobiography of Upton Sinclair (1962), p. 126.

the yards, and my friends would risk their jobs to show me what I wanted to see. I was not much better dressed than the workers, and I found that by the simple device of carrying a dinner pail I could go anywhere.[36]

The Macmillan Company offered to publish Sinclair's manuscript if he would remove much of the "blood and guts" and other material editors considered either objectionable or fanciful, but Sinclair refused to be censored. Instead, after five other publishers turned down the manuscript, and following the publication of excerpts in the radical magazine *Appeal to Reason* in 1905, he printed a limited number of copies himself. About then Doubleday, Page and Company expressed interest, provided it could verify the book's essential veracity. Editor Isaac F. Marcosson in fact visited Chicago, where he interviewed Dr. W. K. Jacques, the former head of the meat-inspection unit of the U.S. Bureau of Animal Industry, who had recently been fired when he had refused to pass diseased meat. Jacques contended that Sinclair had not misrepresented conditions in meatpacking. Marcosson later wrote, "I was able to get a Meat Inspector's badge, which gave me access to the secret confines of the meat empire. Day and night I prowled over its foul-smelling domain and I was able to see with my own eyes much that Sinclair had never even heard about."[37]

Sinclair's revelations revolted the reading public. One passage among many that might be selected from *The Jungle* should suffice as illustration:

> . . . it was the custom, . . . whenever meat was so spoiled that it could not be used for anything else, [that] they [packers] either can it or else chop it up into sausage. . . . It was only when the whole ham was spoiled that it [was] cut up by the two-thousand-revolutions-a-minute flyers, and mixed with a half ton of other meat, [so that] no odor that was ever in a ham could make any difference. There was never the least attention paid to what was cut up for sausage; there would come all the way back from Europe old sausage that had been rejected, and that was mouldy and white—it would be dosed with borax

[36] Ibid., p. 109.
[37] Isaac Marcosson, *Adventures in interviewing* (1919), p. 283.

and glycerine, and dumped into the hoppers, and made over again for home consumption. There would be meat that had tumbled out on the floor, in the dirt and sawdust, where the workers had trampled and spit uncounted billions of consumption germs. There would be meat stored in great piles in rooms; and the water from leaky roofs would drip over it, and thousands of rats would race about on it. It was too dark in these storage places to see well, but a man could run his hand over these piles of meat and sweep off handfuls of dried dung of rats. These rats were nuisances, and the packers would put poisoned bread out for them; they would die, and then rats, bread, and meat would go into the hoppers together. This is no fairy story and no joke; the meat would be shovelled into carts, and the man who did the shovelling would not trouble to lift out a rat even when he saw one—there were things that went into the sausage in comparison with which a poisoned rat was a tidbit. There was no place for the men to wash their hands before they ate their dinner, so they made a practice of washing them in the water that was ladled into the sausage. There were the butt-ends of smoked meat, and the scraps and corned beef, and all the odds and end of the waste of the plants, that would be dumped into old barrels in the cellar and left there. Under the system of rigid economy which the packers enforced, there were some jobs that it paid to do once in a long time, and among these was the cleaning out of the waste-barrels. Every spring they did it; and in the barrels would be dirt and rust and old nails and stale water—and cart load after cart load of it would be taken up and dumped into the hoppers with fresh meat, and sent out to the public's breakfast. Some of it they would make into "smoked" sausage—but as the smoking took time, and was therefore expensive, they would call upon their chemistry department, and preserve it with borax and color it with gelatine to make it brown. All of their sausage came out of the same bowl, but when they came to wrap it they would stamp some of it "special," and for this they would charge two cents more per pound. [38]

The sensational book quickly became a best-seller.

Marcosson and Sinclair separately sent advance copies of The Jungle to Theodore Roosevelt. Peter Finley Dunn, a journalist and

[38] Upton Sinclair, The jungle (1906), pp. 160–62.

leading social satirist of that day, eventually had his popular Irish character "Mr. Dooley" imagine the president's reaction:

> Tiddy was toying with a light breakfast an' idly turnin' over th' pages iv th' new book with both hands. Suddenly he rose fr'm th' table, an' cryin'; "I'm pizened," began throwin' sausages out iv th' window. Th' ninth wan sthruck Sinitor Biv'ridge on the head an' made him a blond. It bounced off exploded, an' blew a leg off a secret-service agent, an' th' scatthred fragmints desthroyed a handsome row iv ol' oak-trees. Sinitor Biv'ridge rushed in, thinkin' that the Prisidint was bein' assassynated be his devoted followers in th' Sinit, an' discovered Tiddy engaged in hand-to-hand conflict with a potted ham. Th' Sinitor fr'm Injyanny, with a few well-directed wurruds, put out th' fuse an' rendered th' missile harmless. Since thin th' Prisidint, like th' rest iv us, had become a viggytaryan.[39]

Reportedly inundated with letters from concerned Americans, Roosevelt soon invited Sinclair to the White House to discuss his allegations. According to Sinclair, the president expressed no great admiration for the packers, for he "ate the meat they canned for the army in Cuba."[40] Indeed, Rough-Rider Roosevelt, like many other veterans of his day, had testified before the Dodge Commission, appointed in 1898 by President William McKinley to investigate assorted complaints about the military's handling of the war with Spain, including the alleged procurement of tainted meat from Armour and the others. Erstwhile rancher and future president Roosevelt reported in 1899 that army rations of "canned fresh beef" were "exceedingly bad. I don't think that more than a quarter of it, more than a tenth of it," he amended his statement upon reflection, "was eaten. When the men got very hungry and ate it, it nauseated the men at the worst, and at the best it was tasteless and insipid. . . ."[41]

The Dodge Commission heard repeated horror stories from first-hand observers, including some soldiers who, having worked in slaughterhouses, had rejected the army's meat rations out of hand. G. W. Stokes, of New York, a former Eastman employee, swore that

---

[39] Quoted in Robert V. Downs, "Afterword," Upton Sinclair, *The Jungle* (1960), p. 346.
[40] Quoted in Sinclair, *Autobiography*, p. 118.
[41] *Report of the commission appointed by the president to investigate the conduct of the war department in the war with Spain* (8 vols.; 1900), V (Serial 3863), p. 2259.

he had seen "thousands of sick, lame, aged, and repulsive-looking animals driven in for slaughter. . . . Such beef was boiled and canned as corned beef. . . ."[42] Army Chief of Staff General Nelson Miles claimed that in some instances canned meat had been pickled with formaldehyde, giving rise to the what the press soon called "the embalmed beef scandal." Yet Harvey W. Wiley, a physician and chief of the USDA's Bureau of Chemistry, upon analyzing specimens furnished by the Dodge Commission, reportedly "uncovered no samples in poor condition and no trace of any preservative except a very small amount of saltpeter in corned and luncheon beef. He thought that the trouble in the army had come from rapid deterioration of the canned meat after opening in the tropics and from serving meats without proper ration balance. He was convinced that at least nine-tenths of the reports condemning the meat supplied were 'purely sensational and without foundation.'"[43] Allegations of substantial adulterations thus parried by a credible scientist, the "embalmed beef scandal" soon faded from the front pages. No public action ensued.

Indeed, historian Thomas Bailey has observed,

> Between January 20, 1879, when the first bill designed primarily to prevent the adulteration of food was introduced in the House of Representatives, and June 30, 1906, when the Pure Food and Drug Law was signed, 190 measures relating to specific foods were introduced. These met with various kinds of opposition: . . . those who objected on the grounds of constitutional interpretation, those who were not aware of the seriousness of the problem and believed there were more pressing questions, and those who were personally interested in the perpetuation of frauds that would be illegal under a pure food statute.[44]

Of the 190 bills, 8 became law (including the Export Meat Inspection Acts of 1890 and 1891, passed to calm the trichinosis scare in Europe), 9 passed one house but not the other, 23 were reported

---

[42] Ibid., VIII (Serial 3866), p. 414.

[43] Oscar Anderson, Jr., *The health of a nation: Harvey W. Wiley and the fight for pure food* (1958), p. 128.

[44] Thomas Bailey, "Congressional opposition to pure food legislation, 1879–1906," *American Journal of Sociology*, Vol. 36 (1930), p. 52.

favorably by respective committees but failed passage, 9 were reported back adversely, and 141 others, following introduction, passed into oblivion. While it has become fashionable among some revisionist historians to denigrate and superciliously dismiss "the twelfth-hour impact of Upton Sinclair's muckraking novel, *The Jungle*,"[45] the sensational book unquestionably riveted public attention on the appalling conditions in meatpacking.

In rebuttal J. Ogden Armour wrote a series of articles for the *Saturday Evening Post* (whose editor had once had been Armour's secretary) and later compiled them into a book, lest "in the public mind a feeling that the traditional corporation policy of silence under attack is sometimes a tacit confession brought about by hostile and mistaken agitators." Armour vigorously denied product adulteration and countered that "criticism of the large packing houses, on the score of cleanliness and sanitation, springs largely from persons who are entirely irresponsible, and who, like the 'yellow' periodicals, have something to gain by attracting attention to their sensationalism." He insisted that "meat and food products, generally speaking, are handled as carefully and circumspectly in large packing houses as they are in the average home kitchen," arguing, "It is *good business* for the packer to be careful. There is a positive dollar-and-cents benefit to him in being able to assert . . . this if it were not true, [for] he would be found out, and the damage he would suffer would overwhelm any monetary profit. . . ." As proof he pointed to existing federal meat inspection, without noting that packer compliance was wholly voluntary save for specified exports and that troublesome government inspectors, such as Dr. Jacques, in Chicago, were often fired. He pointed to contemporary accounts in the *Daily Live Stock Reporter* claiming that the advent of a centralized packing industry "had practically eliminated in so far as the cattle, hogs and sheep slaughtered at the big plants . . . [are concerned] the dangers which may arise from consumption of unwholesome meats"[46]—without noting, as did the Federal Trade Commission as few years later, that the *Live Stock Reporter*'s parent Reporter Publishing Co. of Fort Worth was 46.4 percent owned

[45] R. James Kane, "Populism, progressivism, and pure food," *Agricultural History*, Vol. 38 (1964), p. 161.

[46] J. Ogden Armour, *The packers, the private car lines, and the people* (1906), pp. v, 368, 379.

by Armour and 42.4 percent by Swift and hardly a disinterested observer.

Notwithstanding Armour's spirited defense, President Roosevelt ordered two separate investigations. The first, conducted by the USDA (and dismissed by Sinclair as "like asking a burglar to determine his own guilt"[47]), reported that The Jungle was a willful misrepresentation to discredit inspectors; however, the department did concede that the meat-inspection service under existing law was virtually powerless to prevent condemned meat from entering interstate commerce. The second investigation, conducted by labor commissioner Charles P. Neill and lawyer James B. Reynolds, "obtained evidence," Sinclair said, "of practically everything charged in The Jungle, except that I was not able to produce legal proof of men falling into vats and being rendered into pure leaf lard."[48] Although the meatpackers tried to suppress the highly critical Neill-Reynolds report and to block reform legislation introduced by Indiana senator Albert Beveridge, a mounting public outcry mandated action, and on June 30, 1906, President Roosevelt signed into law a sweeping Pure Food and Drug Act, which banned from interstate commerce any adulterated or mislabeled food and drugs (such as dangerous patent nostrums which were laced with alcohol and narcotics).

Roosevelt that day also signed a Meat Inspection Act. An extension of the enactments of 1890 and 1891 that mandated federal inspection of pork exports, the new legislation extended ante- and postmortem inspection to all classes of livestock and red meats in interstate and foreign commerce. The USDA was "empowered further to require sanitary equipment, conditions, and methods in the slaughtering and packing establishments, to prevent the use of harmful chemicals and preservatives and of misleading labels, and to regulate the transportation of meat in interstate and foreign commerce. . . . Poultry, fish, and game were not subject to inspection."[49]

Appropriations to the USDA were augmented by about $3 million to cover the costs of inspection, for which a packer engaged in interstate commerce must apply. On receipt of the application the

[47] Sinclair, Autobiography, p. 118.
[48] Ibid., p. 120.
[49] Clemen, The American livestock and meat industry, p. 329.

USDA dispatched sanitary experts to make recommendations concerning the maintenance of outdoor yards, pens, alleys, and chutes
and indoor lighting and ventilation of processing rooms, cleaning
procedures for work areas, and toilet and dressing-room facilities for
workers. The fattening of hogs or other animals on slaughterhouse
refuse was strictly forbidden, as was the employment of anyone suffering from tuberculosis or any other communicable disease.

The actual inspections were to be made either by "professional" employees (veterinarians, laboratory technicians, and the
like) or by "lay" civil-service employees (persons specifically trained
to pass on meat products, originally categorized as either grade 1 or
grade 2 workers, depending on experience). The inspections began
in October, 1906, with a visual check of livestock gathered for
slaughter. According to the procedures specified, when an inspector
found an animal

> that to his mind is not perfectly sound and healthy, he, or his
> assistant, affixes to its ear a numbered metal tag bearing the
> words "U.S. Suspect." Such animals are segregated and slaugh-
> tered separately. . . . If the post-mortem examination does not
> confirm the inspector's suspicions, and no lesions of disease are
> found, the tag is taken off . . . and the carcass is sent along as
> edible meat. If lesions which warrant condemnation are found,
> the carcass is sent to the tank. . . .
>
> Animals which have been found by the inspector to be
> sound and healthy . . . are not marked, but proceed by runways
> into the slaughter house itself and to the killing floor, which for
> cattle usually is at the top of the building.[50]

A worker called a "knocker" stunned a steer with a sledgeham-
mer and hooked it onto a moving chain that dragged it hind leg first
to the killing bed, where a "sticker" severed the carotid artery to
bleed the beast to death. The head was skinned and removed at that
station even as the overhead traveler carried the carcass forward. In
fast order a string of butchers and meat cutters disassembled it. A
"legger" severed the hind legs at the hooves and the forelegs at the
knees. A "sider" began the skinning process, yanking the hide
downward but not off the carcass, and a "caul puller" split the belly

[50] Ibid., pp. 331–32.

from throat to anus, removing and tagging the greater caul (the peritoneal fold that covers the stomach and colon) for eventual random microscopic examination.

Another butcher meanwhile loosened the trachea and sawed through the sternum. A "skinner" pulled the hide from the buttocks, sometimes but not always cutting off the tail and tagging it for future identification. The carcass was then hoisted clear of the floor, and another skinner, called the "backer," yanked off more hide, while a "gutter" removed the viscera. A "rump sawyer" divided the carcass from coccyx to lumbar vertebrae. A "splitter," wielding a cleaver, continued the bifurcation to the base of the neck. A "hide dropper" removed the rest of the skin, and a "neck man" split the cervical vertebrae, separating the two sides. "Trimmers" removed ragged pieces of flesh and the spinal cord and pumped blood out of the forequarters by rapidly moving them up and down.

The severed heads underwent preliminary postmortem. The glands at the base of the skull were visually checked by a grade 2 inspector for evidence of tuberculosis. Suspected glands were removed for closer scrutiny up to but not always including microscopic examination. Grade 2 inspectors mostly oversaw the work of gutters: "The law requires this inspector to handle the viscera, and if necessary, to cut into them. This is rapid as well as exacting work, and the head and viscera inspectors frequently exchange places, or the viscera inspector is relieved by another after two hours' work." [51]

Examiners tagged suspect carcasses with "U.S. Retained" labels and diverted them into a registered, ratproof, locked, and government-controlled "retained room," where the meat underwent more expert scrutiny by grade 1 inspectors or even by professionals. When examination confirmed disease, the whole carcass might go into the offal tank. "The inspectors here have a good deal of personal discretion," observed meatpacking authority Rudolf Clemen in 1923. "Certain definite rules are laid down by the Bureau [of Animal Industry], but something must be left to the judgment of inspectors. They must pass upon the question of the extent of the affection and decide whether or not the whole carcass or only part of it should go to the tank." [52]

[51] Ibid., p. 337.
[52] Ibid., p. 334.

Just before an approved side of beef slid along the chain hoist into the chill room, a senior grade 1 inspector tattooed it five times (on the loin, rib, chuck, plate, and round) with the small purple dye stamp, U.S. INSPECTED AND PASSED, required of red meat in interstate and foreign commerce. Passed beef usually remained in the 36°F cooler for about forty-eight hours before being shipped, usually by rail but, after World War I, increasingly by refrigerator truck. The process for sheep and goats was virtually identical, sheep often being killed at one end of cattle-killing floors.

Pork operations and inspection routine were separate and distinct. Early-twentieth-century pork packers were far more mechanized than contemporary beef plants, and federal techniques for guarding against trichinosis and other dangers peculiar to pork preparation were more than a decade old by the time interstate beef inspection began in 1906. About then a large pork plant—one processing three hundred to five hundred hogs an hour—typically herded visually inspected and passed swine tightly into a small pen, one side of which contained a huge wheel with stout hooks set about its outer rim. Workers in the pen deftly attached the loop of a chain to the hind leg of a live, squealing animal and secured the other end of the chain to a hook on the slowly turning wheel, which hoisted the squirming swine to an inclined rail. The hog, hanging head down, passed by continuously moving chain to a "sticker," who severed the carotid artery.

The carcass was dropped into a huge vat of scalding water, dragged through from one end to the other, and hooked onto another chain hoist that pulled it through an automatic scalping machine called the "dehairer." Once shaved, the carcass was skidded onto a moving platform that carried with it a butcher who almost but not quite severed the head to expose glands for inspection, which revealed most cases of swine tuberculosis. Grade 2 inspectors either marked suspect remains with a black × on the forequarter or severed the foreleg ligaments. Gambrels were attached to both passed and suspect carcasses alike, and they were all hooked to overhead rails that transported them for further washing and scraping. Marked carcasses then received U.S. RETAINED metal tags and were sent to a "retained room" for scrutiny, to be either passed or condemned, in whole or in part, to the tank. Unmarked carcasses proceeded down the rail to "gutters," who disemboweled them. The viscera underwent visual and hand inspections by grade 2 inspec-

tors. Approved carcasses were ultimately split, washed, stamped
U.S. INSPECTED AND PASSED, and placed in a chill room for temporary storage.

The inspection act of 1906 further required the USDA to oversee meat curing, pickling, smoking, cooking, canning, and sausage making in interstate or foreign commerce. Chemicals, drugs,
and coloring agents were banned, as were all preservatives save
salt, sugar, vinegar, woodsmoke, and a few others, including
borax—when used exclusively for export to Great Britain. Canned
and other prepared meats were subjected to reagent checks and
even to random microscopic examination. Contamination sometimes caused whole batches, amounting to several tons of meat, to
be "tanked."

Inspection also curtailed widespread mislabeling. Before 1906
many American packers touted their canned output as "Westphalia
ham" or "York ham," leading consumers to infer that these products
were prepared in German or English locales renowned for fine meats.
Thereafter packers were required to amend their labels to read
"Westphalia-style" and the like. Similarly, after 1906 products labeled "potted tongue" by regulation had to contain tongue, which
often had not been the case. Under the new law the secretary of
agriculture or his agents were required to destroy all condemned
meat tankage. It was usually rendered into industrial grease at high
temperature and pressure. Reported Clemen, "All possible precau-
tions are taken to prevent this grease, some of which looks about as
good as lard, from going into trade as edible product."[53]

Enforcement of the Pure Food and Drug Act and the Meat Inspection Act, as the Outlook reported two years later, was spotty.
During the first eighteen months of their existence the USDA collected more than 7,000 food and drug samples, finding 176 of them
to be in violation of the law and referring those cases to the Department of Justice for action. Of these cases only ten (dealing with
apple cider, molasses, wheat flour, coffee, and patent medicines
that "possess none of the remarkable virtues ascribed to them on the
label"[54] were prosecuted or settled out of court.

Not until 1909 did federal inspectors find much amiss in the

[53] Ibid., p. 342.
[54] The Outlook, Vol. 89 (1908), p. 779.

meatpacking industry, against which much of the drive for pure-food regulations had been directed. Indeed, as Mary Yeager wrote, "Meat inspection easily became a handy public relations tool. . . . When consumers began to complain about rising meat prices in 1908 and 1909, the packers simply blamed TR and the new regulations" for increases of between three and five cents a pound in retail meat prices and "sighed with relief when William Howard Taft became President."[55] Taft, however, proved not to be a great friend of the packers, for, as already mentioned, his administration pressed antitrust proceedings against National Packing Co., which voluntarily dissolved in 1912.

In 1920 the Meat Inspection Division of the Bureau of Animal Industry maintained inspectors in 891 establishments in 265 American towns and cities. Its personnel consisted of 800 professional and 1,000 lay (700 grade 1 and 300 grade 2) inspectors, with another 150 administrative and clerical support staff, mostly in Washington, D.C. In that year it examined 62.3 million animals, 190,000 (0.3 percent) of which were condemned. The division's cost to the taxpayer amounted to $3.7 million a year or about six cents per inspected carcass, an insignificant sum that had a negligible impact on the cost of red meat.

Government intervention nevertheless irritated the meat-packers. "More than any other event," says J. Russell Ives, onetime director of marketing for the American Meat Institute, "the passage of the Meat Inspection Act of 1906 was responsible for the organization of the American Meat Packers Association, the first general trade organization in the meat packing industry."[56] About the time of World War I, under the leadership of Thomas Wilson, of Wilson & Co., AMPA became especially aggressive in resisting further government intervention by creating a bureau of public relations and by opening lobbying offices in Washington, D.C. The Department of Justice nevertheless actively pursued alleged antitrust violations by the beef trust, culminating in 1920 in the consent decree that served as a blueprint for the dismantling of an oligopsony-oligopoly. Indeed, despite vigorous opposition from the industry, the interstate red-meat trade was by then the most regulated of American business endeavors.

[55] Yeager, *Competition and regulation*, pp. 212–13.
[56] J. Russell Ives, *The livestock and meat economy of the United States* (1966), pp. 95–96.

5

Depression and War, 1920–1945

Between 1920 and 1945 livestock raising and meatpacking in the United States underwent wrenching economic shocks, as did much of the nation's other business enterprise. In the severe postwar depression of 1921, bloated wartime prices collapsed along with much of the foreign market for commodities, while equally bloated mortgages shouldered to achieve additional productive capacity remained intact. Animal husbandry suffered too, but not as painfully as much of the rest of the agrarian sector. Recovery was slow throughout the balance of the decade and was dashed to pieces by the crash of 1929 and the subsequent Great Depression.

Meatpackers successfully resisted intense pressure from a restive labor force to accept collective bargaining until the New Deal era and World War II, when they were forced by government regulation to concede to unionization in some plants. The larger companies were simultaneously successful in weakening the impact of public regulation by securing modifications in the Packer Consent Decree of 1920. For the stalwart oligopsonists-oligopolists of the past century such concessions were vital, for by then they faced vigorous competition within and outside the industry, which was rapidly changing because of the development of advanced techniques in processing, new products, and modern modes of transportation.

American agriculture was suffering hard times a full decade before the industrial sector tumbled over the economic abyss. A million farmers and ranchers—one in seven—lost everything between the first and second world wars. A cost-price squeeze pinched farmers, including all livestock raisers, following World War I. Expenses, while eroding slightly, remained remarkably stable relative to general commodity prices, which plummeted. Net farm income stood at a record high $7.1 billion in 1920, slid to $6.3 billion in 1929, and collapsed to $1.9 billion in 1932. Not until exaggerated wartime demand caused commodity prices to climb in 1942 did net farm income surpass the 1920 mark.

When measured by parity—that is, when their income is compared with the generally prosperous period 1910 to 1914, relative to prices paid by the agrarian community for all goods and services, including interest—farmers and ranchers lost 18 percent to a ratcheting economy between 1920 and 1929, and another 44 percent following the crash, reaching the bottom of the abyss in 1932. Ten years later, when both gross receipts and net income finally topped 1920 levels, the typical farmer netted merely 105 percent of parity, thereby surpassing the 1910–14 benchmark by only 5 percent and the 1920 record by 6 percent.

Actually livestock raisers were relatively well off during the two-decade-long agrarian depression. Aggregating some $6 billion in gross income in 1920, 6 million stock farmers and ranchers saw their total receipts decline by fully one-third the following year. Even so, livestock producers lost less ground than their crop-raising counterparts, whose revenues dropped by 48 percent. Thereafter slaughter-animal prices inched upward until 1929, when gross receipts of $6.2 billion slightly surpassed the record 1920 level. The livestock-raising component of mixed farming subsidized the typical agriculturalist; only during the worst years of the Great Depression (1933–34) did stock raisers see their revenues plummet below those of sodbusters.

Livestock raising's relative bullishness came despite continuously shifting consumer tastes and preferences for food, especially red meat. By 1920 annual per capita red-meat consumption in the United States had declined to 136 pounds (49.3 percent beef and veal, 46.7 percent pork, and 4 percent lamb and mutton) from the peak in 1908 of 163.3 pounds per capita (48.6 percent beef, 47.5 percent pork, and 3.9 percent lamb). The typical jazz-age American also ate 13.7 pounds of store-bought poultry (for which the USDA began compiling figures in 1910), 4 pounds of cheese (a quantity that had not markedly changed since the government began gathering data in 1849), and 18.2 pounds of fish (for which there is scattered information). During the postwar recession of 1921–22, Americans ate less of everything, per capita consumption of all foods declining to about 1,500 pounds (retail weight), from approximately 1,550 pounds the previous year and from a peak of 1,620 pounds in 1911. Quick economic recovery and general urban prosperity whetted appetites to consume between 1,550 and 1,600 pounds per capita a year for the rest of the decade. Red-meat consumption did not rise proportionally, however, increasing by merely 4 pounds (about 3 percent) over 1920 figures.

While all food consumption declined during the unprecedented hard economic times of the Great Depression (to reach a record low of about 1,480 pounds per capita in 1934), red meat's share of the total food basket dropped disproportionately, to bottom at 7.9 percent—a nadir of 117.4 pounds per capita (52.6 percent beef and veal, which, because of the New Deal pig kills, were more abundant and, uncommonly, cheaper than pork, which slid to 41.1 percent, a low mark for the century, and lamb and mutton, which rose to 6.2 percent, a record high). By 1940, before World War II distorted gross-consumption figures, red-meat eating had increased substantially, to 142.2 pounds per capita (thereby accounting for approximately 9.2 percent of the food basket). Pork led with 51.6 percent, followed by beef and veal at 43.8 percent and lamb and mutton at 4.6 percent. The market share of substitute commodities such as fish and poultry decreased proportionally.

Geographic patterns of livestock production established during the previous century were well entrenched by the middle 1920s. Texas led the nation in total cattle production, followed by Iowa, Nebraska, Kansas, Wisconsin, Minnesota, South Dakota, California, Oklahoma, and Colorado. Except for its rank order of production, that list did not change throughout the ensuing two decades. Similarly, Iowa led in swine output in 1924, followed by Illinois, Nebraska, Missouri, Indiana, Minnesota, South Dakota, Ohio, Georgia, and Texas. Texas moved up to fifth among producing states, and Kansas replaced Minnesota; otherwise, the list did not appreciably change before the end of World War II. Texas led in sheep production in 1924, followed by California, Wyoming, Utah, Colorado, Montana, Ohio, Oregon, Idaho, and New Mexico. Again, save for the order among states, no significant shifts in ovine husbandry had occurred by the end of World War II. An interesting comparison is chicken- and egg-producing states during the inter-war period: Iowa, Missouri, Illinois, Ohio, Pennsylvania, California, Kansas, New York, Idaho, and Texas; except for a dramatic increase in Texas' output, which raised it to fourth place in 1945, the positions of the states remained essentially unchanged.

Texas ranchers, the largest and most successful of all cattlemen, who in turn were among the most prosperous of American livestock raisers, first felt the pinch soon after the Armistice. They held surplus animals, which they had bred to fill exaggerated wartime demand. Rising postwar unemployment (an average of 2.3 percent in 1919 and 11.9 percent in 1921), consumer resistance to skyrocketing retail prices (consumption of beef and veal declining by 12.7 pounds per capita during that period), and a virtual closing of the export market for beef (down to 46 million pounds in 1922 from 711 million in 1918) choked off demand. Wholesale prices for grass-finished slaughter beeves, $14.50 a hundredweight in 1918, dropped to $8.80 in 1920. In 1922 they averaged $6.00 a hundredweight in auction arena.

"The depression of 1922 intensified," cattle-industry authority John Schlebecker has observed, "when Texans dumped their cattle on an already demoralized market. By then cattlemen were against the wall. In New Mexico and Colorado, cattlemen spent an average of $27.98 to produce a calf which sold for $21.50."[1] For a time plainsmen unloaded to cornbelt feeders who, given low prices for both livestock and grain, finish-fed the beasts for an increasingly discerning urban palate, but the number of feedlots (fewer than a hundred capable of carrying a thousand cattle or more) limited this market. Moreover, as consumers decreased their red-meat consumption during hard times, meatpackers reduced their purchases from feedlots, which diminished the number of range animals they bought for finishing. The cattle market collapsed.

Many ranchers were already debtors. During the war the federal War Finance Corporation had lent cattlemen up to 75 percent of the value of their herds, and by war's end Texans alone owed $10 million. Most Great Plains ranchers were still deep in debt in 1920, by which time beef prices were softening. Specialized livestock financiers in Chicago, Denver, Fort Worth, Kansas City, St. Joseph,

[1] John Schlebecker, *Cattle raising on the plains, 1900–1961* (1963), p. 74.

San Francisco, and St. Paul who had collectively lent stock farmers and ranchers $100 million were wary of further loans in depressed times. After 1920 local banks that traditionally provided financing for livestock raisers were forced by Federal Reserve Board rediscount policies to assess progressively higher interest rates: the larger the loan, the higher the interest.

Ranchers, who were ineligible for assistance under the Farm Loan Act (1916), through their spokesman, the powerful American National Livestock Association, demanded government help. An eastern bank consortium announced the creation of the Stock Growers' Finance Corporation, with assets of $50 million, hoping to forestall unwanted government competition in lending. Nevertheless, in 1921, Congress authorized the War Finance Corporation to lend livestock raisers up to $1 billion through any of thirty-three agencies. Cattlemen had borrowed $100 million by August 1, 1921, when the Federal Reserve Board of Governors canceled its progressive rediscount policy, thereby signaling slightly easier credit for livestock producers nationwide.

"Those on the Great Plains" says historian Charles Wood, "had the most severe problem; 9 percent of all Kansas farmers and 28 percent of those in Montana reported losing their farms or other property. Mortgaged indebtedness for Kansas farmers and ranchers reached an all-time high for the interwar period in 1924, when the figure was reported to have reached $535 million."[2] Not even during the worst days of the 1930s did Kansas agrarian indebtedness surpass the 1924 figure. Montana used idle school funds to help its hard-pressed livestock raisers, ultimately recovering only about 25 percent of the indebtedness.

Cattlemen, like most other American businessmen when facing economic adversity, continued to look to Washington for assistance. Schlebecker has observed:

> In a period when the spirit of free enterprise and self-reliance supposedly dominated the American scene, cattlemen appeared singularly free of any doctrinaire opposition to government aid. Cattlemen not only endured, they actively sought government intervention in their affairs. They wanted federal

[2] Charles Wood, *The Kansas beef industry* (1980), pp. 196–97.

help in controlling tick fever and foot-and-mouth disease. When credit was hard to get, cattlemen appealed to the government for help, and when packers threatened, cattlemen again turned to the government. The federal government did not always respond adequately, but that was not the fault of the cattlemen. On the other hand, the government brought the railroads under fair control for the cattlemen. As trucks became more important, cattlemen insisted on federal and state subsidies for road building, that is, subsidies for truck transportation. The plainsmen even demanded more federal supervision of the public domain. In short, the trends of the previous decades continued unabated as cattlemen turned to the government for help.[3]

The American National Livestock Association, the largest organization of cattlemen in the United States, saw tariff protection as a panacea. While taxes had long been imposed on live-cattle imports, not until the twentieth century did the rate truly become protective. Under the Tariff of 1910, duty was levied on imported cattle: $2.00 a head on calves less than a year old, $3.75 a head on all animals more than a year old but valued at less than $14.00 each, and on animals of higher value, 27.5 percent ad valorem. When in 1913 livestock raisers experienced increasing difficulty in supplying urban America's demand for slaughter beeves, cattle were admitted duty free, a policy that did not change until the Emergency Tariff of 1921, which summarily imposed a 30 percent ad valorem tax on live cattle.

The following year Congress answered the anguished cries of cattlemen affected by plummeting demand and enacted an import tax of one and a half cents a pound on animals weighing less than 1,050 pounds and two cents a pound on heavier beasts. According to Lynn Ramsay Edminster:

> Under the act of 1909 the specific rates on cattle had amounted to about 20 per cent [the generally accepted minimum for protection] on animals under one year and 28 per cent on animals over one year and valued less than $14 per head. Under the Act of 1922 the specific duties have been equivalent to about 33 per

[3] Schlebecker, *Cattle raising on the plains*, pp. 102–103.

cent on light, and 43 per cent on heavy animals. It will thus be seen that, barring the Act of 1913, each of those tariff acts imposed higher rates of duty on cattle than did the preceding one.[4]

Throughout the twentieth century Canada and Mexico—until "Revolution struck Mexico with a force that paralyzed her cattle industry"[5]—had been the principal live-cattle suppliers of the United States, but by the middle 1920s it was apparent that Argentina and Australia also offered American meatpackers an abundance of cheap beeves, giving rise to widespread demands for higher tariff barriers to protect American cattlemen.

Relentlessly upward-spiraling red-meat prices became a matter of such intense public concern that the Carnegie Corporation's Institute of Economics (the present Brookings Institution) carefully studied and consequently pronounced against protective tariffs for the American cattle industry. The think tank asserted that the domestic cattle industry "was failing to keep pace with the growth of our population. . . . As a result, the exportable beef surplus of the country, previously large, so rapidly dwindled that at the time of the outbreak of the war [in 1917] imports of beef, live and dressed, exceeded exports." While global war stimulated beef-cattle production in the United States, it "only obscured for a time the underlying trend from national beef-surplus to beef-deficit." The declining importance of cattle raising, the study said, was due to the passing of the frontier, which was forcing the cattle industry to give way to more intensive uses of the land. "While it does not necessarily follow that the production of beef in the United States will continue to decline, . . . there is little reason to suppose that as the industry is now prosecuted production can be increased except at increasing costs."[6] The Brookings Institution concluded that, aside from raising consumer costs, the several tariffs of the early twentieth century had neither substantially increased the income of cattle raisers nor augmented the domestic supply of slaughter beeves.

Coupled with tariff policy in the minds of thoughtful agriculturalists was the controversial McNary-Haugen Bill, which was before Congress on several occasions during the 1920s. The legisla-

[4]Lynn Edminster, The cattle industry and the tariff (1926), p. 116.
[5]Manuel Machado, Jr., The north Mexican cattle industry, 1910–1975 (1981), p. 8.
[6]Edminster, The cattle industry and the tariff, pp. 264–65.

tion would have provided for the creation of a government agency to purchase specific commodities (wheat, cotton, tobacco, and others), which would be dumped on the foreign market. Assorted drafts of the legislation included neat cattle, sheep, and swine, but the version that cleared both houses in 1927 contained no assistance for ranchers. "Plains cattlemen apparently favored the McNary-Haugen Bill," Schlebecker says, "although they supported it half-heartedly"[7] on the theory that what was good for part of the agrarian sector was good for all. Historians Theodore Saloutos and John Hicks, on the other hand, contend that the measure found universal support throughout the rural United States, especially among mixed farmers who belonged to "the American Farm Bureau and numerous state farm bureaus, the National Board of Farm Organizations, which consisted of sixteen different associations, the national Grange, and countless other farm groups,"[8] as well as commercial clubs, merchant associations, and bankers sensitive to the farmers' plight.

Despite the bill's widespread support, President Calvin Coolidge charged in a ringing veto message that it "singles out a few products, chiefly seasonal, and proposes to raise the prices of those regardless of the fact that thousands of other farmers would be directly penalized. If this is a true farm-relief measure, why does it leave out the producers of beef cattle, sheep, dairy products, poultry products, potatoes, hay, fruit, vegetables, oats, barley, rye, flax, and the other important agricultural lines?"[9] He rejected similar legislation the following year, that time pointing to its "socialistic" implications.

The postwar agricultural depression seemingly bottomed out about then, especially for cattlemen. Beef and veal consumption had gradually increased since the Armistice to 68.1 pounds per capita in 1927, up from 61.1 in 1918; moreover, the beef eaters' pool grew, the nation's population having increased by about 9 million persons during the same period. During the mid-1920s cattle prices advanced by one-third on improved consumer demand, grass-fed animals from the Great Plains still finding ample demand even in

[7]Schlebecker, *Cattle raising on the plains*, p. 117.

[8]Theodore Saloutos and John Hicks, *Twentieth century populism: agricultural discontent in the Middle West, 1900–1939* (1951), p. 381.

[9]Quoted in George McGovern (ed.), *Agricultural thought in the twentieth century* (1967), p. 128.

competition with meatier grain-finished animals. "Although prices averaged less than during the war," Schlebecker says of their peaking in 1928 at $10.59 a hundredweight, "they were undeniably high. American consumers resisted the high beef prices. In December, 1927, popular discontent led to a formal beef boycott in Boston."[10] Beef and veal consumption abruptly declined nationwide, to a low of 55.2 pounds per capita in 1928, indicating widespread consumer resistance to higher prices; nevertheless, wholesale and retail prices dropped only slightly. By 1928 many livestock raisers who had taken advantage of generally rising prices to cull their herds of inferior breeding cattle found themselves in the best overall position since the war, their aggregate income at a near-record level.

Successful cattle-raising techniques varied. On the Great Plains, where during the mid-1920s 52 percent of the nation's cattle were bred and raised, if not finish-fed for slaughter, operators increasingly abandoned large-range operations for smaller pastures. Some of the better-known large ranches (the Cowder 6, Higginbotham, James Brothers, Jeter, Slaughter Lazy S, and Yellow House, to list but a few) were broken up and sold to smaller ranchers, farmers, and even speculators. Other ranchers retrenched. In 1921 the Matador Land and Cattle Co., which since 1905 had shipped Texas-bred beasts to leased pastures in Saskatchewan for grass-finishing, found itself trapped between American and Canadian tariff policies and consequently reduced its gigantic international business to merely huge interstate operations in Texas, Montana, and South Dakota, aggregating 70,000 cattle on 837,621 acres it either leased or owned.

Most Great Plains ranches were far smaller. A 1924 USDA study found that while two-thirds of all northern plains stockers owned their own land, they held on an average fewer than four thousand acres each, and between 5 and 16 percent of the total was in crops, usually alfalfa. Three-fourths of all southern plainsmen, on the other hand, leased all or part of a hypothetical three-thousand-acre operation, one acre in twenty devoted to row crops such as feed grains. The technique, termed "ranch farming" or "pasture farming," involved intensive applications of animal husbandry. Cattlemen grew feed (grain or hay), often under irrigation, and

[10]Schlebecker, Cattle raising on the plains, p. 104.

regularly winter-fed their animals, which reportedly reduced weather losses by 12 to 14 percent a year.

The livestock they produced was far improved over the predominantly "native" animals prevalent at the turn of the century. "By 1900," Wood observes,

> a number of producers were well along in their upgrading programs, but there was still much to be done. In this work, Herefords played the lead role; Shorthorn and Angus cattle were understudies. By 1920 the *American Hereford Journal* reported that 41 percent of the cattle in the West were whitefaces, while a decade later the same journal boasted that the "great range sections of our country are now at least 90 percent Hereford-using districts." Another claimed only 75 percent for the Hereford during the 1930s, but either figure represented a considerable change in the complexion of range cattle during the preceding few decades. [11]

While beefier whitefaces appeared on northern American ranges and pastures, southern stockers found them unsatisfactory because they lacked resistance to insects and because they generally fared poorly on semitropical forage under an unrelenting sun. Some southerners experimented with Zebu cattle, which, although they tolerated the heat and insects better, "did not meet requirements as to carcass and were deficient in reproduction and rate of growth in many places in the South. The American Brahman was created by breeders in this country from an amalgamation of several Indian Zebu breeds." [12]

Several crosses were far more exotic. In 1910, almost on a whim, Robert J. Kleberg, of the King Ranch, crossed range-bred whitefaces and Zebus, producing "the best range cattle for hardihood, size, and ability to fatten yet seen on the ranch." Serious experimentation followed, resulting in 1920 in the birth of Monkey, a five-eighths Shorthorn and three-eighths Brahman that became the prototype of Santa Gertrudis cattle, which was officially recognized a breed (rather than a strain) by the USDA in 1940. The King Ranch sold Monkey's sons for upwards of $40,000 each to southern

[11] Wood, *The Kansas beef industry*, p. 98.
[12] Everett Warwick, "New breeds and types," in USDA, *The yearbook of agriculture, 1962* (1962), p. 280.

cattlemen who, like the Klebergs, wanted beefy, climate-resistant livestock. Ten years later the Santa Gertrudis Breeders International was organized by 169 cattlemen who had found that "the calf will usually outweigh a Hereford of the same age by from one hundred to two hundred pounds." Not only was the resulting steer "bigger to begin with, but repeated tests show that the Santa Gertrudis will outgain other breeds on the same feed." [13]

Similar considerations led erstwhile Texas rancher Thomas Lasater of Colorado during the late 1930s to perfect a three-way cross of Shorthorn, Hereford, and Brahman cattle, which the USDA in 1954 recognized as the Beefmaster breed. Another, featuring French Charolais and American Brahman, resulted in the Charbray. A joint USDA and Louisiana Agricultural Experiment Station crossing of Angus and Brahman cattle produced Brangus. Notwithstanding such a notable government-sponsored achievement, says USDA authority Everett Warwick, "the development of polled types within existing breeds, Hereford and Shorthorn, since 1900 has been an outstanding achievement of private American breeders. . . ." [14]

Product improvement, however, failed to offset the horrendous impact of the Great Depression. By 1933 one American in four was unemployed, and as urbanites naturally adjusted food budgets to economize, red-meat consumption declined, beef and veal totals dropping to 52.9 pounds as early as 1930, from 58.9 pounds the year before. Live-cattle prices consequently dropped, thereby reducing ranch and farm equity upon which loans, increasingly difficult to secure, were based. Compounding the disaster was a devastating drouth that not only seared the grassy plains but also hurt the usually well-watered Missouri, Mississippi, and Ohio valleys. Livestock raisers and feeders alike dumped cattle on an already glutted market, and prices tumbled by 25 percent, to reach a new twentieth-century low of $4.14 per hundredweight.

That fall, plowed plains farmland literally blew away in huge black clouds that obliterated the noontime sun. Sand drifts buried sheds and machinery and scattered cattle like winter snowstorms, reminiscent for some of the blizzards of 1886–87. Hordes of grasshoppers set upon what remained, stripping fields of feed crops from

[13] Tom Lea, *The King Ranch* (2 vols.; 1957), II, 692.
[14] Warwick, "New breeds and types," USDA, *The yearbook of agriculture, 1962,* p. 280.

Texas through Montana. "On all fronts, cattlemen faced disaster, and as usual, they wanted the government to help them," Schlebecker observes. "The New Dealers did what they could without hurting the general public."[15]

Legislation included both oblique and direct assistance to cattlemen. The Emergency Soil Conservation Act of 1933 sought ways to control and eliminate fires, floods, insects, and diseases; while the act applied primarily to state and federal lands, private property also benefited. Congress also created the Farm Credit Administration under whose aegis existing Federal Land Banks and the Intermediate Credit Banks as well as the new Production Credit Corporation operated. The Production Credit Corporation assisted by providing feed loans throughout the weather-buffeted prairie and plains states.

To assist the agrarian community by inflating all commodity prices, Congress also enacted in 1933 the first Agricultural Adjustment Act, but, according to Schlebecker,

> most [large-scale] cattlemen opposed all efforts to have cattle included as a basic commodity [along with wheat, cotton, field corn, hogs, rice, tobacco, and dairy products]. Plainsmen asserted that the proposed production limits were unsound because lower beef output would only force consumers to use other kinds of meat. Apparently, most cattlemen believed this. They wanted help, but not controls; they hankered after a handout without regulation. Anyhow, at first cattlemen lobbied for their traditional programs: (1) higher tariffs on beef, fats, and hides (2) lower interest rates (3) lower freight rates, and (4) agencies for more orderly marketing and advertising.[16]

Far more to the liking of ranchers was the Federal Surplus Relief Corporation (later the Federal Surplus Commodities Corporation), which purchased beef as well as corn, dairy products, flour, fruits, poultry, and vegetables and distributed them to state welfare agencies for allocation among the destitute. Congress also created the Federal Emergency Relief Administration, which in 1933 bought 15 million pounds of beef, paying relatively high prices for mostly

[15] Schlebecker, *Cattle raising on the plains*, pp. 135–36.
[16] Ibid., p. 136.

young cows purposely purchased to deplete breeding herds. Thereafter, even though FERA was allowed to die in 1935, ongoing Federal Surplus Commodities Corporation purchases amounted to approximately 8 pounds of beef and veal for each family on relief,
which as late as 1940 aggregated 288 million pounds annually.

The U.S. Forest Service, however, resisted all pleas to reduce
fees for grazing livestock on the public domain; moreover, Secretary
of the Interior Harold Ickes enforced an 1885 law, ordering lessees
to remove all fences from government land. Meanwhile, the drouth
and savage dust storms continued to devastate the Great Plains.
Flowing streams dried up, ponds evaporated, and grasshoppers, rabbits, and other pests gorged themselves on wilting crops. Unable to
water livestock adequately by hand, many midwestern farmers and
ranchers dumped more cattle, further depressing prices. Cattlemen
cried for help. In 1934 the Jones-Connally amendment to the Agricultural Adjustment Act added cattle along with rye, flax, barley,
grain sorghums, and peanuts to the list of basic commodities and
appropriated $50 million for government purchases designed to sup-
port prices of these items.

Additionally, in June, 1934, the Drought Relief Commission,
headed by Secretary of Agriculture Henry Wallace, began buying
cattle in the dust-bowl region and by year's end had paid $525 mil-
lion (about $60 each) for 8.3 million head nationwide. In this New
Deal experiment, which often was derided and sometimes exaggerated by administration critics, one animal in ten was slaughtered on the farm and the meat destroyed to nudge prices upward.
"Government emergency programs literally saved the cattleman,"
Schlebecker has observed. "For this salvation, many cattlemen
never forgave the government. Large numbers of them resented the
help." Some cheated with one ploy or another to inflate their support checks. "Instead of seeing their fellow citizens as saviors, many
cattlemen saw the people as suckers." Yet some fully acknowledged
the public sector's help, as did one Texan who admitted, "If it hadn't
been for the government, I never would have come through. . . ."[17]

Western herdsmen, through the Taylor Grazing Act of 1934,
also finally gained freer access to the public domain. Since 1885,
when Congress forbade fencing of public lands, ranchers increas-

[17] Ibid., pp. 139, 141, 142.

ingly had been forced to deal with government bureaucrats to graze public grass. By the late nineteenth century cattlemen understandably favored the gradual but persistent withdrawal of land from homestead entry by the Department of Interior's Division of Forestry, but they groused over grazing fees and the permit procedures of the foresters. Along with lumbering interests ranchers favored the reorganization of the division as the Forest Service and its transfer to the Department of Agriculture, which was popularly perceived as more supportive of its constituencies than Interior, which exuded conservation and regulation. The shuffle failed, as far as herdsmen were concerned, for foresters retained rigid controls and, during the 1920s, even raised grazing fees by 200 percent. Moreover, the Forest Service refused to liberalize its policy of granting priority leases to area stockmen or to modify its fee structure even when widespread drouth during the early 1930s caused plainsmen to apply for grazing permits in unprecedented numbers.

Edward Taylor, a Colorado congressman, introduced legislation to move the land to Department of the Interior control. Modified substantially by the legislative process, the Taylor Act as signed into law by Franklin D. Roosevelt authorized the creation of fifty grazing districts on 80 million acres of western public land. It gave preference to operators living near the districts and set monthly fees of five cents a head on horses and cattle and one cent on sheep and goats. Long-term leases (up to ten years) were permitted for the first time. Twenty thousand mostly temporary permits were awarded under the law the first year, allowing 1.6 million cattle and 9.2 million sheep access to public grass, while the new Grazing Service surveyed the range to determine carrying capacity.

When the Department of the Interior meanwhile tried to collect fees on revocable temporary permits, the Nevada State Cattle Association sued in federal court, which agreed that the government was not authorized under the Taylor Act to assess temporary fees. Historian Edward Wentworth asserts, "This decision in 1940 hastened practical regulation under the Taylor Act, although it left a feeling of unfair treatment among men whose fees had not been returned."[18] Probably because of the competition with the new grazing districts, in 1935 the Forest Service also reduced its fees in line

[18] Edward Wentworth, *America's sheep trails* (1948), p. 513.

with Interior's for its remaining lands, but it also reduced by 50 percent the number of animals it allowed to browse in National Forest meadows.

Overall, however, the government helped rather than hurt cattlemen, assisting big and small operators alike. The Bureau of Animal Industry, infused with New Deal appropriations, increased its effort to eradicate brucellosis and tuberculosis in cattle, both of which infected an estimated one head in eleven in the United States. Also welcomed, especially by western ranchers, was an Emergency Relief Administration–sponsored Bureau of Biological Survey predator-control program, which concentrated on the bane of herdsmen—bears, cougars, wolves, and coyotes. Senator Tom Connally of Texas also bottled up in the Committee on Foreign Relations a proposed Sanitary Convention with Argentina, under the Reciprocal Trade Act of 1934, which would have thrown open the United States to South American beef.

Assistance also came through the combined efforts of various agencies that planted stands of trees, called shelterbelts, on the plains at right angles to prevailing winds to reduce soil erosion. Unintended aid for big operators even came from the Resettlement Administration, which exchanged land with some destitute farmers, trading irrigable acreage principally on the Great Plains for worn-out tracts farther east. Many of these transplants failed to take root on the plains. "A few livestock farmers [also] failed, but they usually raised very little feed. The most successful farmers combined their enterprises, or else concentrated on livestock. . . . As the defeated farmers left the Plains, the cattlemen came to take over, but the newcomers came as ranch or pasture farmers, not as herdsmen."[19]

Mother Nature—ongoing drouth on the prairies and plains, back-to-back ferocious winters with killer storms, a plague of grasshoppers, and a horde of rabbits—helped Washington bureaucrats reduce the nation's cattle herd by 11 percent, to 66 million head between 1935 and 1939, when war fever began to influence the economy and its commodity markets. Before wartime demanded affected values, slaughter beeves advanced in price by $1.50 a hundredweight, doubling in value to an average of $40.60 each. During the

[19] Schlebecker, *Cattle raising on the plains*, p. 149.

same period per capita beef and veal consumption declined by 10 percent. Conservation also caught on, especially when encouraged by the second Agricultural Adjustment Act (1938) and actively sustained by the Civilian Conservation Corps, in spite of objections by some who believed "it to be the first step in the regimentation of their industry."[20]

Big-pasture cattlemen wanted from the government not regulation but help: more demonstration stock farms; better roads over which to market their livestock in inexpensive, versatile trucks; advances against animal diseases; and research related to breed improvement. Cheating by cattlemen on assorted federal programs was allegedly widespread. An estimated 44 million acres of public land were illegally grazed; inaccurate head counts to alter subsidies and fees reportedly were widespread during the New Deal era.

The outbreak of war in Europe in 1939 invigorated the American economy, and cattlemen achieved unparalleled prosperity in the process. As employment increased and affluence returned, Americans rediscovered their taste for fresh beef. When the Department of War entered the meat market in 1942 to feed depression-gaunt youths in uniform, cattlemen were hard pressed to fill demand. The story was much the same throughout the national economy. Pared back because of depression, business in general initially had so much difficulty meeting wartime needs that Congress created the Office of Price Administration to regulate wages and prices lest they skyrocket during the emergency. In 1943, President Roosevelt ordered an across-the-board price freeze, pending implementation of regulations.

Many cattlemen grumbled about price regulation, and some reportedly engaged in black marketeering. Controlled though they were, wholesale prices for beeves crept upward anyway, reaching a peak of $12.41 in late 1945, up from $11.50 in precontrolled, prerationed 1943. Forced by a bizarre point system to compete against other scarce foodstuffs, beef purchases nevertheless were stacked high in the public shopping cart, and consumption rose by 12 percent overall during regulation. By mid-1944 livestock raisers had expanded their herds sufficiently to meet most of the demand, and all cuts but beefsteak and roasts were removed from rationing. All

[20] Ibid., p. 159.

meat rationing ended late in 1945, and price controls were dismantled soon thereafter. Meanwhile, retail meat prices had actually
declined by 4 percent by war's end. Most cattlemen therefore looked
forward to a promising postwar economic environment, even though
the importation of foreign beef and veal had climbed to 127 million
pounds annually, up from 2.4 million pounds in 1940. Domestic
production, which amounted to eighty times that of total imports,
seemed fully capable of withstanding foreign competition.

Sheep and swine producers underwent similar experiences during the interwar period. Sheep raisers continued a trend toward
commercial feeding begun during the nineteenth century. Plagued
with predator problems and sometimes shut out of rangeland by
competing cattlemen, sheepherders over the years had found commercial feedlots a feasible alternative to migratory grazing. During
the 1880s an average of 1.8 million sheep (mostly lambs) were
recorded on feed (primarily corn), principally in the Platte and
Arkansas river valleys of Nebraska and Kansas. By World War I the
number of feedlot sheep had swelled to 4 million; the total slowly
grew to 5.7 million head on the eve of World War II.

This growth, however, was not accompanied by an expansion
of market demand for lamb and mutton. "Per capita consumption of
mutton and lamb in the United States," a 1930 study reported, "indicates but little flexibility, principally because of competition of
beef, pork, poultry, fish, and other meat and meat products."[21]
Since the turn of the century consumption patterns had remained
remarkably stable, the demand for mutton and lamb holding firm at
between 5 and 7 pounds per capita a year for four decades. Most
ranchers raised sheep for their fleece, as had been the practice from
colonial times, and if sheep had not seriously competed with cattle
for western grazing land, they might be almost wholly ignored in
this book.

Hogs, on the other hand, held their own in the red-meat
trade. For most of the first half of the twentieth century pork consumption in the United States usually equaled and sometimes exceeded that of beef and veal. In 1900 the typical American ate 71.9
pounds of pork, 72.3 pounds of beef and veal, and 6.5 pounds of

[21] George Lewis, *An analysis of shipments of Texas sheep and goats* (1930), p. 23.

lamb and mutton; in 1920, 63.5 pounds of pork, 67.1 pounds of beef, and 5.4 pounds of lamb; in 1940, 73.5 pounds of pork, 62.3 pounds of beef, and 6.6 pounds of lamb; and in 1945, 66.6 pounds of pork, 71.3 pounds of beef, and 7.3 pounds of lamb. Hog raisers nevertheless often lagged in income, during the 1920s, for example, earning only about two-thirds that of their counterparts in cattle raising.

Early twentieth-century pig farmers tended to be far more diversified than cattlemen and hence were much more sensitive to a number of variables, from fluctuating grain prices to alleged trader-manipulated squeezes on the Chicago Mercantile Exchange. By World War I swine production naturally bulked in the Midwest (Illinois, Indiana, Iowa, Missouri, Nebraska, and Ohio), where mixed farmers played the market, feeding cheap grain to hogs when corn prices were low. The ploy worked essentially because, unlike a grass-fed calf, which required a minimum of two years to reach marketable age and profitable size, a litter of pigs could be fattened to slaughter weight (or to breeding age) within six months on almost any inexpensive variety of feeds, including swill.

Consequently, swine raisers seemingly held an ideal position to expand (or reduce) output in response to fickle market demand for red meat. As often as not, though, most pig farmers missed the peaks and plunged into the valleys. About World War I swine expert George E. Day remarked:

> When, owing to scarcity in the supply of hogs, we find the price for hogs goes up, we find farmers increasing the number of breeding sows, and in a very short time the supply of hogs coming to market increased to such an extent that the price is likely to break. If the decrease in price is very severe, the farmer becomes disgusted, and the chances are that many farmers will sell their breeding sows and practically go out of the business. This unloading process adds to the burden of the market, and general demoralization is apt to follow. By and by, after the market has absorbed the excessive supplies thrown upon it, a scarcity occurs again, . . . and the history of the hog market repeats itself.[22]

[22] George Day, *Productive swine husbandry* (1913), p. 3.

Yet pigs are not as readily raised to marketable age as is generally supposed. They contract everything from influenza to roundworms, and, closely confined, they easily infect one another; epidemics sometimes wipe out thousands of animals virtually overnight. Lacking sweat glands, swine also literally die of heat prostration unless provided with shelter or cooling mud in which to wallow. Nor do hogs take to the cold, often becoming antisocial. According to Iowa swine raiser Larry Watt, in cold weather hogs "take a nip out of one another just to be doing something." In the wintertime they also lose interest in breeding: "Pigs will often say to hell with it and go off in a corner."[23] From time to time swine raisers must have been similarly tempted to chuck it all.

Convinced that the livestock market at the Chicago Union Stock Yards as well as the futures market at the city's Mercantile Exchange favored the buyer, some American Farm Bureau Federation hog farmers in 1921 devised a cooperative marketing scheme. The plan "called for a system of terminal livestock commission associations with a central administrative organization, the livestock commission associations to be supplied by producing members bound together through local cooperative shipping associations."[24] Merely a rope of sand, the system worked no better than had some of the railroad pools of the previous century. Independent farmers too often dumped hogs whenever it was advantageous to them.

Dumping, of course, caused wide swings in prices and in the fortunes of pig farmers. Having reached a historic high of $16.39 a hundredweight in 1919, hog prices slid by 22 percent the next year and another 22 percent the year following. Once the short postwar depression bottomed out in 1921, swine prices advanced slowly, cresting late in 1926 at $11.70 a hundredweight; thereafter the trend was a long, bumpy descent to an interwar low of $3.34 in 1932, merely one-fifth the record high at the end of World War I. Prices recovered quickly during the New Deal era, to reach $9.37 a hundredweight in 1936; thereafter the market fluctuated mildly until wartime demand in 1942 and price controls in 1943 combined to set $13.00 a hundredweight as a floor for wholesale pork prices. Un-

---

[23] Quoted in David Garino, "Ralph Shiver's pigs often die trying to avoid the cold," *Wall Street Journal*, February 16, 1982, p. 1.

[24] Saloutos and Hicks, *Twentieth century populism*, p. 280.

like quotations for beef and veal, which by then had duplicated World War I levels, pork prices did not surpass their historic high until 1946, a year after the war ended.

Swine raisers might have fared better during the interwar period if some of their champions in Congress had had their way. The McNary-Haugen Bill, according to President Coolidge's veto message, "contemplates that the packers may be commissioned by the Government to buy hogs enough to create a near scarcity in this country, slaughter the hogs, sell the pork products abroad at a loss, and have their losses, costs, and charges made good out of the pockets of farm taxpayers."[25] In 1933 the New Deal's first Agricultural Adjustment Act actually created a "pig-buying program." It authorized the USDA to purchase potentially millions of pigs weighing under a hundred pounds and at least 1 million sows due to farrow in fall. Designed to reduce swine supplies by 15 percent and to provide some food to the destitute through the Federal Emergency Relief Corporation, the program commissioned the principal pork packers in the Chicago, Kansas City, Omaha, Sioux City, St. Joseph, and St. Paul livestock markets to process pigs weighing thirty pounds or more into dry salt pork and to render smaller beasts (about 90 percent of the total) into inedible grease and fertilizer tankage.

On August 24, agriculture secretary Wallace ordered the six stockyards opened and announced the integration of others into the program as soon as possible. It was not soon enough. The following day all six yards were glutted with pigs, clogged to a standstill. It took Armour, Cudahy, Swift, Wilson, and the other packers a full week to digest them all. "The country was horrified by the mass matricide and infanticide," says historian William Leuchtenburg. "When piglets overran the stockyards and scampered squealing through the streets of Chicago and Omaha, the nation rallied to the side of the victims of oppression, seeking to flee their dreadful fate."[26] To regulate the flow, the Agricultural Adjustment Administration decreed that henceforth dealers must have permits before shipping swine to market, but this gave dealers who held the coveted paper

[25] Quoted in McGovern (ed.), *Agricultural thought in the twentieth century*, p. 128.

[26] William Leuchtenburg, *Franklin D. Roosevelt and the new deal, 1932–1940* (1963), p. 73.

unfair leverage. Some unscrupulous dealers also bought pigs cheap from uninformed farmers, selling them dear to the government.

Farmers participating in the AAA program theoretically were required to reduce commercial hog production 25 percent, but there was little inspection and less enforcement. The swine surplus nevertheless was steadily reduced. In 1934 the Federal Surplus Relief Corporation bought several million fat hogs for distribution among the needy, and by 1935 the number of swine in the United States had been cut by 36 percent, to 37.2 million head from 58.3 million in 1930. New Deal programs were controversial even among their beneficiaries. Some decried the meddling, others the seemingly wasteful, inhumane slaughter of millions of small squealing animals, but by 1936 the substantial reduction in the swine herd had tripled wholesale swine prices and undoubtedly saved many pig farmers from bankruptcy.

Government action also regularized the pig cycle. Massachusetts Institute of Technology economist Dennis Meadows insists:

> It is not corn prices, but the hog-corn ratio which determines the level of hog production. This ratio measures the amount of corn in bushels equal in value to 100 pounds of live hogs. When the ratio decreases, it becomes relatively more profitable to sell corn directly to consumers. When the ratio increases, it is more profitable to feed the corn to hogs and then sell the resulting pork products. The [various] corn programs [of the USDA, originating with the second Agricultural Adjustment Act of 1938] affected only the denominator of the ratio, leaving the price of hogs still free to fluctuate. Short-run changes in the demand for pork still were possible as temporary imbalances between supply and demand brought changes in the price of hogs and pork. Moreover, the inventories of corn created by the program permitted the stock of hogs to be expanded and contracted more quickly in response to these demand changes.
>
> As a consequence, hog fluctuations were not decreased. But as their source shifted from exogenous random factors [such as weather, war, and business cycles], to the endogenous characteristics of the system itself, the cycles did become more regular. A periodicity of about four years began to emerge.[27]

---

[27]Dennis Meadows, *Dynamics of commodity production cycles* (1970), pp. 38–39.

This cycle, shorter than that for cattle, has led to a volatile pork price structure.

The USDA continued its traditional assistance to pig farmers. The market had changed significantly since the Civil War, when lard-type beasts were in demand. After the turn of the century packers increasingly preferred meatier animals containing a higher proportion of lean cuts. In 1934 researchers in quest of the perfect pork chop imported Danish Landrace boars to breed to Berkshire, Chester White, Duroc, Hampshire, Poland China, Tamworth, and Yorkshire dams. Federally sponsored research conducted at agricultural colleges and experiment stations in a dozen states, principally in the pig belt, produced a number of new strains. Private breeders bred back some of these new strains to produce the American Landrace, one-sixteenth to one-fourth Poland China. Although there was relatively little market incentive, swine producers successfully developed leaner, more muscular hogs. Ironically, some of these animals developed Porcine Stress Syndrome: extremely muscular hogs proved to be susceptible to even the slightest stress, sometimes dropping dead without warning.

The federal government also paid for research work on more than a dozen swine diseases and parasites that cost farmers millions of dollars a year. Hog cholera, first reported in Ohio in 1833, soon became a recurring enzootic disease that killed one beast in ten in 1887, 1896, 1919, and 1926. Already facing hard times in 1938, farmers also lost an estimated $10 million worth of animals to the malady. In 1907 scientists at the University of Iowa had developed a crude but moderately effective vaccine; however, nothing but slaughtering was known to contain an outbreak. Continuing work at the National Animal Disease Laboratory in Ames, Iowa, during the depression and war years ultimately resulted in the identification of an RNA-type virus as the cause of the cholera and, in 1951, the development of a more effective live-virus serum. Swine influenza, contracted from human beings in the great pandemic of 1918 that killed an estimated 20 million persons worldwide, became "fixed" in swine because lungworms eaten along with other filth in contaminated pigsties served as the virus's intermediate host during the usually dormant spring and summer months. It never became as virulent among pigs as it did among people, however.

Most of all, pig farmers, like cattle raisers, wanted the government to constrain the meatpackers. As noted earlier, in 1920, to avoid further antitrust prosecution, Armour, Cudahy, Morris, Swift, and Wilson signed a consent decree whereby they agreed to divest themselves within two years of all holdings in public stockyards, terminal railroads and facilities, private railroad cars, cold-storage warehouses, and market newspapers; however, in the words of economist Harry Laidler, "they neglected to obey it. They asked instead for an extension of time."[28] In 1925 the FTC reported to the U.S. Senate that Armour's acquisition of Morris in 1923 had probably violated the consent decree and had unquestionably decreased competition in meatpacking. Moreover, while the surviving Big Four had disposed of about one-quarter of their stockyards holdings, they "still monopolize the meat-refrigeration service of the country."[29]

In 1925, Armour and Swift separately filed suits in federal court to have the consent decree modified. They contended that they were "at a disadvantage as compared with other packers" not covered by the decree and that "chain stores were pushing back their activities to sources of supply and were both preparing and distributing meat and other products."[30] Evidence supported their contention, for the Big Four had seen their market share shrink to 60 percent of all interstate red-meat trade, from more than 70 percent at war's end. Some business had been lost to aggressive small packers, such as century-old John Morrell & Co., lately of Ottumwa, Iowa, which in 1929 grossed $100 million in sales, about 7 percent of the market.

In the decades that followed, improved transportation facilities—along with widespread use of mechanical refrigeration at all links in the red-meat chain—revolutionized meat distribution in the United States. Motor vehicles freed meatpackers and distributors alike from the static facilities of railroads, and during the interwar period the red-meat industry increasingly adapted this new mode of transportation to their needs. While early refrigerated trucks were crude (usually sawdust-insulated tin bodies cooled by salted ice packed in barrels), they were vastly more flexible than trains. For instance, one Detroit packer at the end of World War I reduced its

[28] Harry Laidler, *Concentration of control in American industry* (1931), p. 205.

[29] U.S. Congress, Senate, *Packer consent decree*, Document No. 219 (68th Cong., 2d Sess., 1924–1925) Serial 8413, p. 17.

[30] Laidler, *Concentration of control in American industry*, p. 206.

transportation time to Toledo to six hours, from two and a half days, by using trucks rather than rail.

Statistical data on truck transport before 1950 are fragmentary, but the rate of growth was obviously phenomenal. As Robert Aduddell and Louis Cain have pointed out: "Before the coming of the truck refrigerated rail transport was the only means of shipping meat. Insofar as the major packers owned 92 percent of such specialized transport in 1917, they had an important advantage in shipping their products. When trucks were substituted for rail cars, the advantage declined."[31] By 1946 the red-meat industry was utilizing 100,000 trucks—two-thirds of which were mechanically chilled—one-third of the total being owned by large interstate transport firms not associated with meatpackers and by independent truckers. By then about half of all fresh meat was hauled over highways, but most of the trips were a hundred miles or less; longer journeys continued to be by rail until well after World War II and the introduction of the long-haul tractor-trailer refrigerated rig.

Even so, between the Great Crash and the end of World War II improved transportation allowed the packers to reduce the number of branch houses by 35 percent, thereby substantially increasing the volume of trade passing through independent processors and jobbers, and even that moving directly from packers to retail warehouses or even retail markets. The principal beneficiaries of change were "breakers," "boners," and "peddlers," whose refrigerated warehouses, processing rooms, and delivery trucks were handling one-fourth of all the red-meat trade by the end of World War II. Breakers brought whole beef, veal, and lamb carcasses from independent slaughterhouses and meatpackers and "broke" (or divided) them into primal, wholesale, and, to a limited extent, retail cuts. Most of their output went to independent peddlers, especially to "meat purveyors." "Boners" were processors who specialized in providing boneless cuts for further processing by bulk users, such as canners and pet-food manufacturers; much of the meat used was of lower grades. During World War II boners also processed USDA Good and Choice beef for the armed forces.

About one-fifth of all jobbers of the period were meat purveyors

[31] Robert Aduddell and Louis Cain, "The consent decree in the meatpacking industry, 1920–1956," *Business History Review* 55 (1981), p. 361.

who supplied the steadily expanding urban food-service industry—
restaurants, hotels, hospitals, and other institutional users—primarily with superior grades of red meat, especially beef. Originating
during the nineteenth century, when they hauled fresh meat about
in horse-drawn carts, purveyors become important distributors following the advent of refrigerated trucks in the twentieth century,
especially after World War II. The rest were independent peddlers,
usually small, one-man proprietor-operator businesses that specialized in buying cut meat from processors and selling it to independent retailers and small restaurants.

Purveyors and peddlers also sold to meat markets and grocery
chains. Meat markets dominated the retail scene until the end of
World War II, but few of these enjoyed sufficient volume to buy a
whole carload (30,000 pounds) of meat directly from the packer;
however, grocery chains could and did buy in sufficient quantities
to deal directly with the packer. By 1929 the Great Atlantic & Pacific Tea Company operated four thousand stores nationally; the
Kroger Grocery and Baking Co. had a thousand outlets in the Midwest; and the Skaggs Safeway Grocery Co.'s twelve hundred shops
stretched from southern California to Idaho. In addition to purchasing from meatpackers carlots and even multiple carlots of meat,
which was further broken into cuts suited to the retail trade at regional warehouses operated by chains, A&P, Kroger, and Safeway
developed their own meat-processing operations, relying far more
on refrigerated truck transport than on the railroads.

Meatpackers were not always so progressive. Basic plant design
had changed very little since the 1880s, most facilities remaining
multistoried structures that relied on animal power to move the raw
material to the top floors, where the beasts were killed, and gravity
to propel the chains that carted carcasses along disassembly lines.
While electricity-generated mechanical refrigeration became increasingly common after World War I, packers expanded refrigerated areas beyond the storage room to include areas in which carcasses were boned and broken into retail cuts. Other intermediate
steps in the disassembly process remained unchanged until well
after World War II. There were a few technological advances—de-
hairing devices for hogs, specially shaped knives for "pulling" loins,
and the like.

All was not well within the old beef trust. Armour's acquisition of Morris in 1923, even the FTC conceded, prevented the latter's outright bankruptcy and probably many plant closings. Wilson & Co., saddled with a huge takeover debt dating to Schwarschild & Sulzberger days, underwent corporate reorganization in 1924 to avoid bankruptcy. Public investigations continued to disclose sporadic collusion, especially between Armour and Swift, to share territory and fix prices, but even so throughout the 1920s the Big Four averaged only 1.09 percent profit on sales, while their competition, the smaller packers and the new grocer-processors, reported 2.17 percent.

Finding that size alone did not afford the Big Four unreasonably high profits, the U.S. Supreme Court in 1932 modified the consent decree to allow the packers to retain their fleets of refrigerator cars and trucks; however, retail activities continued to be proscribed, for such probably "would result in the complete annihilation of the independent retail grocer, already a minority in volume of business."[32] The Court also affirmed the other provisions of the consent decree, ordering meatpackers to sell off forthwith their remaining stockyards, terminal railroads, warehouses, grocery lines, and market newspapers.

Because the Big Four were eager to be rid of stockyards, Congress had enacted the Packers and Stockyards Act in 1921 to facilitate the corporate divorce. In essence a code of fair practices laid down by law and enforced by the secretary of agriculture, the enactment made stockyards quasi-public utilities and, anticipating the Securities and Exchange Act a dozen years later, required yard officers, agents, and employees to register with the government. Stockyards, which might offer their services at fixed fees, were forbidden to deal in the livestock they handled. Yards were directed by law to maintain orderly accounts and proper weights and measures and to pay their shippers regularly. For their part packers were henceforth forbidden to own stockyards, to apportion supply among themselves, or to "engage in any course of business or do any act for the purpose of with the effect of manipulating or controlling prices in commerce, or of creating a monopoly in the acquisition of, buy-

[32] *Swift & Co.* v. *U.S.*, 286 US 106 (1932).

ing, selling, or dealing in, any article in commerce, or of restraining commerce."[33] Livestock raisers were placated, and the packers seemingly constrained. "To the majority of packing industry leaders," says Bertran Fowler in a sympathetic treatment of the industry, "the divorce was a welcome one."[34]

By 1940 the government had also promulgated an official livestock and meat-market vocabulary. Cattle were graded as Fancy, Choice, Good, Medium, Common, Inferior, Canner, or Cutter according to "conformation" (shape of animal) and "finish" (quantity and distribution of fat on the beast). Similarly, carcass beef was termed Prime, Choice, Good, Commercial, Utility, Cutter, or Canner based upon the conformation, maturity, and "marbling" (flecks of fat in the muscle). The USDA likewise classed feeder and slaughter sheep and lambs from Fancy to Inferior, or Cull, and the resulting meat from Choice to Cull. Slaughter swine were graded Fat-Type Choice, Meat-Type Choice, Good, Medium, or Cull. Poultry and eggs, increasingly significant rivals of red meat for the protein dollar, were also categorized by the government before World War II to provide buyer and seller similar information in the marketplace. In 1942 the Prime grade designation was suspended for the duration of the war, Choice becoming the top grade of beef during that era of shortages, and the Meat Inspection Division of the USDA was temporarily transferred to the War Food Administration.

The Meat Inspection Division also administered the provisions of the Meat Inspection Act (1906), which mandated continuous federal supervision of interstate red-meat preparation. The law required ante- and postmortem inspection of interstate carcass meat and the stamp U.S. INSPECTED AND PASSED affixed to approved products. Transportation of unpassed product was made punishable by fine of not more than $10,000 and/or two years in jail. The USDA might withdraw inspection service from any establishment that violated the law or agency regulations. "A withdrawal of inspection privileges," says Arthur Herrick, "is tantamount to closing the channels of interstate commerce to the packer, at least so far as products within the purview of the statute are concerned."[35] Fur-

[33] *Packers and Stockyards Act, 1921* (42 Stat. 159), p. 202.
[34] Bertram Fowler, *Men, meat and miracles* (1952), p. 204.
[35] Arthur Herrick, *Food regulation and compliance* (2 vols.; 1948), I, 35.

thermore, by 1940 separate Food and Drug Administration regulations forbade "the addition of substances which impair the product's
wholesomeness or which are not approved by the chief of division."[36] Aside from salt, sugar, woodsmoke, and the like, meat additives were specifically enumerated in quantity (as with benzoic
acid, which might not exceed 0.001 percent per volume), allowed
only if later purged from the product (as with the heavy metal nickel,
which was used in the hydrogenation of lard) or proscribed altogether (as with the embalming fluid formaldehyde).

Most meatpackers welcomed inspectors "into their plants and
cooperated with them in every way possible to fulfill the provisions
of the law," says business historian Lawrence Cheever. "If for no
other reason, this Act must be considered of prime importance to
the industry because it aided the packers in clearing up a lot of mis-
understanding on the part of the general public. Likewise, it assured
this same public they need have no fear of meat products coming
from federally inspected plants."[37]

However much meatpackers welcomed federal inspectors, they
resisted further regulation. The American Meat Packers Association
(the American Meat Institute after 1940), the lobby organized about
the turn of the century by Thomas Wilson to counter adverse publicity associated with the muckrakers, became especially active following the FTC's recommendations in 1919 to nationalize much of
the industry. Wilson gave the trade association the job of "launching
a real program of public relations," Bertram Fowler says. "Through
the Institute, Wilson saw, the packers could enter into conferences
with livestock producers, retail dealers and trade associations, government officials and all the organizations formed to aid and further
the advancement of livestock production and agriculture,"[38] without automatically running afoul of antitrust law.

Through the trade association Wilson offered the stock raiser
the packer's hand in cooperation to debunk what both believed were
harmful myths spread during the roaring twenties by vegetarians
and food faddists about red meat, especially beef. The meatpackers
collectively lost $100 million in 1921, much of which they ascribed

[36] Ibid., II, 718.
[37] Lawrence Cheever, *The house of Morrell* (1948), p. 139.
[38] Fowler, *Men, meat and miracles,* p. 140.

to adverse publicity. Together with the American National Livestock Association, the American Meat Packers Association created the National Live Stock and Meat Board, consisting of eleven representatives of cattlemen and two each from AMPA, the commission merchants, and retailers. The Live Stock and Meat Board, Fowler insists, was "an organization in which they [the packers] could meet producers for the purpose of open discussion and co-operation, and not an organization which the packers could dominate."[39]

The American Meat Packers Association also sponsored an independent research laboratory, endowed with a half million dollars by 1940, at the prestigious University of Chicago. Some of its findings, as well as those from collateral, AMPA-funded research at Rochester and Columbia universities, tended to refute the era's wildest exaggerations about red meat—that it caused high blood pressure and damaged the kidneys and other organs. All favorable information on red meat was widely disseminated by the packers' association. Scientific research, particularly that at the University of Chicago, also naturally uncovered improved methods of curing and handling meat, technological advances in which all members of AMPA shared—as with synthetic sausage casings developed by the Mellon Institute.

At a time when hams routinely were harshly cured—reaching the consumer as chunks of meat that had to be parboiled in progressively fresher water to be edible—European meat processors developed a five-day curing process that offered far more palatable pork. Wilson & Co. independently developed a process that resulted in two new retail hams, respectively trademarked Certified, "guaranteed to reach the table with a maximum of flavor and tenderness without parboiling," and Tender Made, which "offered the housewife a mild and precooked" ham. "The improved methods of curing," Fowler says, "elevated ham to a place on the family table with prime ribs of beef and the festive roast turkey."[40] Indeed, per capita pork consumption climbed slightly between the wars, while that for beef and lamb remained unchanged.

The rest of the industry developed competitive lines. About 1940 the USDA accepted nitrite as a pork curative, and Geo. A.

[39] Ibid., p. 161.
[40] Ibid., pp. 169, 171.

Hormel & Co. quickly introduced a semisterile canned ham. Using iceless refrigeration, increasingly available to industry and to consumers following World War I, Wilson & Co. also marketed sliced, cellophane-prepackaged bacon to compete with butcher-shop slab that, often as not, became rancid in primitive iceboxes unless it was quickly consumed. Wilson's technique was soon copied and in time adapted to popular cuts of beef, pork, and lamb, and to viscera (such as liver), which once had been treated as tankage by most packers, and was often given to preferred customers by retail butchers.

In 1930, Cudahy & Co. discovered low-temperature quick freezing to be an efficient method of extending the storage life of meat, and with the shelf life of their products further extended by mechanical refrigeration, meatpackers broadened their trade lines. They offered more succulent sausages, such as that of Chicago processor Oscar Mayer, whose family recipe remains today a closely guarded corporate secret. In 1940 the American Meat Institute kicked off a nationwide advertising campaign in *Life* magazine featuring sausage. About then packers transformed luncheon meats from a specialty sideline for a few firms into a vigorously competitive struggle between large firms and small for the rapidly expanding urban fast-food market. Armour's Treet, Cudahy's Tang, Swift's Prem, and Wilson's Mor became nationally recognized trade names. So too did Hormel's Spam, which became a staple of GI's during World War II.

Big packers or small, they all had labor problems. In 1918, Federal Judge Samuel Alschuler, a wartime arbitrator appointed by the Wilson administration, had imposed industrial peace on the industry by ordering the packers to reduce the workday from ten to eight hours, without a reduction in pay, and to pay up to time and one-half over forty-eight hours a week, with forty hours guaranteed. The Amalgamated Meat Cutters and Butcher Workmen of North America, while not then officially recognized by any of the packers as the sole bargaining agent for its workers, provided spokesmen for employees in establishing grievance procedures mandated by Alschuler, which by law were to remain in force no more than one year following the end of the war.

Because the Senate failed to ratify the Treaty of Versailles, a joint congressional resolution, signed by President Warren G. Harding on July 2, 1921, was required to proclaim peace and to deregulate the national economy, including meatpacking. By then the United States was suffering the worst economic times of the century to date and the deepest industrial depression in its history. The crisis had thrown 5 million Americans, 11.9 percent of the labor force, out of work. Red-meat sales lagged. In 1921 Armour & Co. lost $31.7 million and, released from the Alschuler edict in November, unilaterally slashed wages between 6 and 16 percent, the larger drawbacks taken from the least skilled, the employees easiest to replace in an era of widespread unemployment.

A clash was inevitable. Labor unrest was widespread in meatpacking, and had been since the Chicago race riot of 1919. When Armour slashed wages, Amalgamated counted 40,000 dues-paying members, about one-third of the industry's work force, three-fourths of whom labored in Chicago. Strike fever was also reportedly high among many nonunion workers. The union consequently called for a walkout in mid-November. Strikers were enthusiastic at Denver and at several of the river points—Kansas City, Omaha, Sioux City, and South St. Paul. The strike was weak in St. Louis and inconsequential in St. Joseph. Police, deputy sheriffs, and even National Guard were called out to suppress sporadic outbursts of violence during the initial days of the walkout. In Ottumwa the militia was mobilized to protect the property of John Morrell & Co., and in St. Paul troops with fixed bayonets patrolled the stockyards. In Chicago the meatpackers claimed that fewer than 10 percent of their workers walked off the job. The union insisted that there were far more, perhaps as many as 20,000 altogether, most of them from the plants of the Big Five.

Armed with injunctions based on the contemporary American Steel Foundries case, the Chicago police soon reduced the impact of pickets to almost nothing, and allied trade guilds throughout the stockyards—engineers, firemen, and teamsters—while promising sympathy strikes, often refused to honor those picket lines that Amalgamated was able to man. "The big packers, all of whom began to recruit strikebreakers, experienced little difficulty in finding replacements," says labor historian David Brody. "The suffering of the strikers and their families grew intense as the winter deepened. Relief committees drew on local support, but they could not provide adequate assistance. . . . the strikers were forced by privation to return to work in increasing numbers."[41] Amalgamated appealed to the Department of Labor for assistance, and it offered Armour and the other packers use of its Conciliation Service, which was curtly declined. The meatpackers also refused to discuss wage cuts or any other issue with the union. Amalgamated, with three-fourths of its members back at work on company terms anyway, had little choice but to declare a formal end to the strike on February 1, 1922.

Once more the union was virtually broken. Meatpackers re-hired selectively during the years that followed, and Meat Cutters and Butcher Workmen members were not popular during open-hiring calls. During the interwar years Amalgamated was far more successful in organizing at the retail level. During the late 1920s and early 1930s it took on Kroger and Safeway at several urban places, in 1935 even signing a master agreement with the latter chain store whereby contractual negotiations would begin whenever the union had 55 percent of the meat cutters within twenty-five miles of a union local's headquarters; however, the open shop prevailed. Following the Supreme Court's approval of the Wagner Act in 1937, many butcher locals sprang up. In Buffalo, New York, four were formed and inducted 2,000 new members within three weeks of the decision. By mid-1940, Amalgamated held contracts with A&P covering sixty-three localities, including Baltimore, Philadelphia, Pittsburgh, and Washington, D.C. By then two-thirds of the company's 9,200 butchers were union men.

Nothing of the sort could be said for packinghouse employees. "Only government intervention," Brody says, "could redress the balance that favored the packers."[42] It began early in the New Deal with the enactment of the National Industrial Recovery Act (1933), the idea for which had originated in the U.S. Chamber of Commerce to suppress ruinous cutthroat price slashing that had set in with the panic of 1929. Under the new law the government agreed to suspend antitrust enforcement and allow American industry and commerce to suppress "unfair competition" through cartellike apportionment of output and markets and, to a degree, to eliminate price competition—provided business agreed to shorten hours, raise wages, and attempt to increase employment.

[41] David Brody, *The butcher workmen* (1964), p. 105.
[42] Ibid.

On August 5, 1933, the American Meat Packers Association on behalf of its membership signed an agreement with the National Recovery Administration whereby it would draw up a code of "fair competition" for the red-meat industry; however, like several other business groups, AMPA received concessions from the NRA which, pending promulgation of a formal code, suspended the law's Section 7(a), which assured workers in participating industries "the right to organize and bargain collectively through the representative of their own choosing." When Amalgamated, swollen with 50,000 new members recruited during the last three months of 1933, presented demands (an eight-hour day, time-and-a-half over forty hours a week, grievance procedures, seniority, shop committees, arbitration, and restoration of 1929 wage rates, with fifty cents an hour minimum), packers separately and collectively through AMPA declined to bargain.

Following the labor strife of the early 1920s many meatpackers had developed representative councils, or conference boards, to open dialogue with their workers to forestall the resurrection of unionist tendencies. Some, such as Swift & Co., always the most enlightened of the packers with respect to labor relations, had introduced grievance procedures, paid vacations, group insurance plans, and other benefits and was genuinely surprised to learn that its workers were unhappy. The NRA invited the packers to Washington to meet with Amalgamated in April, 1934. The packers declined, and the NRA, which by law had the power to fix hours, wages, and working conditions, was unable to force compliance. Some packers claimed that they already carried on collective bargaining through their representative councils. Brody says that even those "forced to acknowledge that the unions did indeed represent their employees took a very narrow view of 'collective bargaining.' The standard practice was to listen to the union's demand and then either assent or decline. But the packers did not bargain; they did not make counter-offers; nor did they sign contracts."[43]

Mostly, they stalled. In mid-1934, AMPA presented the industry's formal opposition to any regulatory code promulgated by the NRA, saying that the industry was already adequately regulated by

[43] Ibid., p. 158.

the Packers and Stockyards Act of 1921. Sporadic strikes flashed, as at Hormel's Austin, Minnesota, plant, where the National Guard was called out; nevertheless, even there an Independent Union of All Workers forced company recognition. Too, communists continued to be active in the Chicago stockyards, as they had been since World War I, especially when it became evident among the rank-and-file that Amalgamated's moderate leaders (President William Green and Secretary-Treasurer Patrick Gorman) opposed strikes, particularly since national unemployment stood at 18 percent. The union's membership dropped to fewer than 15,000 by year's end. Relying primarily upon Washington to force packers to the bargaining table, Amalgamated was stunned when in 1935 the U.S. Supreme Court declared the National Industrial Recovery Act an unconstitutional transfer of legislative power into private hands, as well as an illegal attempt at regulating business in intrastate commerce.

Congress then enacted the National Labor Relations Act, or Wagner Act, which created a three-person board to administer labor relations in interstate commerce. The law established the right of workers to organize and bargain collectively and outlawed as "unfair labor practices" such management tactics as blacklisting, yellow-dog contracts, company unions, and other coercive measures commonly used by employers. When the Supreme Court upheld the law in 1937, Amalgamated rolls swelled to 71,000. "Collective bargaining began," Brody says, "but the reality was little different from before April 1937; there was rarely genuine negotiation or signed agreements, and activities were limited mainly to grievances."[44] This time packers claimed that they did not know with whom to bargain: the Amalgamated Meat Cutters of the American Federation of Labor; the new Packing House Workers Organizing Council (PWOC), sponsored by the Congress of Industrial Organizations; or perhaps some independent group.

Frustrated by the timid approach of the craft-dominated Amalgamated, many workers had been attracted to the PWOC, which initially relied primarily on rank-and-file participation for its vigor. Unlike Amalgamated, the PWOC believed in strikes. On the last day of 1938 shop stewards in Cudahy's Sioux Falls plant blew whistles,

[44]Ibid., p. 170.

whereupon workers stopped production altogether for fifty minutes in a variation of the CIO's generally successful sitdown strike the year before at the Fisher Body Works of General Motors. This device was significantly limited when in 1937 the Supreme Court ruled that the dismissal of sit-down strikers was not an unfair labor practice. Spoiling for a fight anyway, a national PWOC conference in 1939 voted to strike Armour & Co. unless it signed a national agreement. The membership was astounded when union Chairman Van Bittner instead accepted Armour's counteroffer to negotiate on a plant-by-plant basis. A high-handed autocrat who had entrenched himself through cronyism, Bittner was soon ousted and replaced by J. C. Lewis, late of the United Mine Workers.

Denied the facade of pliable company unions by the Wagner Act, packers soon preferred the relatively tame Amalgamated to the strike-prone PWOC. In July, 1939, Amalgamated signed a contract with Kingan & Co.'s Indianapolis plant, which was extended the following year to all other Kingan facilities. It became the basis of a pact in 1938 with Oscar Mayer & Co. Of the Big Four, Cudahy was the most receptive to Amalgamated. While avoiding a national agreement, it nevertheless signed contracts covering its plants in Los Angeles, New York City, and Portland, Oregon—sites where organized labor was strong and consumer boycotts were especially popular.

PWOC began challenging Amalgamated's representation in many plants, and in National Labor Relations Board–sponsored elections workers increasingly voted to switch to the more radical CIO affiliate. By the end of World War II the PWOC represented a plurality of packinghouse workers. Packers nevertheless resisted master agreements with the PWOC, insisting instead on plant-by-plant pacts. For example, Armour & Co. refused to sign an agreement with PWOC that would have covered thirteen of eighteen plants nationwide in which the union had been certified following worker elections, insisting instead on the tedious local negotiations which the unions contended amounted to foot dragging by management. Not until it was ordered to do so by the wartime National Defense Mediation Board in 1941 did Armour sign a master agreement with PWOC. The agreement provided for a five-cent-an-hour increase to raise the minimum wage to seventy-two and a half cents an hour and grievance procedures that eventually allowed disgruntled workers access to federal mediation.

Cudahy and Swift soon signed similar pacts. To avoid a threatened national strike, the Mediation Board early in 1943 also ordered Wilson & Co. to negotiate a master agreement, and shortly thereafter the War Labor Board froze wages for the duration of the conflict—the minimum rate being highest on the West Coast (seventy-seven and a half cents per hour) and the lowest in the Deep South (fifty-two and a half cents). While they were generally exempted from the overtime provisions of the Fair Labor Standards Act (1938), by 1941 most meatpackers were voluntarily paying time-and-a-half after forty hours a week. By August, 1945, collective bargaining had apparently been established throughout the industry, even though most union members believed that the packers "at the first opportunity . . . [would] tear up the Agreement and go back to the old days."[45]

[45] Ibid., p. 210.

Above: Preparing cattle for market was a complex undertaking, the first step being branding, as on the Garst Ranch in south central Kansas during the 1890s (Courtesy, Kansas State Historical Society, Topeka). *Below:* Dehorning, somewhere in west Texas (Courtesy, Southwest Collection, Texas Tech University, Lubbock).

Above: While cattle awaited railroad shipment to assorted national markets from Lubbock, Texas, during the 1950s, buyers and sellers surveyed the livestock from boardwalks (Courtesy, Southwest Collection, Texas Tech University, Lubbock). *Below:* Buyers and sellers meet at livestock auction arenas, such as this one in Lubbock, Texas, ca. 1955 (Courtesy, Southwest Collection, Texas Tech University, Lubbock).

HOGS FEEDING ON ALFALFA ONE MILE FROM CANYON CITY, TEXAS.

Above: Typical of late nineteenth-century swine raisers was this unidentified small farmer in Barton County, Kansas (Courtesy, Kansas State Historical Society, Topeka). *Below:* During the late nineteenth century, large herds of hogs were allowed to run free on some open ranges, as with these alfalfa-fed porkers near Canyon, Texas (Courtesy, Panhandle-Plains Historical Museum, Canyon, Texas).

Above: An itinerant shepherd and his flock near Abilene, Kansas, at the turn of the twentieth century (Courtesy, Kansas State Historical Society, Topeka). *Below:* A large-scale sheep-feeding operation in Finney County, Kansas, about the turn of the twentieth century (Courtesy, Kansas State Historical Society, Topeka).

Above: Frontier farmer-butchers were commonplace in the American tradition from the earliest colonial times, until nationally integrated meat-packing companies using railroad "peddler cars" took their products to even the most remote rural regions (Courtesy, Southwest Collection, Texas Tech University, Lubbock). *Below:* Frontier meat markets were hardly more sanitary than contemporary slaughterhouses deplored by Upton Sinclair (Courtesy, Southwest Collection, Texas Tech University, Lubbock).

Above: A late nineteenth-century hide yard at Canadian, Texas (Courtesy, Panhandle-Plains Historical Museum, Canyon, Texas). *Below:* Interior of A. A. ("Jack") Drummond's Sand Springs, Oklahoma, beef-packing plant, 1934 (Courtesy, Oklahoma Historical Society, Oklahoma City).

Above: Beef (boxed and unboxed) in Excel Corp. coolers, Dodge City, Kansas (Courtesy, Mr. and Mrs. S. H. Marcus, Wichita, Kansas). *Below:* Excel Corp.'s fleet of refrigerated trucks haul boxed beef from coast to coast (Courtesy, Mr. and Mrs. S. H. Marcus, Wichita, Kansas).

Advertising targeted at the fast-paced postwar American lifestyle (Courtesy, Mr. and Mrs. S. H. Marcus, Wichita, Kansas).

6

Prosperity and Inflation, 1945–1983

Forced by World War II rationing into some abstinence, prosperous Americans ate much more red meat once government controls were removed. Indeed, for a time it seemed that the whole United States was alit coast to coast with backyard barbecues. According to the United States Department of Agriculture, at war's end red-meat consumption averaged 145.2 pounds (170.3 pounds, including poultry) for every man, woman, and child in America, a total that virtually replicated the trend since the turn of the century; in 1976, it averaged 193 pounds (232.9 pounds, including poultry); moreover, the population had increased by 64 percent, to an estimated 218 million persons, from about 132.5 million in 1945. Thus, not only had the number of red-meat eaters increased, but, individually, they ate more red meat; however, thereafter, even though the population continued to grow to more than 225 million by 1983, red-meat consumption ebbed, declining to merely 144.7 pounds (210 pounds, including poultry) per capita.

Beef was the principal beneficiary of the post-war red-meat boom, as well as the primary victim of recent changes in tastes and preferences. In 1945, Americans consumed an average of 71.3 pounds of beef and veal, 66.6 pounds of pork, and 7.3 pounds of lamb, mutton, and goat (and an additional 25.1 pounds of poultry); in 1976, the most gluttonous postwar year of red-meat consumption in the United States, they averaged 129.8 pounds of beef, 61.5 pounds of pork, and 1.7 pounds of lamb (and an additional 39.9 pounds of poultry). Thereafter, the market for red meat began to erode, per capita beef consumption slipping in 1983 to 78.2 pounds and pork to 61.9 pounds; lamb, mutton, and goat consumption actually increased slightly, to 4.6 pounds per capita, and the poultry market made huge gains, consumption rising to 65.6 pounds per capita.

As early as 1947 the early postwar trend was apparent. Per capita consumption of red meat had jumped 6.9 percent overall since the end of the war, the lion's share (90 percent) of that 10.1-pound increase being beef. Livestock production, however—especially of cattle for the booming fresh-beef trade—did not immediately expand. Says historian and ranching authority John Schlebecker:

> Unquestionably, cattlemen and others intentionally created a meat shortage before controls ended. Producers held their cattle off the market as they waited for the end of controls; when controls did cease, they expected prices to shoot up. They were right, and they did not have to wait long. In October, 1946, all meat controls ended, and prices immediately rose. Stimulated by price incentives, producers sold all they could, but they could not market enough beef to satisfy consumers. The postwar inflation had begun.[1]

By the end of 1947 live-cattle quotations had vaulted by 58.8 percent to an average of $23.29 a hundredweight, from $14.66 in 1945. Retail prices climbed 40 percent virtually overnight, causing many consumers to curtail all meat purchases, especially beef. In 1948 outraged housewives boycotted meat markets, and during the height of Korean War inflation red-meat consumption in the United States declined to 138 pounds per capita (46.4 percent beef, 52.1 percent pork, and 1.5 percent lamb), a post-depression low. Even as beef consumption declined, prices for slaughter beeves rose, reflecting the inherently slow buildup of cattle herds commonly called the "ten-year cycle," to peak in 1951 at a record of $29.69 a hundredweight. By then cattle raisers received 146 percent of parity, while the typical farmer netted 107 percent; however, most cattlemen soon became too ensnared in the general business cycle to manipulate their market very much. Oversupply popped the cattle-price bubble in 1952, quotations deflating to a low of $14.90 a hundredweight in 1956, nine years following its previous nadir.

[1] John Schlebecker, *Cattle raising on the plains, 1900–1961* (1963), p. 186.

The cycle peaked once more in 1962, at an average price of $21.30 a hundredweight, before a glutted market again depressed quotations for live cattle to a low of $17.22 in 1967. Thereafter, prices generally advanced on Vietnam War and energy-related inflation, which tripled the consumer price index between 1967 and 1983. Average prices for cattle steadily advanced to a seemingly astronomical $66.10 a hundredweight in 1979 before receding slightly the following year to $62.40, a level nevertheless three times the previous historical high. A new price cycle crested at $72.50 in mid-1983. Similar price movements at the retail levels—the cost of virtually all cuts of beef doubled between 1945 and 1960 and then tripled again by 1983—caused new consumer boycotts. Meanwhile, health reports cast considerable suspicion on meat-rich diets in which Americans had increasingly indulged since World War II.

Repeatedly warned of a multiplicity of possible carcinogens in beef and increasingly perplexed by relentlessly upward-spiraling retail prices, Americans abruptly shifted consumption patterns about 1979. Beef eaters thereafter apparently dieted, and consumption bottomed in 1980 at 105.5 pounds per capita (57.7 percent of all red meat), the lowest level since 1965. Pork consumption meanwhile rose to 74.8 pounds per capita (41.1 percent), up from 54.5 pounds (30 percent) in 1975, its postwar nadir. Demand for lamb, however, remained anemic, averaging about 3 pounds per capita (about 2 percent) for the whole postwar period. Overall, despite consumer resistance to retail-price rises and increasing concern over both its wholesomeness and its nutritional value, beef remained king.

This dominance has continued despite controversy concerning quality. When compulsory meat grading ended in October, 1946, the percentage of federally rated meat in interstate commerce dropped from 100 to 22 percent. A few packers claimed to be unable to afford even the modest fee charged by the USDA to station graders in their plants. Some, such as Armour and Swift, had already launched expensive nationwide campaigns to tout their respective copyrightable trade names for succulent meats. One, the ultraconservative Wilson & Co., Inc., rejected the purple government stamp as an unacceptable intrusion into private enterprise. Too, the big packers undoubtedly realized that universal use of USDA grades for meat, especially for beef, would allow small independent packers to compete more effectively.

Congress nevertheless reimposed mandatory grading of beef, veal, and lamb in 1951 as part of Korean War price regulation. By 1953, when controls were lifted, about 90 percent of the interstate red-meat and poultry trade had come under government classification. By then many beef packers used USDA Prime and Choice designations in their advertising, and only about half of the packers dropped out of the grading program. In 1955, 50 percent of interstate beef, 40 percent of lamb, and 20 percent of veal were stamped with the purple dye of USDA graders. In 1960, 78 percent of all interstate red meat was graded; in 1970, 89 percent; in 1978, 93 percent; and in 1983, about 96 percent.

Beef-grading standards, originally promulgated in 1926, were revised by the USDA in consultation with livestock raisers and meatpackers in 1939, just before the war, and again in 1950 in large measure to alleviate the postwar beef shortage. The former Prime and Choice categories were combined into Prime, and Good was upgraded to Choice. The top one-third of what had previously been lower-grade Commercial beef (often sold to bulk users, who turned it into assorted prepared foods) was reclassified as Good, the rest retaining the old Commercial designation. Other categories (Utility, Cutter, and Canner) remained unchanged. In 1956, Commercial was divided once more, based strictly on maturity, into Standard (young) and Commercial (old).

The combined impact of these changes allowed leaner beef to qualify as a better grade of meat at a commensurately higher price at each link in the red-meat chain. Many consumers were outraged and boycotted beef, action which was usually countered by a publicity campaign on behalf of livestock raisers launched by the National Livestock and Meat Board. Except for minor changes in 1965 and in 1973, the USDA did not tinker much with grade standard until 1976, when it again reduced the amount of marbling required for better classes of beef. Once more consumers objected; beef consumption declined by 2.7 percent, the first significant drop in a decade.

In 1981 the American National Cattlemen's Association, on behalf of its mostly western, big-spread ranching membership, asked the USDA to consider further modifications that would allow even leaner, grass-finished beasts to qualify as the grades of beef affluent Americans preferred: Prime and Choice. While the consumption of generally more expensive Prime has remained remarkably stable since World War II (averaging about 4 percent of all beef), that for Choice almost doubled (to 53 percent from about 34). Good's market share shrank to 18 percent from 26, and the lower grades of beef that provide bulk for everything from canned soup to pet food also declined, to 25 percent from 37. Grass-finishing cattlemen, who were eager to upgrade their mostly Good beasts, therefore suggested Choice Light and Choice Lean as new USDA designations or changing Good to Lean, designations which might appeal to diet-conscious Americans. Unorganized consumers, as well as affected retailers such as those represented by the National Restaurant Association, vigorously objected, as did many cattle raisers (principally represented by the Iowa Livestock Association, the Kansas Livestock Association, and the Texas Farm Bureau) who grain-finished their beasts; they contended that the proposed changes would confuse consumers, who inevitably would pay top-grade prices for second-class meat. The USDA shelved the idea.

Moreover, meat standards were being corroded by government corruption. During the 1970s a series of unrelated investigations including CBS's "60 Minutes" uncovered widespread evidence that

> federal meat graders were accepting bribes of up to four hundred dollars a week to mark beef USDA Choice that was of inferior quality. They [the investigators] found that supermarket buyers who accepted this inferior meat were the recipients of lavish gifts from packinghouses. They found numerous abuses within packinghouses involving mislabeling and relabeling of beef. . . . And the packer makes a nice profit on the mistake. Just one carcass graded choice that should only be good, the packer [in 1982] makes about $47, or about 6.7 cents per pound. At the supermarket, the consumer pays 15 to 20 cents per pound more, and the yearly overcharge to consumers runs to the hundreds of thousands of dollars.[2]

Relatively little of this windfall profit has accrued to western cattlemen, such as those who have advocated assorted lean-meat designations. Indeed, ranching authority Harold Oppenheimer once believed himself compelled to

[2] Wayne Swanson and George Schultz, *Prime rip* (1982), pp. 14, 20.

dispel the fiction of the millionaire rancher who made it on operations. Outside of possibly the dozen in the United States
who have consistently been able to "buy low and sell high," the
rest are making their money . . . from their oil and mineral
revenues, [or from] selling off portions of their ranch for suburban
developments or to "city ranchers." Having inherited enormous
tracts of land from their grandfathers who got it at fifty cents an
acre, they forgot to throw in a normal return on the [fair] market value of their land into their operating costs for analysis purposes, [and] they neglected to consider their own managerial
abilities or the wages of their sons at market value as part of
their operating costs.[3]

Stringent cost-accounting practices, Oppenheimer insists, frequently
reveal losses instead of profits.

In addition to rising operating costs and often depressed livestock quotations, ranchers since World War II have also faced keener
foreign competition. As the Brookings Institution forecast in 1926,
the United States became a net importer of red meat, especially
beef. By 1955 the trend was apparent. In that year the United
States exported 195 million pounds of red meat (34.9 percent beef
and veal, 64.6 percent pork, and 0.5 percent lamb and mutton); it
imported twice as much, 406 million pounds (56.4 percent beef,
43.1 percent pork, and 0.5 percent lamb). In 1964 it exported 315
million pounds of red meat (35.1 percent beef, 62.9 percent pork,
and 2 percent lamb), and imported five times as much, 1.5 billion
pounds (68 percent beef, 24.3 percent pork, and 7.7 percent lamb).
In 1980 it exported 645 million pounds of red meat (34.6 percent
beef, 64.7 percent pork, and 0.7 percent lamb) and imported 2.7
billion pounds (78 percent beef, 20.6 percent pork, and 1.4 percent lamb).

Since the turn of the century cattlemen—especially those represented by the American National Cattlemen's Association—had
lobbied for protection, which peaked in 1930 with the depression-
era Hawley-Smoot Tariff that placed a 20 percent ad valorem tax
on beef imports. The Roosevelt administration lowered that as-
sessment slightly under the authority of the Reciprocal Trade Agreement of 1934, as did President Harry S Truman, in accordance

[3] Harold Oppenheimer, *Cowboy arithmetic: cattle as an investment* (2d ed.; 1964),
pp. 205–206.

with the United Nations General Agreement on Trade and Tariffs (GATT), which the United States ratified in 1947. The Trade Expansion Act of 1962, which gave the president authority to reduce rates by as much as 50 percent, was vigorously applied, ironically, by President Lyndon B. Johnson, a cattle rancher.

Through a combination of these measures prevailing duties on carcass beef and pork had declined to 5 percent ad valorem by 1964. Responding to vehement protests from cattlemen who demanded protection from a veritable flood of cheap Argentine, Australian, Brazilian, Canadian, and Mexican beef, Congress that year enacted the Meat Import Act (revised in 1979), which mandated quotas whenever red-meat imports exceeded target levels, which in 1982 amounted to 1.3 billion pounds a year. Even so, enforcement has been spotty. The Carter administration, for example, in 1978 incurred the ire of cattle producers of all sizes when, having imposed quotas, it suspended them to allow the entry of another 200 million pounds of beef.

It is remarkable not that some ranches failed during this period but that so many survived. In 1980 the USDA estimated that 60,000 businesses in America were loosely classified as ranches, down from about 70,000 in 1945. By contrast, 58 percent of the nation's mixed farmers (about 3.5 million enterprises) went out of business during the same period. America's 67,159 ranches, as surveyed by the USDA in 1959, constituted merely 1.8 percent of the nation's 3.7 million agrarian endeavors and yet utilized 41 percent of its land mass, some 944 million acres. About one-third was leased public domain (mostly western forest and grassland), the balance being privately held. Such enormous landholdings, as ranching authority James Gray observed, explain "the extraordinary political power wielded by this group. . . ."[4]

Approximately 150,000 men, women, and children labored on ranches in 1959 (65,000 owner-operators, 54,000 hired hands, and 31,000 unpaid family members), constituting a minute 0.2 percent of the civilian labor force of 65.6 million persons. Ranching's labor pool was shrinking even then, in large part because of abysmally low wages—about one-third the national average. Consequently, the work force increasingly was composed of part-time employees,

[4]James Gray, Ranch economics (1968), p. 9.

mostly local youths who commuted from town. "Most of the real cowboys I know," says sixty-four-year-old Jim Miller, cow boss of the Fain Land & Cattle Co. of Arizona, "have been dead for a while."[5] In 1959, 1,650 ranches (2.5 percent of the total) were owned and operated by women, mostly widows—a trend that has continued. In 1982 the USDA calculated the female participation rate at 5 percent of all farming and ranching, the latter amounting to 3,300 spreads. Many of these women—such as Jane Glennie, of the 30,000-acre Two Dot Ranch in central Montana—rope and brand cattle, castrate calves, and string barbed wire. "Women worked harder to settle the West than any man ever did," she once commented. "We've been liberated forever. We're indispensable."[6]

Among the 10,000 or so American ranches that went out of business during the third quarter of the twentieth century were some notable historical enterprises. By 1950 the Matador Land and Cattle Co., a Scottish corporation established in 1882, was running 50,000 head of purebred Hereford cattle on 1.5 million acres of owned and leased pastures (mostly in Texas). The company was nettled by the "blight of double taxation"[7] peculiar to alien enterprises operating in the United States and finally liquidated in 1951. It retained half the mineral rights to its land and transferred them to the Toreador Royalty Company, a Delaware corporation, ownership of which was apportioned among Matador stockholders. It then sold for $18.9 million the balance of its holdings—approximately 800,000 acres of Texas Panhandle rangeland, assorted improvements, and about 47,000 cattle to the Lazard Brothers and Co., Ltd., of London, which acquired the spread on behalf of itself and several American interests. After suitable tracts totaling 10,000 acres were resold directly to farmers, the balance was divided into fifteen ranches varying in size from 16,000 to 96,000 acres. New owners included R. J. Fulton, of Lubbock, whose purchases along the Canadian River aggregated 100,000 acres; Coyal Francis, of Wichita Falls, whose syndicate acquired about half the land surrounding the south ranch headquarters; and the Rock Island

---

[5]Quoted in William Blundell, "Life on the job: the days of a cowboy are marked by danger, drudgery, and low pay," *Wall Street Journal*, June 10, 1981, p. 1.

[6]Quoted in Carrie Dolan, "True grit: rancher Jane Glennie carries on the tradition of women of the West," in ibid., November 18, 1982, p. 1.

[7]W. M. Pearce, *The Matador Land and Cattle Company* (1964), p. 212.

Oil and Refining Co. of Wichita (today Koch Industries, a privately held conglomerate that in 1980 was America's 134th-largest corporation, with aggregate sales of $4.3 billion), which bought much of the rest and the rights to the Matador name.

Similarly, the Swan Land and Cattle Co., Ltd., a Scottish firm founded in 1883, was reorganized in 1926 as a Delaware corporation, and by the time of World War II was running 70,000 head of livestock (mostly sheep) on 420,000 acres of Wyoming grasslands. The company grew weary of profits that "would not have amounted to more than 2.5 per cent a year." According to historian Harmon Ross Mothershead:

> The decision to stock the range with sheep in 1904 was not particularly successful. Sheep fared no better than, if as well as, cattle. The only reason the board offered for running sheep was that the range was no longer open and it was easier to take care of sheep than cattle. . . . It took four to five years for cattle to mature sufficiently for market and only a year for sheep. Sheep were marketable twice each year, once for wool, once for meat. But the wool market was more unpredictable than the dressed-meat trade, and mutton was never as popular as beef in the United States. It appears that the company missed a great opportunity in not capitalizing on what [founder Alexander] Swan had begun, namely improved stock and selective breeding of cattle.[8]

In 1943 the company began liquidation by selling for $2.22 to $17.05 an acre blocks ranging from 2,000 to 60,000 acres; the last slice was disposed of in 1950. All told, stockholders received $2.2 million, a $1.6 million capital gain that amounted to an annual return of merely 4.4 percent on their sixty-seven-year investment.

Absurdly high land values led some spreads to abandon ranching altogether. The 100,000-acre Irvine Ranch near Newport Beach, California—midway between Los Angeles and San Diego—yielded to potentially enormous revenues after World War II, when heirs of nineteenth-century Scotch-Irish immigrant James Irvine reorganized as the Irvine Co., a realty-development firm that owned one-

---

[8] Harmon Mothershead, *The Swan Land and Cattle Company, Ltd.* (1971), pp. 163, 164.

sixth of sun-drenched Orange County on California's gold coast. Leasing to builders who adhered to its master plan, the Irvine Co. fixed rents for twenty-five years at 6 percent of the initial fair-market value of the luxury homes, condominiums, shopping centers, and office towers that soon sprouted. In 1977 a private investor group headed by A. Allan Taubman, a Michigan shopping-mall magnate, bought the Irvine Co. for $377.4 million. Not long thereafter the new owners began reappraising some property for the first time since the mid-1950s. Rents subsequently were raised by as much as 4,150 percent, leading several outraged leaseholders to sue. At this writing, litigation continues.

El Rancho de las Colinas, 12,000 acres (18.75 square miles) of rolling north Texas grassland owned by the heirs of Lone Star Steel Corp. founder John Carpenter, is similarly parlaying its proximity to the Dallas–Fort Worth Airport into a billion-dollar real-estate complex designed to contain by the year 2000 some 50,000 residents of luxurious homesites, marina-side condominiums, and apartments, which, appropriately enough, will be within walking distance of the Dallas Cowboys' Texas Stadium. Rancho Colinas expects its office parks, with a skyline to rival that of downtown Dallas, and its shopping malls (to include a $12 million film and video center already touted as the Hollywood of Texas), to attract upwards of a quarter of a million persons a day.

Other spreads have been successful, as a west Texas rancher once wryly phrased it, "crossing cows with oil."[9] The most celebrated example is the fabled King Ranch. Saddled with substantial inheritance taxes and inevitable dismemberment following the death of Mrs. Richard King, in 1933 her heirs sold to Humble Oil and Refining Co. (now Exxon) exploration rights to 1.2 million acres of land in south Texas (then the largest oil-and-gas lease in the world) for loan guarantees amounting to $3 million and for the usual one-eighth mineral royalties on whatever extractable resources were discovered. Not long thereafter the ranch was divided, the largest block (825,000 acres) passing to scions of Richard Kleberg, who incorporated the King Ranch. Humble did not drill there un-

[9] Quoted in Seymour Freedgood, "The spectre at Lambshead Ranch," *Fortune*, Vol. 61 (1960), p. 129.

til 1945, yet within two years its annual royalty payments to the Klebergs exceeded $3 million. By 1980 the ranch contained 2,730 oil-and-gas wells, more than had been drilled in all of Saudi Arabia.

In 1958 the King Ranch and Humble renegotiated their agreement. In return for permission to erect what eventually became the world's largest natural-gas processing plant, Humble increased the ranch's royalty to one-sixth. According to William Broyles, Jr., "By 1969 the ranch was producing, Fortune magazine estimated, $120 million a year in oil and gas, making its one-sixth share worth $20 million, or about fifteen times the profit from the entire ranching operation." [10] With these enormous revenues the King Ranch steadily increased its capital investment. Its cattle herds, amounting to 50,000 head during wet years, over time became almost exclusively Santa Gertrudis. It also built a computer-controlled feedlot capable of handling 20,000 animals. It strung more than 2,000 miles of expensive mesh (rather than barbed) wire around its constantly patrolled perimeter. By 1980 its labor force, known locally as Kineños—vaqueros, cooks, blacksmiths, farmers, laborers, secretaries, heavy-equipment operators, accountants, and pilots— numbered 563.

Most postwar American cattle ranches were far more modest. More typical was E. Wayne Hage's Pine Creek Ranch, a hardscrabble two-thousand-head cow-calf operation sprawled over 2,500 square miles of semiarid federal rangeland in Nye County, Nevada. Hage nevertheless turned a profit more years than not (even during the difficult 1970s, "while the King Ranch lost as much as $15 million a year" [11]) by resorting to anachronistic open-range techniques. Avoiding such expenses as vaccination, dehorning, artificial insemination, and supplemental feed, he reduced Pine Creek's costs by 30 percent. "You want those cattle to make their own living," Hage once explained. "We don't want to support that cow, we want her to support us." [12] Watkins Reynolds Matthews, operating partner in the historic 51,000-acre Lambshead Ranch of north Texas, practiced a similar range-management philosophy after World War II, preferring

[10] William Broyles, Jr., "The last empire," Texas Monthly, Vol. VIII (1980), p. 256.
[11] Bryan Burrough, "Lawsuits offer peek at Texas family's feud over wealth of world's largest ranch," Wall Street Journal, June 18, 1982, p. 21.
[12] Eric Larson, "Old West: at vast Nevada ranch, roped calves still bawl and still get branded," in ibid., January 22, 1982, p. 1.

not to winter-feed any of his expensive, registered Hereford cows—disdaining Santa Gertrudis as "boloney factories"—unless it literally faced starvation: "She gets to depend upon handouts and won't rustle for herself." [13]

More typical in technique is Bob Cooper's Green Valley Cattle Co., a 10,000-head stocker-feeder ranch situated on 5,000 acres of well-watered grasslands near San Marcos, Texas. Established in the 1950s as a finish-feeder, it bought freshly weaned calves, such as those produced by Hage's Pine Creek Ranch, and carried them through the generally mild winters of central Texas on grass and some supplemental feed before selling them, usually to buyers for feedlots. Cooper claimed that in 1972 he "grossed about 12 percent. . . . That was unusual—usually it's more like half that much." [14]

Kansas rancher Jim Gilliland, who runs Hereford-Angus crossbreeds near Leon, sees himself foremost as a businessman: "I'm a cowman. . . . I'm in it for the beef. I try to use management instead of cowboying as much as possible." [15] So too do his neighbors Harold and Tony Frankhauser, father and son, who practice intensive grazing on 400 of the 4,000 acres of Kansas Flint Hills they own and lease. By placing as many cattle as possible on sweet spring grass and by selling them to feedlots in mid-July, months before traditional fall marketing—just as the pasture's carrying capacity breaks down—says Tony, who holds a degree in animal science from Kansas State University, "I think you get more pounds of beef per acre." [16]

For all their supposed glamour, popular mystique, and real or imagined political clout, the nation's 60,000 or so great and small cattle ranches together have accounted for merely one-tenth of total American beef-cattle production since World War II. As historically had been the case, most of the slaughter-beef supply has originated with small farmers who own fifty head or less, most of them operating on fewer than 180 acres. In the tradition of American agriculture they are mixed farmers who hedge economically by

[13] Quoted in Freedgood, "The spectre at Lambshead Ranch," *Fortune*, Vol. 61, pp. 130, 210.

[14] Quoted in Everett Groseclose, "Following cattle herd to market helps show why meat's so costly," *Wall Street Journal*, May 24, 1973, p. 1.

[15] Quoted in Dirck Steimel, "Management is all to Flint Hills cow-calf producer," Wichita *Eagle-Beacon*, August 29, 1982, p. 1G.

[16] Quoted in Dirck Steimel, "The payoff: break with grazing tradition is reaping rewards for father-son partnership in Kansas Flint Hills," in ibid., September 12, 1982, p. 1G.

diversifying. Livestock in general and cattle in particular have out-performed crops with respect to parity throughout much of the period. While the overall ratio has eroded precipitously since 1952, the year it last stood at 100 percent—to 82 percent in 1957, 91 percent in 1973, 66 percent in 1977, and 54 percent in 1982—the ratio for livestock has generally held higher than average. In 1982, during unquestionably depressed times for United States agriculture, slaughter-cattle prices averaged 54.4 percent of parity, hogs a whopping 62.9 percent; however, sheep quotations had collapsed to 46.1 percent of parity. By contrast, wheat stood at 48.3 percent of parity; corn, 45.4 percent; sorghum, 42.2 percent; and soybeans, 47.2 percent. Times were so bad that in 1982 Dallas billionaire Nelson Bunker Hunt, who for fifteen years had owned mixed operations in Mississippi, Oklahoma, and Texas, decided that farming was not a moneymaking proposition and announced his abandonment of it. "He hired the top cowboys, the top farmers and bought the latest equipment," a spokesman said, "but the returns weren't there. It's a discouraging turn of events."[17] Hunt's agrarian investments, estimated at between $5 million and $10 million, were expected to bring half their value at auction.

The most spectacular change in American beef-cattle production following World War II was the increased significance of feedlots, livestock's growth industry since the 1960s. Although first appearing in the central corn belt as early as the 1840s, most commercial feedlots were merely small pens operated part-time by sod-busters eager to find an outlet for surplus grain. Most nineteenth-century operations were like Morris Case's in Waterloo, Iowa, which had "150 head of cattle in rows of stalls facing a track used to distribute feed ground by a steam engine. Others built troughs or feed bunks 3 feet off the ground and 10 to 14 feet long for snapped ear corn and hay, and a few advocated the use of oil cake meal, bran, oats, and even turnips as supplements."[18] While the size and scope of these entrepreneurial experiments expanded over the ensuing century, as late as the Great Depression the vast majority remained situated in the corn belt and were capable of feeding fewer than

[17] Quoted in David Stipp, "Bunker Hunt, down on his luck, says it's time to close business," *Wall Street Journal*, December 3, 1982, p. 25.

[18] James Whitaker, *Feedlot empire: beef cattle feeding in Illinois and Iowa, 1840–1900* (1975), p. 115.

1,000 head at a time. Indeed, in 1935 the USDA reported only 2.2 million (5.1 percent) of the nation's 42.8 million beef cattle on feed.

Then, at the end of World War II, to lure into their stores a rapidly expanding, affluent, and taste-discriminating urban population, California retail grocery chains such as the Safeway Stores, Inc., began demanding for their meat markets USDA Choice cuts and, as soon as controls ended, Prime cuts, which required corresponding grades of cattle. Grass-fed beasts rarely qualified under the standards then imposed. So few grain-finished cattle were available locally that entrepreneurs such as Dwight Cochran sallied forth to fill the demand. He resigned as Safeway's marketing vice-president, organized the publicly held Kern County Land Co., and built at Bakersfield a complex capable of handling 50,000 animals a year, feeding "the most advanced nutritional formulas plus beet pulp, citrus rinds, and other local byproducts to fatten up to 35,000 at a time, . . . maturing beef according to rigid specifications."[19]

By the mid-1960s huge commercial feedlots had similarly sprouted throughout southern California and spread into Arizona and onto the Great Plains, appearing first in Colorado, then in Texas, Oklahoma, Kansas, and Nebraska. In 1963 the USDA reported 9 million cattle (11.1 percent) on feed, representing two-thirds of the steers and heifers slaughtered in the United States that year. About 40 percent of those originated in these highly automated "beef factories" of the West.

On the Texas high plains, for example, interest in feedlot finishing intensified in the 1950s, when a drouth withered the grasslands; however, the area's irrigated farms produced an abundance of relatively inexpensive feed grains, and half a dozen small yards opened. "None of the farmer-feeder businesses of this era, however, attracted as much attention as the Lewter Feed Yard near Lubbock," says agricultural historian Gary Nall: "Constructed in 1955 by Durward Lewter, a former county agent, and Clint Murchison, Sr., a Dallas investor, the 125-acre feedyard included a feed mill, storage tanks and pens with space for 10,000 (later 34,000) head of company-owned cattle. It was the region's first large-scale [commercial] feeding operation."[20]

---

[19]"The new cattle business," *Fortune*, Vol. 61 (1980), p. 228.

[20]Gary L. Nall, "The cattle-feeding industry on the Texas high plains," in Dethloff and May, Jr., (eds.), *Southwestern agriculture: pre-columbian to modern* (1982), p. 108.

Most big operations began more modestly, as at the Hitch
Ranch, in the Oklahoma Panhandle, where in 1953 Henry Hitch,
Jr., erected four pens in which to fatten a few ranch cattle on home-
grown ensilage cut from tall grain sorghums and grain threshed from
milo maize. In the late 1950s he hired an experienced feeder to su-
pervise the works, increased the capacity of his yards to 5,000 head,
and, on the recommendation of the nationally respected Doane's
Agricultural Service, eliminated his cow-calf herd entirely in favor
of feeder cattle bought elsewhere and run on ranchland grass before
120 to 150 days of finishing in the feedlot.

When the boom in commercial feedlot construction hit the
Great Plains during the mid-1960s, Hitch "enlarged the ranch
feedlot to 20,000 head, making it into probably the largest non-
custom yard in the nation. . . ."[21] He also began building custom
lots in which to feed other people's cattle to specifications. In 1965,
Hitch led several investors to build the 50,000-head Texas County
Feedlot near Guymon, in the Oklahoma Panhandle. Two years later
he headed another syndicate that erected the 22,000-head Master
Feeders' complex near Hooker, Oklahoma, followed in 1969 by
Master Feeders' II, south of Garden City, Kansas. These huge feedlots
eventually lured major meatpackers into the area.

During the early 1960s, before the idea of buying cattle and
having someone else feed them caught on, financing feedlots
throughout the cattle country of the southern Great Plains was uncertain. Nall writes:

> With an average accommodation cost of $35 per head, most
> feedlot developers spent between $250,000 and $500,000 ini-
> tially. Since area lenders had no experience with such enter-
> prises, the early organizers found it extremely difficult to secure
> either long-term loans for construction or short-term loans for
> operating expenses. Indeed, most developers depended upon
> sources outside the region. The investors in the Hereford Feed
> Yards [of Texas], for example, secured $180,000 from the federal
> Small Business Administration by convincing agency officials
> that their operation was a service industry rather than an agri-
> cultural firm.[22]

[21] Donald Green, *Panhandle pioneers: Henry C. Hitch, his ranch, and his family* (1979),
p. 217.

[22] Nall, "The cattle-feeding industry on the Texas high plains," in Dethloff and May
(eds.), *Southwestern agriculture*, p. 109.

Southern plains feedlots—which usually finished their cattle on rations of processed local milo; some silage; the minerals salt, calcium, and phosphorus; and, as was then common throughout the whole industry, the growth hormone diethylstilbestrol (DES)—had to overcome the prejudice of meatpackers long accustomed to corn-fattened beasts. To popularize its product among buyers, the Lewter Yards of Lubbock entered its slaughtered steers in carcass shows throughout the country and in so doing won a contract with the A&P grocery chain and ready acceptance of its beef on the East Coast. Eventually five large packers—American Beef, Iowa Beef, Missouri Beef, Swift, and Wilson—opened facilities in the region to process southern Great Plains feedlot cattle.

Feeders everywhere hired nutritionists and full-time veterinarians and installed computers to systematize their beef factories. Sustained by what for a time seemed to be a perfectly elastic demand for Prime and Choice beef, the feedlot industry expanded on eager investment further encouraged by federal tax codes. During the early 1970s affluent, mostly professional Americans by the untold thousands, including actor John Wayne, poured money into limited partnerships such as the Amarillo-based Western Beef Cattle Fund, which bought livestock, placed them in feedlots, and then sold them for club members. Tax incentives led conglomerates such as the Mesa Petroleum Co. of Amarillo to buy the 50,000-head Swisher County Cattle Co. near Tulia, in the Texas Panhandle, and the privately held agribusiness giant Cargill, Inc., of Minneapolis, to acquire several yards on the Texas high plains.

The market began to fluctuate early in 1973. A bitter winter killed tens of thousands of animals, and the Food and Drug Administration banned further use of DES in animal feed for fear it was a carcinogen, as recent research had indicated. Consumer demand for beef nevertheless remained strong, leading to skyrocketing retail prices, well-publicized meat boycotts by disgruntled housewives, and, in the spring of 1973, a freezing of beef prices by President Richard M. Nixon. When controls were relaxed that fall, feeders held their cattle off the market in anticipation of rising prices, in the process adding both weight to their animals and expenses to their total costs. A mild winter and moderate grain prices further stimulated weight gain throughout the feeder industry, which produced a surplus of beef that depressed prices. Then a sudden increase in grain exports virtually doubled the price of feedstocks overnight.

In 1966 the typical cattle feeder paid 22.8 cents for every pound gained in feedlots; in 1974 he paid 50 cents. Boardroom cowboys quickly vanished. "Even though the industry lay in shambles," Nall says, "it did not die; instead, major adjustments were made. Local stock farmers, cattlemen, and packers resumed their earlier dominant role by placing livestock in the feedyards where outside investors once searched for quick profits and tax benefits."[23] The shakeout was severe. By 1977 the number of large feedlots on the Texas high plains, for example, reportedly had diminished by one-fourth, and those remaining in business were only 20 to 40 percent full. Market prices for live cattle subsequently recovered to 68 cents a pound in 1979, before fluctuating once more between 63 and 72 cents a pound, wholesale; even so, feeders claimed that there was little profit, for by 1982 the average cost of adding one pound of beef to a steer in a feedlot had climbed to 66 cents.

Meanwhile, the number of sheep and lambs in feedlots peaked during World War II at about 7 million animals, declining thereafter to approximately 4 million head in 1951, a figure that remained reasonably constant until the early 1970s, when a further decline set in, which by 1983 had slowly eroded the total to 1.6 million beasts, or about 10 percent of all sheep and lambs in the United States. Intended for slaughter and fed on a ration of grain or other concentrates or run on succulent grasses, feedlot sheep and lambs produce carcasses that grade Good or better: "Lambs are fed by large numbers of farmer-feeders in the North Central region and in various areas of the West. The bulk of the commercial feedlot lambs, however, are usually concentrated in a relatively few hands, and partly for this reason, the lamb feeding industry is characterized by considerably more stability than is true of the fed cattle sector."[24] Even so, sheep production has steadily slipped since 1940, when the USDA counted 52.1 million head in the United States, to 11.3 million in 1981. During the same period lamb and mutton production plummeted from 876 million pounds a year (6.6 pounds per capita) to 303 million pounds in 1981 (1.8 pounds per capita). This decline was especially disastrous to producers who had come to depend on the red-meat trade for approximately 85 percent of their revenues.

[23] Ibid., p. 115.
[24] Willard Williams and Thomas Stout, Economics of the livestock-meat industry (1964), p. 292.

Not only had lamb and mutton consumption declined in the United States, but during the early 1970s the wool market collapsed as well, compounding the sheep raiser's woes. During the cold war of the early 1950s wool was designated a strategic commodity and its price supported by Washington to ensure a sufficient supply during any national emergency. "The bottom dropped out of the wool market in 1971, largely because of the surge in popularity of polyester fabrics. In that year, average prices fetched a meager 17 cents a pound, 55 cents below the federal incentive payment—the amount guaranteed by the government to take up the slack in lean years."[25] In 1973 extraordinarily large Japanese wool purchases on the Australian market, which serves as bellweather for the world, pushed prices upward once more to a dollar a pound; thereafter, in the face of double-digit inflation for much of the ensuing decade, fine wool prices merely doubled, to about two dollars a pound, in 1980, leaving American sheepmen no better off than before. The wool clip in 1980 totaled 106 million pounds, less than half that of 1955; moreover, net imports of 500,000 pounds by 1980 amounted to half the total national output.

Aside from ongoing price-support payments amounting to $46.6 million in 1982 (and aggregating about $2 billion since 1955), the public sector, many sheep ranchers contend, has been insensitive to their plight and in at least one instance actually destructive of their industry. During the 1970s at the insistence of environmentalists sheepmen on public lands were shorn of the right to use poisons indiscriminately against eagles, coyotes, and other predators; a few producers were even prosecuted for hunting eagles and coyotes from airplanes. The recent animosity between environmentalists and sheepmen, according to west Texas rancher Monte Noelke, is an aberration: "We used to be brothers. Then somewhere along the line we had a family fight, and it turned into a big battle. Now I don't think we'll ever get back together. We need an environmental program, but we also need to make a living."[26]

During the early 1950s, Utah sheep raisers contended with unprecedented environmental pollution by their own government, which was conducting atomic-weapons testing in the atmosphere

[25]Mike Tharp, "Monte Noelke loves the sheep business, worries about future," *Wall Street Journal*, January 21, 1974, p. 1.
    [26]Quoted in ibid., p. 22.

over the state. Resulting radiation, they contended in a 1953 law-
suit, caused the deaths of thousands of their animals. Dismissed
in 1955 for lack of evidence by Federal District Judge Sherman
Christensen, the case was reopened at his order in 1979. At that
time Christensen disclosed that the military had perpetrated a fraud
on the court by suppressing evidence in the original trial. Litigation
on the suit and on related issues continues at this writing.

During the same period swine raisers, facing a remarkably inelastic market demand for pork, suffered severe attrition rates. "In Indiana," Frankfort farmer William Rothenberger said in 1972, "the
number of producers of hogs has steadily decreased from 80,000
(100 head per farm) in 1959 to 50,000 (160 per farm) in 1964, to a
possible 25,000 (320 per farm) in 1974. More significant is the
probability that 2,000 of the 25,000 producers in 1974 will supply
half of the 8 million Indiana hogs.[27] The Pork Industry Committee
of the National Livestock and Meat Board and the National Pork
Producers Council, organized after World War II along the lines of
the Beef Industry Council to promote pork consumption, have had
little impact. While per capita pork consumption has varied between 75.8 pounds in 1946 and 54.8 pounds in 1975, it has averaged 63.1 pounds for the entire thirty-eight-year postwar period,
which is approximately the mean for the whole twentieth century.

This flat demand curve has sorely distressed many knowledge-
able observers. Arval Erikson, vice-president of Oscar Mayer &
Co., noted in 1972:

> I am . . . concerned that the demand for pork has not kept pace
> with beef, or that we have not been able to cut costs as much as
> has been the case for another strong competitor, namely poul-
> try. As a result, pork, which in 1947–49 commanded 40 per-
> cent of the red meats and poultry market, had a share of only
> 28 percent in 1970. If pork had maintained its 1947–49 share
> of the 1970 total, about 38 million more hogs would have been
> required with all the related services.[28]

[27] William Rothenberger, "Vertical coordination: a producer's viewpoint," in Robert E.
Schneidau and Lawrence A. Duewer (eds.), *Symposium: vertical coordination in the pork industry* (1972), p. 151.
[28] Arval Erickson, "Challenge of a changing pork industry," in ibid., p. 12.

Dismal prices, bottoming near twenty-four dollars a hundred-weight in 1974, caused thousands of farmers to sell off their mature animals, thereby reducing the hog count in 1975 to 49.3 million head, the lowest level since 1954. Prices consequently vaulted to sixty dollars a hundredweight, which led to a veritable orgy in the barnyard. Because a sow gives birth to an average litter of eight piglets about 120 days after impregnation and because those pigs mature fully in another six months, swine producers who had slaughtered much of their herds in the face of declining prices just as readily expanded their output to catch rising market quotations. "You'd think hog farmers would learn from their past mistakes," says Orville Sweet, executive vice-president of National Pork Producers, "but they almost never do. We never seem to get that delicate balance between supply and demand just right."[29]

Keen competition forced many survivors of the hog cycle to adopt a streamlined business strategy popularly called "vertical coordination," whereby farmers focused primarily on slaughter-swine production. They grow their own feed, breed their own beasts, and finish-feed them personally by the tens of thousands a year. The USDA estimated in 1982 that 10 percent of the nation's farmers employing vertical-coordination techniques produced 70 percent of America's hogs; indeed, 40 percent of the United States' 80 million pigs (about 32 million animals) were raised in total confinement best described as "factory farms," where diets were carefully controlled through computer-mixed feeds that included copious quantities of antibiotics to lessen the omnipresent danger of epidemics. Concerned consumers and health authorities alike have questioned the quality of the resulting product and the propriety of inadvertently creating mutant viral and bacteriological strains readily communicable to people.

Typically, factory farm buildings (often prefabricated concrete-floor structures designed to accommodate the breeding, farrowing, and feeding of as many as five thousand swine at a time) and equipment (climate controls, sophisticated sewer systems to flush away feces for treatment or, increasingly, conversion into methane gas,

[29]Quoted in Terri Minsky, "Hog prices currently outstripping cattle, an aberration that worries pig farmers," *Wall Street Journal*, September 1, 1982, p. 1.

and computers to oversee everything) aggregated an estimated 15 to 20 percent of expenses for operators like Rothenberger. Feed costs, which vary primarily according to the size of the grain crop, account for 65 to 80 percent, the balance being labor, interest, and taxes.

Variable costs—whether for big producers or small—become almost meaningless when extraordinary factors intervene, as in early 1982, when an arctic blizzard's winterkill decimated herds just as porkers were bringing a respectable fifty-three dollars a hundred-weight at many corn-belt packing plants. Larry Watt, who owned two thousand swine near Winterset, Iowa, upon seeing one of his frozen hogs, remarked, "I feel like I'm flushing a hundred-dollar bill down the stool."[30]

Others were caught in a credit crunch. In 1979, Gerhard Schramm, of Albert City, Iowa, expanded his facilities to accommodate 15,000 pigs a year only to see interest rates zoom from 9.5 to 17 percent. Corn prices also climbed, by a dollar a bushel in 1980, raising feed costs by one-third—just as hog prices collapsed, tumbling below thirty dollars a hundredweight from about fifty dollars the year before. When an outbreak of hog cholera compounded the situation, Schramm was forced to liquidate to avoid bankruptcy. Not long thereafter he died of a self-inflicted gunshot wound that "was reported as a suicide in the local newspaper. . . ."[31] As late as September, 1982, the situation remained grim, according to the *Wall Street Journal*: "Hog raisers decided to forgo expansion even though prices for their animals are close to record highs and feed is cheap. Most farmers borrow money so they need bankers' cooperation to raise pigs."[32]

Exacerbating the situation for pig farmers were widespread slaughterhouse closings all across the land. For a variety of reasons—ranging from a depressed national economy to fierce competition among meatpackers—between 1979 and 1982, 10 percent of

[30] Quoted in David Garino, "Ralph Shiver's pigs often die trying to avoid the cold," *Wall Street Journal*, February 16, 1982, p. 1.

[31] Claudia Waterloo, "Season of stress: farm life is changed as perilous economics undermines confidence," in ibid., April 9, 1982, p. 13.

[32] "Farmers are raising fewer hogs: supplies of pork to stay tight," in ibid., September 23, 1982, p. 46.

the nation's three hundred pork packers permanently closed their doors, the American Meat Institute claims. For example, in 1982 a sour economy coupled with usurious interest rates caused Hygrade Food Products to shut down its relatively modern Storm Lake, Iowa, packinghouse. Also that year, when the union refused to give back about one-fourth of current wages (as much as eleven dollars an hour), John Morrell & Co. closed what it said was an obsolete facility (Rodeo Meats) in Arkansas City, Kansas, after eighty years of operation, putting eight hundred employees out of work and forcing area farmers to truck their animals as far as San Antonio and Omaha to find buyers. When consumers resisted high pork prices, some firms quickly reacted by reducing their runs, as did Detroit's Frederick and Herrod, Inc., which pared back its slaughtering by one-third, to 3,500 head a day. Others selected 1982 as a propitious time for capital improvements. Farmland Foods closed its Denison, Iowa, facility for sixty days to modify its kill floor. In June the Jimmy Dean Meat Company, specializing in whole-hog sausages, furloughed its Osceola, Iowa, labor force for one week to reduce inventories.

This shakeout in the pork trade reflected a heightened level of competition common in the red-meat industry since World War II. The number of meatpacking establishments engaged in interstate commerce peaked in 1967 at 6,188, up from 3,974 in 1947, before declining further to 4,534 in 1977. Despite such a marked swing— in which one-third of the industry's capital facilities either opened or closed—the mix of plant types remained relatively constant throughout the whole postwar period. About two-thirds were engaged principally in slaughtering animals, either for themselves or under contract with other firms, and the rest were processing plants which manufactured sausages or other prepared meats, mostly from purchased carcasses. Approximately 54 percent of all meatpacking plants specialized in beef, 27 percent in pork, and 19 percent in lamb and mutton.

The market dominance of the Big Four steadily eroded following World War II. In 1948 the Department of Justice initiated antitrust proceedings designed to dismember the beef trust, proposing that Armour & Co. and Swift & Co. be broken into five companies each and Cudahy Packing Co. and Wilson & Co. into two each.

The suit was abandoned in 1954, American Meat Institute executive J. Russell Ives says, "with the somewhat petulant remark [by the government] that '. . . it would insist on obedience to the consent decrees of 1903 and 1920.'"[33]

In 1948 the old oligopsony-oligopoly controlled about 40 percent of the fresh-beef trade (collectively accounting for 38.3 percent of all cattle slaughtered and 43.6 percent of calves), but in 1955 it controlled only 32 percent (30.8 percent cattle and 34.7 percent calves). In pork their aggregate position declined from 40.4 to 36.4 percent, and in lamb from 67.8 to 58.5 percent. Some of this slippage accrued to the next five-largest firms, Hormel, Hygrade, John Morrell, Oscar Mayer, and Rath, which collectively expanded their market share of beef, pork, and lamb. But much of the Big Four's losses went to aggressive companies, such as Iowa Beef Packers, that had entered the trade anew following World War II. Consequently, in 1956 the Big Four asked further relief from the Consent Decree of 1920, petitioning in federal court to be allowed to sell meat and poultry at the retail level and to engage in the production and sale of grocery and dairy products at all market levels. Armour, Cudahy, Swift, and Wilson argued that their combined share of red-meat production had steadily eroded since 1920 and thus competition had been restored to the meat trade and that they therefore deserved relief to allow them to function more effectively in the trade.

Federal Judge Julius Hoffman of Chicago denied the petition. He ruled:

> In the typical case, it might be safe to presume that after forty years the object of the equity decree will have been achieved if it is ever to be. But this is not a case where equity intervened to correct a temporary dislocation or to afford a respite so that competition could be restored, and time alone is not a remedy. Here the defendants were huge and remained huge after the decree. They chose to retain size as meat packers rather than risk further dismemberment, at the price of abandoning the opportunity to extend into other fields. The decree therefore operates as a restraint and a fetter to preserve the bal-

[33] J. Russell Ives, *The livestock and meat economy of the United States* (1966), p. 104.

ance of competitive power. Its usefulness is not exhausted or outworn. . . .[34]

Economists Robert Aduddell and Louis Cain observe that "the industry was still characterized as an oligopoly in 1956, albeit a weaker one than in 1920."[35]

The consent decree was substantially amended fifteen years later when—battered by the new, aggressive beef boxers, such as Iowa Beef Packers—Armour, Cudahy, Swift, and Wilson were permitted to manufacture and distribute at wholesale the nonmeat items originally banned; however, they still were not allowed to sell any item at retail. In 1979 the Department of Justice sought to soften the consent decree further by allowing the old Big Four to acquire retail firms dealing in the proscribed items, provided that these new subsidiaries had annual sales of less than $100 million each and that acquisitions did not result in packer control of more than 50 percent of the market. As of this writing, this proposed modification is still pending court approval.

Of the old Big Four, only Swift remains among the largest meatpackers. The big packers, which had been on the leading edge of the industrial revolution during the last half of the nineteenth century—adapting the latest technology to create moving disassembly lines manned by the most intricate divisions of labor then practical—in the early twentieth century became lethargic. Between 1899 and 1954 the output per manhour for meatpacking increased by only 0.5 percent a year, as contrasted with an average of 2.2 percent for American industry as a whole. Labor historian David Brody observes that after World War II

> a second technological revolution hit meat packing. New methods and machinery began to appear: stunners, mechanical knives and hide skinners, power saws, electronic slicing and weighing devices. At the end of 1955, an engineer told the American Meat Institute that automation—that is, electronic control of fully mechanized production—was a technical reality

[34]Quoted in Robert Aduddell and Louis Cain, "The consent decree in the meatpacking industry, 1920–1956," *Business History Review*, LV (1981), p. 360.

[35]Ibid., p. 366.

in sausage and bacon operations. Labor production rose by 15
per cent from 1954 and 1958. Demand could not keep pace,
and employment began to fall. Total man-hours declined by 13
per cent during the four-year period. That represented nearly
18,000 production jobs.[36]

By 1972 total employment in meatpacking stood at 189,000, down
from 274,000 in 1947.

Simultaneously, innovative architectural design made the old
multistory facilities obsolete. In 1954, Cudahy led the exodus from
Chicago, and within six years most of the large plants there were
idle. In 1970 the Union Stock Yards closed for lack of business. The
principal river-point sites similarly experienced a decline as new,
spacious meat factories began to appear in the rural Midwest, Southwest, and Far West, where initial land costs were invariably lower
than those in crowded eastern cities. The new plants were also usually situated near feedlots made practical by an extensive modern
highway system and by the companion rise of the interstate trucking
industry, which, increasingly since the 1920s, had freed the packers
from near-total dependence on the railroads. They were also frequently situated in "right-to-work" states.

Foremost among the new breed of postwar businesses was Iowa
Beef Packers. Founded in 1960 by Currier Holman and A. D. Anderson and financed with a $300,000 loan from the U.S. Small
Business Administration, the company took Gustavus Swift's original idea to its logical conclusion. It erected its first plant at Denison, Iowa, near an abundant supply of corn-fattened feedlot cattle,
which significantly reduced its transportation costs for raw material.
It installed the latest capital equipment in a sprawling, highly automated one-story facility made practical by cheap energy. Company
executive Dale Tinstman explained that IBP

> refrigerated the entire process [immediately] after the kill be-
> cause the quicker the carcass can be cooled, the less shrinkage
> there is from dehydration. . . . It was a natural progression
> from the efficiencies of shipping carcasses to shipping boxed
> beef. There is a lot of wasted space in a modern truck or rail car
> filled with chilled sides of beef. A side of beef has an awkward

[36] David Brody, *The butcher workmen* (1964), pp. 241–42.

shape—it can't be neatly packed, and a side has a lot of bone and trim that will never go into the meat case. It was logical to move to boxed beef.[37]

In 1967, Iowa Beef Packers opened a second, even more stream-lined plant in Dakota City, Nebraska, especially to produce boxed beef, which was sealed in vacuum bags. The facility was so suc-cessful that it was followed in short order by similar factories in West Point, Nebraska; Luverne, Minnesota; Emporia, Kansas; and, in 1974, what was then the world's largest beef-packing plant in Amarillo, Texas. Seven years later IBP opened an even larger fa-cility at Holcomb, Kansas, near a large concentration of feedlots that had appeared on the high plains of Kansas, Colorado, Okla-homa, and Texas following World War II.

Iowa Beef's Holcomb, Kansas, plant—America's state-of-the-art facility—sprawls over fourteen acres. Every day cowpunchers push 3,700 head of cattle into a chute that feeds its disassembly line with live raw material. As soon as a steer enters the building, it is automatically zapped by a pneumatic gun that fires a yellow pellet into its skull, stunning the animal, which stumbles to its knees, glassy-eyed. A worker hooks a chain onto a rear hoof, and the co-matose beast is mechanically yanked from the platform to hang head down. "The kill floor looks like a Red Sea," a visiting jour-nalist wrote: "Warm blood bubbles and coagulates in an ankle-deep pool. The smell sears the nostrils. Men stand in gore with long knives slitting each steer's throat and puncturing the jugular vein. Each night the gooey mess is wiped away from the red brick floors and galvanized steel as required by federal regulations."[38]

The dead animal, moved steadily by a chain hoist, passes rudi-mentary disassembly stations consisting of whirring machines and sweating men and women. A skinning machine strips off the hide. Then the carcass is decapitated, the tongue split and removed, all parts being placed on hooks attached to the moving chain. The car-cass is gutted, the entrails being inspected and then dropped into stainless-steel containers for eventual use in pet food and other by-

[37]Dale Tinstman and Robert Peterson, *Iowa Beef Processors, Inc.: an entire industry re-vitalized*, (1981), p. 8.

[38]Lynn O'Shaughnessy, "Death comes in assembly line style," *Kansas City Times*, May 11, 1982, p. A-7.

products. Disemboweled, the half-ton carcass is pulled through a mechanical washer, quickly examined by an employee of the USDA Food Safety and Inspection Service (FSIS), and split in two by a team of workers maneuvering motorized saws that rip through bone in seconds. Halves are weighed, washed again, wrapped in sanitary cloth shrouds, and stored overnight in a huge, chilled meat locker.

The next day the halves are moved mechanically into the processing department, where they are set upon by brawny workers with power saws who section the beef into its familiar forms—round, sirloin, short loin, rib, chuck, short plate, and brisket—which are tossed onto conveyor belts, each manned by thirty or forty boners and trimmers with assigned, specific tasks: "As far as the eye can see there are waves of white-frocked workers with knives furiously attacking the meat. Each hour, 250 cows are butchered and boxed in the brightly lit, cavernous expanse. There is no time for idle chatter or daydreams here. A worker devotes the split-second free time between meat slabs sharpening his knife—a dull blade slows production and hurts hands. Concentration is essential as a clean cut."[39] A chunk of meat may be handled by three or four persons working on the conveyor belt before it reaches the end of the disassembly line, where—now resembling the basic cuts of a supermarket display case—it is vacuum-packed, boxed, and hauled into a vast, computer-controlled cold-storage warehouse capable of handling 93,000 fifty-pounds boxes. From there it is eventually trucked to distribution points around the country.

Over the years Iowa Beef Packers also acquired existing plants in Boise, Idaho; Fort Dodge, Iowa; and Pasco, Washington. In 1970 the firm changed its name to Iowa Beef Processors, which it believed more accurately reflected the fabricating role—breaking carcasses into primal and subprimal cuts—it had carved out for itself. IBP's boxed beef also allowed meat wholesalers and supermarkets to reduce labor costs by eliminating most of their skilled butchers, and when IBP trimmed its product virtually to retail specifications, it retained the valuable waste materials, such as fat for tallow and entrails for pet food.

Iowa Beef Processors also minimized its own labor costs by lo-

[39] Ibid.

cating primarily in states such as Iowa, Kansas, Nebraska, and Texas that, under the aegis of the Taft-Hartley Act (1947), had outlawed union shops, thereby allowing the company to ignore master agreements that the unions had hammered out over the years with the Big Four and the small packers. While often paying its employees the highest average wage in the industry, IBP steadfastly refused to grant many costly fringe benefits demanded by the unions, a sore point with workers that repeatedly led to violence-punctuated strikes and, consequently, to open hiring by the company.

Also, Iowa Beef Processors "penetrated a key market in the early 1970s," the *Washington Post* reported in an investigative feature article on the company, "by paying off gangsters and using illegal pricing policies and is still locked in complex antitrust litigation. IBP proudly proclaims itself as a tough and hard-nosed competitor, but it says its stormy, corruption-riddled past—which included the 1974 conviction of its [co-]founder, the late Currier Holman, on a criminal charge of conspiring with a Mafia figure to bribe IBP's way into New York—is a closed book."[40]

So too appears to be the civil antitrust suit brought by about five hundred cattlemen against Iowa Beef, MBPXL Corp. (today Excel Corp. of Wichita, Kansas, a subsidiary of Cargill, Inc., and IBP's closest competitor in the boxed-beef trade), Spencer Foods, Inc. (a subsidiary of Land O'Lakes, Inc.), and ten large grocery chains (including A&P, Jewel, Kroger, Safeway, and Winn-Dixie), which, the cattlemen alleged, had conspired to fix prices by manipulating the *Yellow Sheet*, a meat-price publication issued by the Chicago-based National Provisioner, Inc. In June, 1982, Federal District Judge Patrick Higginbotham of Dallas dismissed the supermarkets as defendants because no direct link between them and livestock producers could be demonstrated. While vowing to appeal the ruling, cattlemen conceded that the decision had substantially weakened their case, which was set for trial in 1984.

Perhaps equally significant was the virtually simultaneous decision by the Federal Trade Commission to end its three-year probe of the same firms and their beef-pricing policies. In July, 1982, the

[40] Thomas Lippman, "Iowa beef makes its move on anxious pork industry," *Washington Post*, April 18, 1982, p. 2.

FTC announced that "no further action is warranted by the commission at this time."[41] Some critics nevertheless have questioned
Iowa Beef's seemingly cozy relationship with federal regulators, illustrated by a USDA Packers and Stockyards Administration staff
investigation of purportedly illegal IBP practices which was reportedly scuttled by Packers and Stockyards Administration head
Charles Jennings, a Carter administration appointee. According to
Congressman Neal Smith of Iowa, whose House small-business
committee investigated the red-meat industry, "the Packers and
Stockyards Administration [under Jennings] 'deliberately' pursued
only a 'limited' action against Iowa Beef that conveniently turned
up evidence so weak that there was no alternative but to drop the
probe."[42] Red-meat industry critics Wayne Swanson and George
Schultz are even more blunt:

> There is more compelling reason to doubt Jennings: he is now
> vice-president for public relations for Iowa Beef Processors, Inc.
> Six months after leaving the meat industry's most powerful regu-
> latory job, he was hired by the most powerful packer. The move
> was branded as cynical at best by outraged consumers, govern-
> ment reformers, and even meat-industry groups.[43]

By whatever methods, Iowa Beef Processors by 1980 had come
to dominate America's boxed-beef business, which accounted for
half the nation's fresh-beef trade. IBP slaughtered 5.7 million cattle
(16 percent of the trade) in ten separate interstate plants, which
netted the company $53.2 million in profits on gross sales of $4.6
billion—approximately three times that of its nearest rival, MBPXL.
"The growth of the boxed beef industry has had a significant impact
on the structure of the meat packing industry and the pricing and
distribution systems in the wholesale beef markets," the U.S. House
Committee on Small Business determined in 1980, following a
lengthy investigation. "In May, 1979, 19 of the top 20 chain stores
purchased about two-fifths of their beef requirements in boxed form,

[41]Quoted in "FTC closes probe of beef industry on price fixing," *Wall Street Journal,*
July 22, 1982, p. 2.
[42]Quoted in Swanson and Schultz, *Prime rip,* 126.
[43]Ibid.

five chains purchasing only boxed beef, while two chains [relied] entirely on carcass beef."[44]

Citing internal IBP documents, the committee charged that IBP regularly resorted to predatory pricing practices to increase its share of the boxed-beef market, which by then amounted to 40 percent of the national output. Other processors divided the balance: MBPXL controlled 13 percent, and Armour, Cudahy, Land O'Lakes, Monfort, Swift, and 49 other firms, mostly on the Great Plains, shared 36 percent; fifty-one one-plant businesses, primarily situated in eastern states, accounted for the balance. The committee also asserted that between 1965 and 1978 the oligopoly of meatpackers annually inflated the retail price of beef by an average of 25.1 cents, thereby accounting for 30 percent of all meat price increases during the period.

In 1981, Occidental Petroleum bought Iowa Beef Processors with an $800 million stock swap designed to acquire a domestic subsidiary to absorb the giant oil company's unused investment tax credits, estimated at $117 million. "That means Iowa Beef will probably pay little or no taxes for several years," *Fortune* magazine postulated, adding: "The mind reels with questions about all this tumult. Why is Oxy getting into the [meatpacking] business just as so many presumably savvy managers are bailing out? And what does this mean to Armour, Wilson, Cudahy, and all the other familiar names that have been lining freezer shelves for years?"[45] Equally unsettling was IBP's entry into the pork trade the following year with the purchase of Hygrade's idle Storm Lake, Iowa, facility; moreover, it announced plans to erect a sophisticated pork-processing plant in either eastern Iowa or western Illinois, deep in hog country. To deemphasize its beef connection and to acknowledge its horizontal move into pork, the company also officially changed its name to IBP.

Wilson Foods, itself for many years the subsidiary of a giant

[44]U.S. Congress, House Committee on Small Business, *Small business problems in the marketing of meat and other commodities: monopoly effects on producers and consumers* (96th Cong., 2d Sess., 1980), Pt. 7, p. 8.

[45]Alexander Stuart, "Meatpackers in stampede: fearsome Iowa Beef's access to oxy-dollars lends new urgency to its competitors' scramble for survival strategies," *Fortune*, Vol. 103 (1981), pp. 67, 68.

conglomerate (the Dallas-based LTV Corp.) and the world's largest hog slaughterer, which handles pork the way IBP does beef—cut up, quick-chilled in vacuum bags, and shipped in boxes—with sales of $2 billion in 1981, was critical of its new competitor. One Wilson Foods spokesman expected that IBP's entry into the pork trade would "accelerate the shakeout of marginal companies and put pressure on a limited supply of hogs. Also, if [as anticipated] they [IBP] have lower wages, it will be hard for others to compete."[46] Indeed, the number of slaughterhouses for beeves had decreased by 34.9 percent between 1972 and 1980, and according to one government study the number of companies in beef packing declined by 32.7 percent, from 855 to 575 nationwide. Wilson had good cause for concern.

Wilson Foods, which as Schwarschild & Sulzberger in 1870 had built its first packing plant in New York on what later became the site of the United Nations headquarters, relocated in Chicago about the turn of the century to be at the heart of the industry. It was renamed Wilson & Co., Inc., in 1916. During the 1930s its superior hams wrested from Swift & Co. leadership of the pork trade, a position it is yet to relinquish. Following World War II, Wilson & Co. marketed leaner hams than those of its competitors under Masterpiece (top of the line), Wilson (medium-priced), and Corn King ("value-priced") brands for an increasingly demanding American palate. In 1967 the company's retail success attracted the attention of conglomerate builder James J. Ling, and he added Wilson & Co. (including its poultry, pharmaceutical, and sporting-goods subsidiaries) to Ling-Temco-Vaught's other celebrated acquisitions of the period, which included Braniff International and Jones & Laughlin Steel.

Suddenly well financed, Wilson & Co. closed obsolete plants in Boston, Chicago, Kansas City, Los Angeles, and Omaha, and in 1970 (the year the Union Stock Yards in Chicago closed for lack of business) shifted its headquarters from Chicago to Oklahoma City. It built new, streamlined plants (as at Marshall, Missouri) and modernized other facilities in Colorado, Illinois, Indiana, Iowa, Kansas, Kentucky, and Minnesota; moreover, it erected slaughterhouses in Auckland and Gore, New Zealand.

[46] Quoted in Lippman, "Iowa Beef makes its move on anxious pork industry," Washington *Post*, April 18, 1982, p. F-3.

The company (sans sporting goods and pharmaceuticals) changed its name to Wilson Foods in 1976. According to its president, Kenneth Griggy, "We wanted to make this into a company with more of a marketing thrust and into more of a food company than a traditional meat packer." Three years later Wilson Foods virtually eliminated its beef operations, explaining: "Our facilities were not as modern as some of our competitors. . . . Specialization [in pork] has worked for us. Our reputation is of being a far more preferred industry [by investors] since we focused our attention on pork."[47] The closing of its four beef plants also reduced Wilson's work force by 17 percent, to about 10,000 persons from 12,000. Even so, disappointing returns from meatpacking, precipitated principally by the heightened level of competition implicit in the rise of the new beef boxers (and their pork-substitute product), as well as pressure from antitrust rulings requiring LTV to divest itself of many of its holdings, led to the spin-off of Wilson Foods in 1981 as an independent firm once more.

Armour & Co., which had once led the industry in corporate acquisitions, was itself gobbled up in 1970 by the Greyhound Corp. Ranked second after Swift & Co. among interstate packers at the end of World War II, Armour pounced on the processed-meat business, in time deemphasizing the wholesale fresh-beef market that IBP eventually came to dominate. In 1978, Armour decided to focus on the fast-food phenomenon by concentrating primarily on "its branded processed-meat lines, where the margins are higher. . . . Armour botched the metamorphosis," *Fortune* magazine reported in 1981, for "processed-meat volume slid and losses mounted into the millions. Then last summer it reversed course, returning to the commodity orientation of yore. Today, Armour has no discernible niche: it's dealing in all meats—beef, pork, lamb, poultry—and operating at every level of the business from dressed carcasses to the Armour Star hot dog. It eked out a slight profit in the first quarter [of 1981], but competitors hardly seem dazzled. Says one: 'Armour's dead in the water.'"[48]

Swift & Co., a wholly owned subsidiary of conglomerate Esmark, experienced parallel woes and in 1981 spun off much of its

[47] Quoted in "Wilson refocuses from production to customers," Wichita *Eagle-Beacon*, August 15, 1982, p. 9G.

[48] Stuart, "Meatpackers in stampede," *Fortune*, Vol. 103, p. 71.

fresh-meat operation (about 65 percent of the business) as the Swift Independent Packing Co. (SIPCO), retaining the rest to guarantee a steady supply for Swift's Soup Starter, Butterball turkey, Swift ham, and Treasure Cave cheese retail lines, among others. SIPCO meanwhile "is pressing hard into the boxed-beef business and had launched a frontal assault on labor costs. Just before SIPCO's birth, Esmark shut down three slaughterhouses and paid the necessary severance costs; then SIPCO reopened the plants. The ploy allowed the company to wriggle out of the UFCW's master agreement and hire workers who would toil at reduced wages and benefits."[49] Cudahy Foods, until 1981 a unit of General Hosts, was similarly cut loose and sold to its managers, who hoped to improve on an abysmal (0.6 percent) return on revenues ($408 million in 1981).

Contrary to the divestiture trend throughout much of the industry is the saga of the Excel Corp. Founded in Chicago as Excel Packing Co. in 1936, it was acquired five years later by erstwhile Swift salesman Samuel Marcus and moved to Wichita, where there was a steady supply of slaughter animals. In 1969 it merged with the Kansas Packing Co., the Circle E Ranch Co., and two small Philadelphia firms and changed its name to Kansas Beef Industries, marketing its boxed beef under the XL label. Five years later Kansas Beef merged with Missouri Beef Packers (whose principal plant was then in Amarillo), creating the MBPXL corporate acronym. It also transferred its Texas operations to Wichita and for a time relied on separate slaughterhouse and fabricating facilities there for its entire output.

In 1978, Cargill Industries, a privately held Minneapolis grain giant, outbid equally mammoth ConAgra, of Omaha, to acquire MBPXL. Infused with capital, the meatpacker the following year built a 250,000-square-foot slaughterhouse at Dodge City to utilize an abundance of local feedlot cattle. Soon thereafter it closed its comparatively antiquated Wichita facility. In 1982, having changed its name once more, this time to the Excel Corp., it broke ground for a huge fabricating facility in Dodge City designed to handle 3,500 carcasses a day and, ultimately, to replace its less modern processing plant in Wichita. By then Excel was the nation's sixth-largest beef packer, accounting for approximately 12.5 percent of all the boxed-beef output, about one-third of IBP's total. Like IBP, Excel had also gained a reputation for hard-nosed labor relations.

Organized labor in meatpacking—for the most part divided by dual unionism and confronted by a generally hostile public sector—overall lost leverage following World War II. A ten-week strike in Chicago in 1948 came to naught, workers ultimately accepting the packers' original offer of an increase of nine cents an hour. Southern independent packers blocked the best organizing efforts of both the Amalgamated Meat Cutters and Butcher Workmen of North America (AFL) and the United Packinghouse Workers of America (CIO). Labor historian David Brody says that there was a "pattern of employer and community resistance [in] small towns, race antagonism, and violence—for instance, the beating of Amalgamated representatives in Gainsville, Georgia, in March, 1951, and the dynamiting of the tourist cabin of an Amalgamated organizer in Center, Texas, in 1954."[50] The discord was not limited to the South. In an especially bitter strike in Boston against the Colonial Provisions Co. in 1954–55 the UPWA was decertified.

The most spectacular postwar labor success came in 1956 against the big packers. The Amalgamated and UPWA together struck Swift & Co. nationwide on September 20. Five days later Armour signed a master agreement with a joint UPWA-Amalgamated bargaining team, granting an increase of twenty-five cents an hour spread over three years, a modified union shop, and other concessions. The strike against Swift was soon settled along similar lines, except that the open shop was retained. Emboldened, the UPWA announced in 1958 that henceforth it would bargain toward a thirty-hour week for all its members, a goal yet to be achieved anywhere in meatpacking, at least in part because of a changed legal environment.

The Labor Management Relations (Taft-Hartley) Act of 1947 had tipped the balance of power away from labor (as had been the case following the passage of the National Labor Relations [Wagner] Act of 1935) and back toward management. The Taft-Hartley Act authorized the president in the interest of national health or safety to impose an eighty-day "cooling-off" suspension of strikes, required unions to bargain with management, outlawed closed shops and secondary boycotts, permitted states to ban union shops (which

---

[50] Brody, *The butcher workmen*, p. 247.

nineteen states did), and required union officials to attest to the National Labor Relations Board that they were not communists in order to obtain the services of the board.

Historically, radicals had abounded in meatpacking. Socialists and even anarchists were allegedly active in the 1882 strike against Armour & Co. The Chicago Stockyards Butchers' Union, which provoked Packingtown's participation in the great Pullman strike of 1894, was openly led by avowed communists. Upton Sinclair claimed to find militants of all stripes among meatpacking workers when he researched in Chicago at the turn of the century, and William Z. Foster, three-time Communist party presidential candidate (1924, 1928, and 1932), led the organizing drive at the Union Stock Yards during World War I. In 1939, Representative Martin Dies of the House Committee on Un-American Activities charged that communists, fellow travelers, left-wingers, and other subversives had infiltrated every aspect of the CIO's Packing House Workers Organizing Committee (later the UPWA). "Left wingers," Brody says in his balanced treatment of the union movement, "had played a significant role in the internal life of the UPWA," until Washington forced the union to purge itself. "By 1956, the Communists were no longer visible, but many [knowledgeable persons] . . . did not doubt that they were still entrenched 'underground.'" [51] UPWA's leadership was even suspected by its own relatively conservative rank-and-file, and membership consequently shrank. UPWA's clout with management thus dwindled.

The far more orthodox Amalgamated Meat Cutters and Butcher Workmen grew steadily throughout the 1950s and even indirectly benefited from the great red scare of the McCarthy era. By 1960, Amalgamated's rolls listed 327,000 dues-paying members, twice the count of 1948 and three times that claimed by the UPWA. Of this increase 50,000 were recruits. About 25,000 who had observed that the Butcher Workmen bargained more effectively with management than did Packinghouse Workers had been proselytized. Another 40,000 came with the enrollment of fish, cannery, and poultry workers. The rest were members of theretofore independent unions absorbed by Amalgamated. The tiny Sheep Shearers' International (AFL) had allied with Amalgamated in 1940 to gain lever-

[51] Ibid., p. 265.

age with the National Wool Growers' Association; eventually it became a semiautonomous division, despite some objections from the
AFL's executive committee, which distrusted jurisdictional growth.
In 1951 the United Leather Workers' International (AFL), with
5,000 members, similarly became a branch of Amalgamated. In
1955 the Stockyards Workers' Association of America, which consisted of four livestock handlers' locals that had bolted the UPWA
over the issue of communism, also joined Amalgamated.

Also in 1951, Amalgamated adopted the 40,000-member International Fur and Leather Workers' Union of the United States
and Canada. The IFLWU was openly dominated by radicals (its
president, Ben Gold, his assistant, Irving Potash, and numerous
local leaders were members of the Communist party), and as a con-
sequence it had been kicked out of the CIO in 1953. Because the
union stood to lose recourse to the National Labor Relations Board,
Gold and the others resigned, and new IFLWU leadership quickly
negotiated a deal with Amalgamated. Although the merger was
soon consummated, it was not recognized by the AFL-CIO until
the end of the decade, largely because union chief George Meany
objected to sanctuary for radicals among the Butcher Workmen.

Thus when in 1955 the United Packinghouse Workers of America approached Amalgamated about solidarity similar to the AFL-
CIO merger of that year, communist influence in the UPWA became a sticking point. Amalgamated's leaders also worried that their
position might be threatened by the addition of yet another left-
leaning block of votes numbering 100,000. Complex discussions between the rival bodies—encouraged by the parent AFL-CIO—
dragged on for months, finally collapsing in 1956. Although the
two unions periodically negotiated a merger for the next dozen
years, it did not occur until July 11, 1968, when the UPWA simply
submitted to total absorption by the bigger, more powerful
Amalgamated.

Even so, jurisdictional squabbles did not end. From its very beginning before the turn of the century, Amalgamated Meat Cutters
and Butcher Workmen had broadly defined its constituency to embrace livestock handlers and clerks in meat markets, which after
1900 placed it in occasional conflict with the then ineffectual Retail
Clerks' International Association (AFL). For its part Amalgamated
most often swept up clerks while organizing retail butchers, as in

the Loblaw grocery chain in Buffalo, New York, in 1937, rather than recruiting them as a group. Then, during the New Deal, when union organizing surged throughout the United States, both the Retail Clerks and the CIO's rival United Retail and Wholesale Employees became more aggressive, regularly soliciting retail butchers, which strained relations with Amalgamated.

Attempting to draw a jurisdictional line between his two affiliates, AFL President William Green said in 1938 that Amalgamated might organize clerks who sold "groceries and food products in connection with their meat selling and meat cutting" while members of Retail Clerks would be those "employed in selling groceries, spices and food products, *other than meats*, handled and sold in grocery stores. . . ."[52] Amalgamated interpreted its mission very loosely to include any retail establishment that sold meat, whereas Green and the Retail Clerks intended to give away only meat-market workers. Raiding between unions sometimes played into management's hands. In 1941, Safeway Stores refused to recognize the exclusive domain of either union unless the other formally ceded its claims. For a time neither union was able to negotiate a nationwide pact with the retailer.

In 1942, with the nation at war, Green imposed an armistice between Amalgamated and the Retail Clerks. Even so, here and there the two skirmished over assorted job classifications—women who wrapped prepackaged meats in markets, poultry and fish handlers, and, in one instance, even those who made sausages in a delicatessen—but for the most part the AFL arbitrated in favor of the larger, more powerful Amalgamated. In 1949, still settling wartime jurisdictional disputes, the AFL gave workers in prewrapped and frozen meat to Amalgamated and workers in canned meat and all checkers, when meat and groceries were purchased together, to the Retail Clerks. A dispute two years later in California, where the Retail Clerks were especially strong, landed before the National Labor Relations Board, which ordered the AFL to arbitrate. President Meany initially gave the territory in question to the Retail Clerks but in 1951, under pressure from Butcher Workmen, modified his decree to allow Amalgamated greater latitude in organizing supermarket employees.

[52] Quoted in ibid., p. 254.

Postwar supermarkets, with their self-service meat counters, wholly unsettled the boundaries. Unlike the rivalry with the CIO's UPWA, which was a matter of dual unionism, Amalgamated's fight with Retail Clerks over the new retail outlets involved exclusive jurisdiction; where one existed, the other clearly could not. As automation reduced the number of jobs in meatpacking, Amalgamated saw supermarkets as a hedge against a declining membership pool. Indeed, between 1955 and 1977 employment in meatpacking nationwide had shrunk by 14.5 percent, to 171,000 jobs from 200,000, even though meat processing and fabricating together employed 23,000 more persons than before. Moreover, the average work week in meatpacking declined to 41.6 hours in 1977, from 42.4 hours in 1955; nevertheless, annual red-meat output had zoomed upward by 47.6 percent, to 39.7 billion pounds from 26.9 billion pounds. While the total number of persons employed in the retail grocery trade had similarly slipped (to 1.72 million in 1977 from 1.82 million in 1955), the substantially larger work force in retailing offered relatively bountiful recruiting prospects. In 1960, Amalgamated broached merger with the Retail Clerks.

The Retail Clerks were attracted by Amalgamated's apparent success at collective bargaining. Since World War II wages throughout the meat trade had risen faster and higher than those in American manufacturing generally, reaching an average of $6.42 an hour for slaughtering, processing, and fabricating in 1977, up from $1.96 in 1955—as contrasted with an average of $5.63 an hour for manufacturing in general in 1977, up from $1.86 in 1955. Moreover, according to the American Meat Institute, union-required fringe-benefit packages (covering paid leave, overtime, holidays, shift differentials, pensions, insurance, and severance pay) and government-mandated contributions to Social Security and to unemployment and workmen's compensation funds added another 22.9 percent to labor costs.

Not mentioned by AMI was the number of job-related accidents in meatpacking. According to a report of the federal Occupational Safety and Health Administration of 1982, the meatpacking industry had an incident rate of 33.5 percent—that is, one chance in three that a worker would be slightly injured, maimed, or even killed at work—and led all other American industries in job-related accidents. By comparison, the average injury rate among steel workers was 26 percent; construction workers, 15.7 percent; miners, 11.2 percent, and petroleum-refining workers, 5.4 percent—persuasive argument that meatpacking workers, however well they might be compensated, were not overpaid.

Retail Clerks, whose wages were 20 percent less than those of meat cutters, but whose working environment was infinitely safer, seemingly had much to gain by the merger. Serious discussions began in 1960 and then dragged on for two decades. Finally, on August 8, 1979, the Retail Clerks' International Association (AFL-CIO) and the Amalgamated Meat Cutters and Butcher Workmen of North America (AFL-CIO) agreed to become the United Food and Commercial Workers International (AFL-CIO), with a total membership of 1.2 million persons.

Despite the power suggested by such vast numbers, organized labor has not dictated to management throughout the red-meat chain. "Before Iowa Beef entered beef-packing in 1961," the *Wall Street Journal* has observed, "the industry was dominated by a few companies using the union's master agreement, which provided wages and benefits generous by today's standards. Iowa Beef turned the industry on its ear by refusing the master contract. . . ."[53] New production techniques that substantially reduced skilled manpower requirements, as well as IBP's stubborn refusal to grant high-cost fringe-benefit packages, led to repeated strikes, some marred with violence.

For example, IBP's boxed-beef facility at Dakota City, Nebraska, was shut down on four occasions between 1969 and 1984, including one fourteen-month strike that ended in 1977. The one that commenced in June, 1982, saw 2,450 members of the UFCW walk off the job rather than swallow a four-year wage freeze (at $9.27 an hour for packinghouse workers and $8.97 for processing-division employees), the elimination of a cost-of-living escalator, and possible wage givebacks tied to competitors. Rock and brick throwing caused Nebraska governor Charles Thorn to mobilize the National Guard. Later he persuaded both labor and management to sit down and talk, but negotiations went nowhere. "After weeks of impasse, the company announced it would start up again. It advertised for

[53] Sue Shellenbarger, "Iowa Beef's effort to slash labor costs at strike site may speed industry trend," *Wall Street Journal*, August 6, 1982, p. 22.

help in all the surrounding states. Out-of-work people responded." [54] After hiring approximately 1,400 strikebreakers, IBP reopened two shifts in July and announced that strikers would return to work on company terms or not at all.

Meanwhile, the *Wall Street Journal* reported that

> workers at the Wichita plant of Excel Corp. . . . surprised other packers by agreeing to concessions that Iowa Beef says include a wage rollback and a 30-month wage freeze. Swift Independent Corp., a streamlined packer spun off last year by Esmark Inc., closed three plants that had been operating under the master agreement and reopened two with cheaper labor rates. And workers at two of the three beef plants operated by Land O'Lakes Inc., Minneapolis, recently agreed to wage freezes. [55]

The situation was similar throughout the rest of the industry. Dubuque Packing Co., an Iowa-based beef packer, closed its Wichita plant in 1981 because workers rejected a wage rollback to $6.30 an hour, from $8.50, but to keep their jobs, the employees of another Dubuque facility in Mankato, Minnesota, agreed to reductions amounting to $2.00 an hour.

Also in Wichita two hundred members of UFCW employed by Dold Foods, Inc., walked out rather than give back $2.43 an hour, or 28.8 percent of the $8.44 wage base. Dold, a privately held pork processor that claimed it could not compete without employee concessions, resorted to open hiring and eventually asked the National Labor Relations Board to decertify the union. For its part the UFCW filed five separate complaints with the NLRB alleging unfair labor practices by Dold Foods, notably its refusal to meet and confer with the union. As of this writing, hearings on the charges and countercharges continue. Dold meanwhile discovered an ample supply of unskilled workers in Wichita, especially among recent immigrants from Southeast Asia. In November, 1982, the UFCW surrendered, asking merely that the company take back the strikers. Dold's president, Stephen Ritter, replied that his firm would rehire only as positions became available. He added that, because of re-

---

[54] Ernest Furguson, "Iowa Beef Processors plays hard ball in Siouxland," Wichita *Eagle-Beacon*, August 10, 1982, p. 3C.

[55] Shellenbarger, "Iowa Beef's effort to slash labor costs at strike site may speed industry trend," *Wall Street Journal*, August 6, 1982, p. 22.

duced labor costs (as little as $5.25 an hour for probationers), pro-
ductivity had surged; Dold Foods finally "had turned the corner" toward profitability. [56]

Many other meatpackers were not so fortunate. Even with unprecedented worker cooperation, survival was far from ensured. A
classic case in point is the Rath Packing Co. of Waterloo, Iowa, a
pork-packing and processing operation whose fifty-year-old four-
story plant by 1980 was obsolete compared with newer, one-story
facilities such as Wilson's in Oklahoma City, which effeciently moves
carcasses continuously along automated disassembly lines. Rath's
labor force was predominantly middle-aged, many workers having
been with the company for thirty years or more, and thus burdened
it with expensive wage and benefit costs. Having lost $22 mil-
lion during the previous five years, the company faced impending
bankruptcy.

"To save the business," the *Wall Street Journal* reported in 1981,

> local 46 of the United Food and Commercial Workers Union,
> which represented most of the 2,000 rank-and-file employees,
> . . . offered to take 10 shares each of Rath common stock a
> week in lieu of $20 in wages. The workers also agreed to forgo
> raises, one-half of their vacation pay, and three days of their sick
> pay. The company, furthermore, was allowed to postpone pay-
> ments into the workers' pension fund. In return, the union got
> control of the board of directors; 10 directors were added to the
> board of six, including three new directors who are members of
> the union. [57]

Rath, like an estimated 250 other worker-owned American companies with ten or more employees, experienced a temporary upsurge in productivity. The hog kill increased by one-third, from 600
to 800 a day. Absenteeism declined by 50 percent, wildcat work
stoppages ceased, and tardiness was not tolerated by workers' committees that meted out discipline. With the help of the citizens of
Waterloo the company secured from the U.S. Department of Hous-
ing and Urban Development a $4.5 million loan for ten years at 3

[56] Bill Hirshman, "Dold strike ends after 34 weeks," Wichita *Eagle-Beacon*, November
13, 1982, p. 4D.

[57] Terri Minsky, "Gripes of Rath: workers who bought Iowa slaughterhouse regret that
they did," *Wall Street Journal*, December 2, 1981, p. 1.

percent interest with which to build a modern bacon-processing plant, the company's first significant capital improvement in two decades.

Following modest profits in 1980, widely attributed to wage and benefit concessions by its worker-owners, Rath reported a $9.6 million loss in 1981, which it claimed was caused by higher hog prices and diminished consumer demand for pork. Too, worker-owners became restive, complaining that they had no real voice in company management, "and some workers are even talking of forming a new union when their contract expires. . . . Once proud that their sacrifice pushed Rath's earnings into the black, workers now feel that they gave up too much. . . . Ordinarily, workers would take their complaints to their union, but Rath employees feel that the union [local] president [Lyle] Taylor has been co-opted by management. He sits on the board of directors, . . . often has lunch with [Herbert S.] Epstein, Rath's CEO, and travels with him to meat-industry shows." [58]

To avoid reorganization under bankruptcy protection, or outright liquidation because of losses of $6.5 million in 1982, Rath terminated three separate pension plans covering 6,300 employees and retirees and sought relief from the federal Pension Benefit Guarantee Corporation, which insures funds for about 36 million American workers. The government agency agreed to assume Rath's pension liabilities, amounting to $38 million, in return for company contributions totaling $13 million spread over sixteen years, and a variable rate of Rath's pretax profits (if any) for ten years, commencing in 1985. After making an initial payment of $1.8 million in 1982, Rath, because of heavy losses, defaulted on $1.7 million due in September, 1983, forcing the Pension Benefit Guarantee Corporation to reschedule the company's payments, its alternative being the attachment of the meatpacker's property, accounts receivable, and inventory, which serve as collateral for the guarantee. Rath's survival at this writing is far from certain.

If a worker-owned meatpacker could be so cavalier toward its own stockholders, conditions were ripe elsewhere for even more high-handed managerial tactics. Rodeo Meats, the Arkansas City, Kansas, subsidiary of John Morrell & Co. (a unit of United Brands

[58] Ibid., p. 10.

Co.), which closed in June, 1982, because of what management claimed were excessively high labor costs, reopened as Ark City Packing Co., a new John Morrell subsidiary wholly unfettered by union contracts. It offered jobs at $5 an hour, as contrasts with $11 paid by defunct Rodeo Meats. With the local unemployment rate in excess of 11 percent, the new meatpacker received nine hundred applications for employment the first day, one hundred more persons than had previously worked at the plant.

In 1983, Wilson Foods Corp. of Oklahoma City—adapting Johns Mansville's ploy to escape liability over the health effects of asbestos—filed for protection under the bankrupty code. It repudiated its contract with the UFCW and slashed wages 40 percent, to $6.50 an hour from $10.69. While the union protested vehemently to the NLRB, workers—keenly aware of high unemployment nationwide—had little alternative but to accept grudgingly the rollback, especially after the U.S. Supreme Court early in 1984 sanctioned bankruptcy as an escape hatch for floundering enterprises. This "union-busting" tactic may have its limitations, however, for it exposed Wilson to a takeover bid by IBP, which offered Wilson's court-appointed receiver $162 million for the pork processor's operating assets—a bargain, according to many market analysts.

Undoubtedly many Wilson and Rath employees, to economize, have reduced their own red-meat consumption, but some critics of the industry contend that meatpacking workers regularly consume less meat than the average American because they are revolted by their own products. One critical study of meatpacking has observed:

> The ingenuity of food chemistry and processing technology long ago overwhelmed the consumer's natural detection devices—seeing, smelling, tasting—which might have protected him from bad meat. Seasoning agents, preservatives, and coloring agents can now serve effectively as cosmetics to mask the true condition of meat products. The use of cheap fillers and additives such as water, cereal, and fat, unless carefully controlled, give the consumer less protein for his dollar. A case in point is the hotdog, the fat content of which increased from 19 percent to 33 percent between 1937 and 1969.[59]

[59] Harrison Wellford, *Sowing the wind: a report from Ralph Nader's Center for Study of Responsive Law on food safety and the chemical harvest* (1972), p. 2.

As early as 1960, Congressman Smith of Iowa called attention to ongoing sanitation problems in American meatpacking notwithstanding the Meat Inspection Act of 1906. A farmer, Smith observed that in his region the same buyers for intrastate packers consistently purchased "4-D livestock"—dead, dying, diseased, and disabled; moreover, there was no foolproof method by which concerned consumers could distinguish between interstate (and inspected) meat and the intrastate (uninspected) variety once the product was prepackaged and displayed in a supermarket. USDA surveys of state plants in 1963 (and kept secret until 1967) confirmed Smith's worst suspicions: many intrastate plants, including some facilities operated by Armour, Swift, and Wilson and totaling 15 to 25 percent of the nation's red-meat trade, were reminiscent of conditions exposed in Upton Sinclair's *The Jungle*.

Twenty-two states did not require both ante- and postmortem examinations of livestock, and eight states had no inspection standards whatever. The situation came to national attention in 1967 when newspaper reporters and consumer advocates secured copies of the suppressed USDA report and made it public. In Delaware, USDA investigators had found "rodents and insects, in fact many vermin, [which] had free access to stored meats and meat product ingredients." In Norfolk, Virginia, federal observers "found abscessed beef and livers, abscessed pork livers, parasitic livers mixed with the edible products." At a North Carolina facility a visitor reported "snuff spit on the floor, sausage meat fallen on the same floor which was then picked up and shoved into the stuffer."[60]

Despite vigorous opposition by the American Meat Institute, the National Independent Meat Packers Association, and the Western Meat Packers Association, as well as by most state departments of agriculture, which objected to federal intrusion into what they contended was states' rights, numerous bills were introduced in Congress to mandate federal inspection of all red meats and also of poultry, which critics contended was equally suspect. The resulting Wholesale Meat Act, which was signed into law by President Lyndon B. Johnson on December 15, 1967, with Upton Sinclair looking on, required states to develop within two years inspection programs equal to USDA Food Safety and Inspection Service stan-

[60] Quoted in ibid., pp. 5–6.

dards (the federal government paying 50 percent of the total cost) or have the FSIS take over intrastate inspection altogether. Moreover, the secretary of agriculture was empowered to order federal inspection of any plant deemed dangerous to public health.

Even so, says Harrison Wellford, a vocal critic of American food-processing standards, "Changes in the technology of food processing have increased the risk of microbiological poisoning, as more fully processed foods are offered to the consumer and as the time span between processing and consumption continues to increase. . . . The hazards from chemical contaminants are both more serious and less easily controlled . . . [because] between 80 and 90 percent of all beef and poultry produced in this country is grown on a diet of antibiotics and other drugs from birth to slaughter."[61] Cattle are regularly fed diethylstilbestrol and other growth hormones and are sometimes inadvertently exposed to pesticides, many of which until recently contained toxins such as dioxin, difficult to detect by regular FSIS inspection techniques. Investigative journalist Lynn O'Shaughnessy adds that "when [in 1981] the Reagan administration solicited from the meatpacking industry on ways to cut down [government] waste, high on its list was the abolishment of the Lawrence [Kansas] office [of FSIS]. The industry considers the review branch a frivolous adjunct to the inspection service, which already has circuit supervisors and area and regional offices to serve as guardians for the consumer."[62]

FSIS inspectors are overworked and reportedly subjected to relentless pressure to approve diseased and spoiled meat. According to veteran FSIS employee John Coplin, "Those [inspectors] who make waves on behalf of consumers face vicious retaliation."[63] Whistle blowers reportedly are harassed by USDA bureaucrats and their careers sometimes stagnated. "The deliberate laxness of USDA in the inspection area also extends to residue testing (for antibiotics, chemical pollutants, etc.) which involves a more insidious and under-reported set of problems," says the Center for Study of

[61] Ibid., pp. 125–26.

[62] Lynn O'Shaughnessy, "Meatpacking industry would like to chain up the watchdog," Kansas City Times, May 10, 1982, p. A-9.

[63] Quoted in Kathleen Hughes, Return to The jungle: how the Reagan administration is imperiling the nation's meat and poultry inspection programs (1983), p. 8.

Responsive Law, a consumer lobby headed by Ralph Nader. It contends that the Reagan administration

> is determined to reduce the frequency of inspections, loosen enforcement standards and sanctions, speed up the time pressure on a dwindling number of inspectors, and place the curtain of secrecy over damaging inspectors' reports on plants that in the past have served to alert the consuming public. . . . if the Reagan administration believes the free market should handle the matter of meat safety, it should not bias the decisions of the market by asserting the meat has been [adequately] inspected by the government. If the government is no longer guaranteeing safety, it should not mislead consumers by putting the USDA INSPECTED AND PASSED stamp on packages of meat and poultry.[64]

Even with inspection there is no guarantee that the public interest is served. A case in point is the ongoing Department of Justice probe of the Cattle King Packing Co. of Denver and its sister firm, Nebraska Beef Processors of Gering, Nebraska, which together process about one-fourth of the ground beef used in the federal school-lunch program and which have been accused of knowingly selling schools contaminated meat. In January, 1984, a former Cattle King supervisor, Bruce Ryan, pleaded guilty in Denver's federal district court to participating "in a scheme to manipulate required meat-testing procedures established to ensure compliance with federal contracts involved in the federal school lunch program."[65] The U.S. Attorney's office announced that other indictments are pending as of this writing.

[64] Ibid., pp. v, 12.
[65] Quoted in Wichita *Eagle-Beacon*, February 1, 1984, p. 6A.

7

Conclusions and Expectations

The imperfect market structure of the red-meat trade of the United States, in which millions of producers funnel livestock through a relative handful of processors to feed hundreds of millions of consumers, ironically provides livestock raisers and meatpackers a more equitable share of the product than is generally the case in food processing nationally. The middleman's share of the consumer's food dollar for all agrarian produce rose to a record 71.9 percent in 1983, up from about 68 percent in 1978. The farmer's average take from fruit, vegetables, meat, dairy products, and poultry and eggs slipped to 28.1 percent in 1983, down from 32 percent in 1968. Nevertheless, the worth of slaughter beasts on farms and ranches hovered at about 50 percent of their retail value, which approximates the overall trend for the past century—since the rise of the large meatpacking firms and the concomitant development of a nationally integrated red-meat chain.

While retail meat prices in the United States have soared spectacularly since World War II, neither livestock raiser nor meatpacker has reaped remarkable profits. According to the USDA, Americans enjoy the world's lowest across-the-board food costs, averaging 12.7 percent of per capita income, whereas Australians typically spend 17.1 percent, Britons 17.3 percent, the French 18.5 percent, the Japanese 21.5 percent, South Africans 25 percent, and Soviets 33.7 percent. Americans pay about 20 percent more for their beef, for example, than South Africans and twice as much as do Australians, but at least 28 percent less than Britons, 50 percent less than the French, and 90 percent less than the Japanese or the Soviets.

The relative prosperity of American livestock producers (as contrasted with crop raisers), however, is small solace to those mixed farmers who are forced out of business. The shakeout in agriculture whereby the number of farms in America declined to 2.37 million in 1983, from 2.40 million the year before, continues unabated, as it has throughout the twentieth century, as does the trend toward larger agrarian units, the average reaching 437 acres in 1983, up from 433 the year before.

Yet averages can be misleading. According to the USDA, between 1978 and 1982 the attrition rate in Kansas (ranked fourth in overall farm output) was greatest among those operators holding five hundred to a thousand acres each, whereas the largest increase in new agrarian units came from persons working fifty acres or less. In the wheat state in 1982 rural Kansans typically received 62 percent of their revenue from livestock production, 35 percent from crops, 2 percent from dairy products, and 1 percent from poultry and eggs. Notwithstanding the enhanced significance of husbandry (and of large-scale meatpacking) in the state's economy, in 1984 the legislature refused to amend its laws to allow corporate ownership of farmlands (which would have allowed agribusiness giant DeKalb to continue to operate a 150,000-head swine farm in southwestern Kansas and perhaps in the process attract a pork packer to an area already bristling with feedlots and beef packers) rather than intensify the level of competition among the state swine raisers, most of whom are small operators.

Not only do livestock producers actually compete with one another—large-scale operators with small, cowmen with pig farmers, and the like—they also regularly suffer the ill effects of economic tremors elsewhere in the agrarian economy. Two recent cases should suffice as examples. The Reagan administration's "payment-in-kind" (PIK) program, whereby farmers received government-stored commodities in lieu of cash subsidies in return for reductions in specified crop acreage, in the short run prompted an increase in livestock production for the red-meat trade, the cattle either grazing idle pastures or munching on grains liberated from government bins, but as adverse weather and the PIK program combined to dramatically decrease the corn supply, feeders of all sorts faced problems. In 1983 pig producers discovered that the hog-corn ratio had abruptly declined to 15.6 bushels per hundred pounds of live porker, from 22.4 bushels per hundred pounds the year before, which represented a 40 percent increase in feed costs. They consequently dumped animals, the swine slaughter rising 7 percent for the year, and reduced their production, which portends higher pork prices for the consumer in the future.

Similarly, when in 1983 giant feedlots on the Great Plains of Texas, Oklahoma, Kansas, and Colorado found corn priced thirty-five cents a bushel more than wheat, they increasingly substituted the latter grain, which is more commonly destined for human consumption and which, because of increased diversion into animal feeds, will probably increase in price for retail consumers. Complicating the situation was the public sector's decision not to grant sought-for milk-price supports for the dairy industry in 1983, which led many dairy farmers to dump their cattle on the slaughter market. The result was that, with beef-cattle production in 1983 up 3 percent over 1982 (and with the average live weight of commercially slaughtered cattle up 7 percent), cattle quotations slid, which usually signals fewer slaughter beeves in the future and inevitably, higher beef prices at the supermarket.

Undoubtedly exacerbating the situation for consumers in the future will be the revised trade agreement with the Japanese—sought by cattlemen and other groups and delivered by the Reagan administration in 1984—that increases the old annual import quota of 30,800 metric tons of high-quality American beef allowed into that nation by 6,900 metric tons every year for four years. Yet American cattle producers cannot meet domestic demand for their product. As has been the case throughout the twentieth century, the United States continues to be a net importer of both live cattle and fresh beef. In 1983 the United States imported 940,000 livestock (700,000 cattle, 155,000 swine, and 85,000 sheep and horses) but exported only 700,000 animals (about 500,000 cattle, 120,000 swine, and 80,000 sheep and horses). Moreover, while the United States that year exported about 70,000 metric tons of fresh beef and veal, it imported 1.25 million metric tons, the limit allowed by law, for a trade deficit of 1.18 million metric tons. Recent projections by agricultural economists James Simpson, of the University of Florida, and Donald Farris, of Texas A&M University, predicted an ongoing production shortfall in the range of 1 million metric tons throughout the 1980s. Therefore, premium-grade American beef sold on the lucrative Japanese market will have to be diverted from domestic American consumption, which will raise the price of Prime and Choice cuts in the United States and, ironically, likely lead to increased importation of these premium grades into the United States.

Such an upsurge in beef imports may well imperil the health of the American consumer, for in 1983 the USDA's Food Safety and Inspection Service advised twenty-three nations, including France, Ireland, Iceland, and all the nations of Central America, that unless they implement significant improvements in meat inspection and processing procedures they will be barred from the American marketplace. Fastidious though United States standards thus appear, it should be noted that almost simultaneously Canadian meat inspectors banned the products from a dozen American plants to which the FSIS had given clean bills of health. While the sanitation standards of American meatpacking unquestionably are infinitely superior to the deplorable turn-of-the-century conditions lambasted by Upton Sinclair and other critics, scandal haunts the industry—as with Cattle King Packing Co. of Denver and Nebraska Beef Processors of Gering, which, as of this writing, are under investigation for allegedly furnishing inferior products to the federal school-lunch programs and for altering the government-required records; and the M&M Packing Co. of New York, which in 1984 pleaded guilty to purposely misrepresenting some of its beef as kosher meat.

Industry critics contend that a far more serious problem plagues meatpacking: the upsurge in industry consolidation (including the absorption of meatpackers by conglomerates) that portends a return to the days of the beef trust. Both Occidental Petroleum's IBP and Cargill's Excel among the new Big Four—including FDL (formerly Dubuque Packing Co.) and the Spencer Beef division of Land O'Lakes—have recently been cited as employing predatory business tactics (IBP by the U.S. House of Representatives' Small Business Committee in 1979 and Excel in federal court in Denver in 1984) for the expressed purpose of driving its competition out of business. By 1983 the Big Four collectively controlled 40 percent of the nation's beef business, up from 29 in 1976. In 1972, 717 beef packers operated nationwide; in 1983, there were only 479. While this attrition cannot be clearly ascribed to predatory practices, many of the firms that have folded cite fierce competition as the reason for their demise, and even some large operations have announced imminent withdrawal from the red-meat trade.

In 1983, Minnesota farm co-op Land O'Lakes tried to spin off its fourth-ranked Spencer Beef division, which it claimed was unprofitable, by selling it to Excel, which announced plans to expand Spencer's facilities. Early in 1984, at the insistence of meatpacker Monfort of Colorado, Inc., the sale was invalidated by Denver Federal Judge Sherman Finesilver, who ruled that the purchase violated antitrust statutes. About the same time that Excel tried to buy Spencer, Greyhound's subsidiary Armour Food Co., which packs both beef and pork, announced that within six months it would close or sell thirteen unprofitable plants across the nation. Quickly ConAgra, the agribusiness giant of Omaha and the nation's largest flour miller and poultry processor, which had lost out to Cargill in 1978 in an attempt to acquire Excel, paid Greyhound $166 million in cash and stock to acquire the whole Armour operation.

A similar trend is under way in pork packing, where the issue of profitability most usually has been linked to allegedly excessive labor costs, as with Wilson Foods' bankruptcy filing to divorce itself from the master agreement and $10.69-an-hour labor costs. Yet such tactics—first used successfully in meatpacking by John Morrell in Kansas in 1982—expose vulnerable firms to takeover attempts, as when Occidental's IBP offered to buy the whole Wilson operation. Wilson executives vehemently objected, claiming that such acquisition would violate antitrust laws by further monopolizing the meat industry of the United States, and, ironically, begged for labor's support to fend off IBP. Miffed though it may have been at Wilson Foods, the United Food and Commercial Workers Union perceived IBP as far worse. Union spokesman John Mancuso predicted, "If they [IBP] follow their past history, they would fire everyone and hire all new workers at lower wages."[1] While trimming its labor costs by 40 percent under bankrupty protection, Wilson at least

---

[1] Quoted in Dirck Steimel, "Wilson and union join to fight IBP," Wichita *Eagle-Beacon*, January 29, 1984, p. 1C.

had retained its same work force. The IBP bid was rejected by the courts.

In August, 1983, citing high labor costs connected to the master agreement, Swift Independent Packing Co. announced the closing of its Sioux City, Iowa, plant and possible termination of operations in Glenwood, Iowa, and National Stock Yards, Illinois. The threat was sufficient to cause an anxious union to accept a 23 percent pay reduction from the master agreement base to $8.25 an hour. With meatpackers doing everything they can to diminish the impact of unions, it is little wonder that labor is again becoming restive in an industry traditionally beset by violence and radicalism—especially as food processors in general report rebounding earnings, profits averaging 13 percent nationally in 1983. Lewie Anderson, head of UFCWU's meatpacking division, predicts: "Workers will say, 'You took it [money] out of my hide. I'm going to get it back or strike you.' These workers are going to come back with vengeance in their eyes."[2] If so, even more firms will undoubtedly seek bankruptcy protection inasmuch as the U.S. Supreme Court upheld early in 1984 the action in the case of Bildisco Manufacturing Co. of New Jersey.

In any event, the issue of profitability in meatpacking seems contrived. One wonders why Esmark, Swift's erstwhile parent, which got out of meatpacking in 1981, reentered by buying Cudahy Specialty Foods Co., a $70 million-a-year sausage and meat operation, if the business was truly unprofitable, as Cudahy claimed. Indeed, Consolidated Foods of Chicago attributed much of its improved returns in 1983 to its acquisition of Standard Meat Co., a specialty processor. Frequently meatpacking plants that are closed because they are reportedly obsolete are soon reopened—sometimes by the same company using different names (as in the case of Rodeo Meats, which metamorphosed into Ark City Packing Co., both John Morrell subsidiaries), usually without a union contract.

Sometimes so-called antiquated plants are miraculously rejuvenated. In 1983 several former Excel Corp. executives, bankrolled by Dallas financier Edwin Cox, Jr., established Val-Agri, Inc., of Wichita, purchased the Kansas Beef Processors plant in

---

[2] Quoted in Joann Lublin, "Embattled unionist: effort to save pay scales in meatpacking brings Lewie Anderson many spats, not all with firms," *Wall Street Journal*, August 4, 1983, p. 42.

Garden City, Kansas, and the idle Amarillo Beef Processors subsidiary of John Morrell & Co., and announced plans to double the daily kill, thereby giving the new firm about 10 percent of the boxed-beef business. At other times rejuvenation requires public assistance. Winchester Packing Co. of Hutchinson, Kansas, closed its doors in 1983 because of reported annual losses of $193,000 that it attributed to labor's refusal to accept a $1.06-an-hour pay cut. Four months later Foley Meats, Inc., a Wichita firm, negotiated to buy the idle plant, provided the city of Hutchinson agreed to issue industrial revenue bonds to finance the purchase.

While Val-Agri and Foley Meats appear to offer hope, in that old plants and jobs are saved through the entry of new firms into meatpacking, the overall trend continues. Each year IBP, Excel, and a handful of others control a larger share of the nation's beef business, and the tendency in pork appears parallel, albeit retarded. The trend unmistakably points toward a new meat trust dominated by a few firms. As Robert Aduddell and Louis Cain noted in a slightly different context, "How much farther history will go in repeating itself remains to be seen."[3]

[3]Robert Aduddell and Louis Cain, "The consent decree in the meatpacking industry, 1920–1956," *Business History Review*, LV (1981), p. 378.

Bibliography

Following is a selected bibliography, a list of the more useful sources on the red-meat trade of the United States from colonial times to the present, including those cited in the text as well as some notable works of fiction that cast light on American livestock raising and meatpacking. Additional references can be gleaned from the bibliographies in many of the volumes that follow. Modern library style is used in the entry format, and to facilitate the location of sometimes obscure public documents, SuDocs (Superintendent of Documents identification) or serial set numbers have been appended where appropriate.

Abbott, Edith, and S. P. Breckinridge. "Women in industry: the Chicago stockyards." *Journal of Political Economy* 19 (1911), 632–54.

Adams, Andy. *The log of a cowboy: a narrative of the old trail days.* Boston: Houghton Mifflin Company, 1903.

Adams, Ramon F. *Burs under the saddle: a second look at books and histories of the West.* Norman: University of Oklahoma Press, 1964.

———. *More burs under the saddle: books and histories of the West.* Norman: University of Oklahoma Press, 1979.

———. *The rampaging herd: a bibliography of books and pamphlets on men and events in the cattle industry.* Norman: University of Oklahoma Press, 1959.

Aduddell, Robert M., and Louis P. Cain. "The consent decree in the meatpacking industry, 1920–1956." *Business History Review* 55 (1981), 359–78.

———. "Location and collusion in the meat packing industry." in Louis P. Cain and Paul J. Uselding, eds., *Business enterprise and economic change.* Kent, Ohio: Kent State University Press, 1973.

————. "Public policy toward 'The greatest trust in the world'." *Business History Review* 55 (1981), 217–42.

Akerman, Joe A., Jr. *Florida cowman: a history of Florida cattle raising.* Kissimmee, Fla.: Florida Cattlemen's Association, 1976.

Algren, Nelson. *Never come morning.* New York: Harper, 1942.

Allen, Lewis Falley. *American cattle: their history, breeding and management.* New York: Tainor brothers & co., 1868.

————. *History of the short-horned cattle: their origin, progress, and present condition.* Buffalo, N.Y.: the author, 1883.

American Meat Institute. *Financial facts about the meat packing industry.* Chicago: American Meat Institute, 1925–1981.

————. *Financial review of the meatpacking industry.* Washington, D.C.: American Meat Institute, 1977.

————. *Meatfacts: a statistical summary about America's largest food industry.* Chicago: American Meat Institute, 1978.

————. *The packing industry.* Chicago: University of Chicago Press, 1924.

Anderson, Oscar E., Jr. *The health of a nation: Harvey W. Wiley and the fight for pure food.* Chicago: Published for the University of Cincinnati by the University of Chicago Press, 1958.

Andrew, John. "Anger in paradise: soaring rents spur a revolt of the rich; Newport Beach's leaseholders sue Irvine Co. to prevent increases of up to 4,150 percent." *Wall Street Journal,* February 24, 1982, pp. 1, 15.

Arant, Willard D. "Wartime meat policies." *Journal of Farm Economics* 28 (1946): 903–19.

Armour, J. Ogden. *The packers, the private car lines and the people.* Philadelphia: Henry Altemus Company, 1906.

Arnade, Charles. "Cattle raising in Spanish Florida, 1513–1763." *Agricultural History* 35 (1961): 116–24.

Arnould, Richard J. "Changing patterns of concentration in American meat packing, 1880–1963." *Business History Review* 45 (1971): 19–34.

Atherton, Lewis. *The cattle kings.* Bloomington: Indiana University Press, 1962.

Atkinson, J. H. "Cattle drives from Arkansas to California prior to the Civil War." *Arkansas Historical Quarterly* 28 (1969): 275–81.

Aveling, Edward, and Eleanor Marx Aveling. *The working class movement in America.* 2d ed. London: S. Sonnenschein & co., 1891.

Bailey, Thomas A. "Congressional opposition to pure food legislation, 1879–1906." *American Journal of Sociology* 36 (1930): 52–65.

Barger, Harold, and Hans H. Landsberg. *American agriculture, 1899–*

1939: a study of output, employment, and productivity. New York: National Bureau of Economic Research, 1942.

Barnes, Will C. *The story of the range: an account of the occupation of the public domain ranges by the pioneer stockmen, the effects on the forage and the land of unrestricted grazing, and the attempts that have been made to regulate grazing practices and perpetuate the great natural forage resources of the open range.* Washington, D.C.: Government Printing Office, 1926. A13.2:R16/6; Y4.P96/1:F76/6

Bennett, Merrill K. "Aspects of the pig." *Agricultural History* 44 (1970): 223–36.

Bergman, Arvid Mathias. *A review of the frozen and chilled trans-oceanic meat industry.* Stockholm: Almqvist & Wiksell, 1916.

Bidwell, Percy Wells, and John J. Falconer. *History of agriculture in the northern United States, 1620–1860.* Washington, D.C.: Carnegie Institution, 1925.

Bischoff, J. P. "Sheep and wheat: the history of flocks in Oklahoma," in *Ranch and range in Oklahoma,* edited by Jimmy M. Skaggs. Oklahoma City: Oklahoma Historical Society, 1978.

Bishop, C. E., ed. *Farm labor in the U.S.* New York: Columbia University Press, 1967.

Billington, Ray Allen, and Martin Ridge. *Westward expansion: a history of the American frontier.* 5th ed. New York: Macmillan Publishing Co., Inc., 1982.

Blundell, William E. "Life on the job: the days of the cowboy are marked by danger, drudgery, and low pay." *Wall Street Journal,* June 10, 1981, pp. 1, 16.

Bogue, Allan G. *From prairie to corn belt: farming on the Illinois and Iowa prairies in the nineteenth century.* Chicago: University of Chicago Press, 1963.

Bonnett, Clarence E. *History of employers associations of the United States.* New York: Vantage Press, 1965.

Branch, E. Douglas. *The cowboy and his interpreters.* New York: D. Appleton and Company, 1926.

Brand, Donald D. "The early history of the range cattle industry in northern Mexico." *Agricultural History* 35 (1961): 132–39.

Branda, Eldon Stephen, ed. *The Handbook of Texas: a supplement.* Austin: Texas State Historical Association, 1976.

Breen, David H. *The Canadian prairie west and the ranching frontier, 1874–1924.* Toronto: University of Toronto Press, 1983.

Brisbin, James S. *The beef bonanza; or, how to get rich on the plains, being a description of cattle growing, sheep-farming, horse-raising, and dairying in the West.* Reprint. Norman: University of Oklahoma Press, 1959.

Brody, David. *The butcher workmen: a study of unionization.* Cambridge, Mass.: Harvard University Press, 1964.

Brown, Leo C. *Union politics in the leather industry.* Cambridge, Mass.: Harvard University Press, 1947.

Broyles, William, Jr. "The last empire," *Texas Monthly* 8 (1980): 150–173ff.

Buck, Solon Justice, and Elizabeth Hawthorn Buck. *The planting of civilization in western Pennsylvania.* Pittsburgh: University of Pittsburgh Press, 1939.

Bunton, Mary Taylor. *A bride on the old Chisholm trail in 1886.* San Antonio: The Naylor Company, 1939.

Burcham, L. T. "Cattle range and forage in California: 1770–1880." *Agricultural History* 35 (1961): 140–49.

Burmeister, Charles A. "Six decades of rugged individualism: the American National Cattlemen's Association, 1895–1955." *Agricultural History* 30 (1956): 143–49.

Burnett, Edmund Cody. "Hog raising and hog driving in the region of the French Broad River." *Agricultural History* 20 (1946): 86–103.

Burns, Robert Homer, Andrew Springs Gillespie, and William Gay Richardson. *Wyoming's pioneer ranches.* Laramie: Top-Of-The-World Press, 1955.

Burrough, Byran. "Lawsuits offer peek at Texas family's feud over wealth of world's largest ranch." *Wall Street Journal,* June 18, 1982, p. 21.

Bushnell, Charles Joseph. *The social problem at the Chicago stockyards.* Chicago: Chicago University Press, 1902.

Butz, Dale E., and George L. Baker, Jr. *The changing structure of the meat economy.* Boston: Harvard University Graduate School of Business Administration, 1960.

Caldwell, Margaret Evans. "The Mudge Ranch." *Kansas Historical Quarterly* 24 (1958): 285–304.

Camp, William. "Reforms in the system of food distribution." *Journal of Political Economy* 29 (1921): 824–25.

Capie, Forrest, and Richard Perren. "The British market for meat, 1850–1914." *Agricultural History* 54 (1980): 502–15.

Carlson, Paul H. *Texas woollybacks: the range sheep and goat industry.* College Station: Texas A&M University Press, 1982.

Caruso, John A. *The Appalachian frontier: America's first surge westward.* Indianapolis: Bobbs-Merrill, 1959.

Casey, Clifford B. *Soldiers, ranchers and miners of the Big Bend.* Washington, D.C.: U.S. Department of the Interior, National Park Service, 1969. 129.2:B48/2.

Castle, Emery N. *Agriculture: economic development in south central Kansas.* Lawrence: University of Kansas School of Business, Bureau of Business Research, 1953.

Chambers, William T. "Edwards Plateau: a combination ranching region." *Economic Geography* 8 (1932): 67–80.

Cheever, Lawrence Oakley. *The house of Morrell.* Cedar Rapids, Iowa: The Torch Press, 1948.

Chevalier, François. *Land and society in colonial Mexico: the great hacienda.* Berkeley: University of California Press, 1963.

Christensen, Alice M. "Agricultural pressure and government response in the United States, 1919–1929." *Agricultural History* (1934): 169–95.

Clark, J. Stanley. "Texas fever in Oklahoma." *Chronicles of Oklahoma* 29 (1951–52): 429–43.

Clarke, Mary Whatley. *The Swenson saga and the SMS ranches.* Austin: Jenkins Publishing Company, 1976.

Clawson, Marion. *The western range livestock industry.* New York: McGraw-Hill Book Company, 1950.

Clay, John. *My life on the range.* Chicago: privately printed, 1924.

Cleaveland, Agnes Morley. *No life for a lady.* Boston: Houghton Mifflin Company, 1941.

Clemen, Rudolf Alexander. *The American livestock and meat industry.* New York: The Ronald Press Company, 1923.

———. *By-products in the packing industry.* Chicago: University of Chicago Press, 1927.

———. *George Hammond, 1838–1886: pioneer in refrigerator transportation.* New York: Newcomen Society in North America, 1946.

Coburn, Walt. *Pioneer cattlemen in Montana: the story of the Circle C Ranch.* Norman: University of Oklahoma Press, 1968.

Colver, William B. "The Federal Trade Commission and the meat packing industry." *Annals* of the American Academy of Political Science 82 (1919): 218–22.

Commons, John R. "Labor conditions in meat packing and the recent strike." *Quarterly Journal of Economics* 19 (1904): 1–32.

Commons, John R., et al. *History of labour in the United States.* 4 vols.; New York: the Macmillan Company, 1935–36.

Connor, Seymour V. "Early ranching operations in the panhandle: a report on the agricultural schedules of the 1880 census." *Panhandle-Plains Historical Review* 27 (1954): 47–69.

———. *Texas, a history.* New York: Thomas Y. Crowell, 1971.

Crawford, C. W. "Technical problems in food and drug law enforcement." *Law and Contemporary Problems* I (1933): 36–43.

Critchell, James Troubridge, and Joseph Raymond. *A history of the frozen meat trade: an account of the development and present day methods of preparation, transportation, and marketing of frozen and chilled meats.* London: Constable and Company, 1912.

Croxton, Fred. "Beef prices." *Journal of Political Economy* 13 (1905): 201–16.

Cuff, Robert D. "The dilemma of voluntarism: Hoover and the pork-packing agreement, 1917–1919." *Agricultural History* 53 (1979): 727–47.

Currie, Barton W. "A city that kills its own meat: Paris, Texas, sets the fashion in the feed-yourself campaign." *The Cattleman* 2 (1915): 19–23.

Dacy, George H. *Four centuries of Florida ranching.* St. Louis: Britt Publishing Co., 1940.

Danhoff, Clarence H. *Change in agriculture: the northern U.S., 1820–1870.* Cambridge, Mass.: Harvard University Press, 1969.

Dale, Edward Everett. *Cow country.* Norman: University of Oklahoma Press, 1942.

———. *The range cattle industry: ranching on the Great Plains from 1865 to 1925.* Norman: University of Oklahoma Press, 1930.

Dana, Richard Henry. *Two years before the mast.* New York: Harper, 1840.

Day, George E. *Productive swine husbandry.* Philadelphia: J. B. Lippincott company, 1913.

Day, Robert. *The last cattle drive.* New York: Avon Books, 1977.

DeGraff, Herrell. *Beef production and distribution.* Norman: University of Oklahoma Press, 1960.

"Denver beef business in quiet demise." Wichita *Eagle-Beacon,* February 26, 1984, pp. 7, 8C.

Dick, Everett. *The sod-house frontier, 1854–1890: a social history of the northern plains from the creation of Kansas & Nebraska to the admission of the Dakotas.* New York: D. Appleton-Century company, 1937.

Dickinson, A. T., Jr. *American historical fiction.* 2d ed. New York: The Scarecrow Press, Inc., 1963.

Dobie, J. Frank. *Cow people.* Boston: Little, Brown and Company, 1964.

———. "The first cattle in Texas and the Southwest: progenitors of the Longhorns." *Southwestern Historical Quarterly* 42 (1939): 171–97.

———. *Guide to the life and literature of the Southwest.* Rev. and enlarged ed. Dallas: Southern Methodist University Press, 1952.

———. *The Longhorns.* New York: Little, Brown and Company, 1941.

———. *Vaquero of the brush country.* Dallas: Southwest Press, 1929.

[Dodge commission]. *Report of the commission appointed by the president to investigate the conduct of the war department in the war with Spain.* 8 vols. Washington, D.C.: Government Printing Office, 1900. Sen. Ex. Doc. 221, 56th Cong., 1st Sess., 1901–02, ser. 3858-66.

Dolan, Carrie. "True grit: rancher Jane Glennie carries on tradition of women of the West." *Wall Street Journal,* November 18, 1982, pp. 1, 22.

Doran, Michael F. "Antebellum cattle herding in the Indian Territory." *Geographical Review* 66 (1976): 48–58.

Douglas, C. L. *Cattle kings of Texas*. Dallas: Cecil Baugh, 1939.

Downes, Randolph C. *Frontier Ohio, 1788–1803*. Columbus: The Ohio State University Press, 1935.

Drago, Harry Sinclair. *The great range wars: violence on the grasslands*. New York: Dodd, Mead & Company, 1970.

Drury, John. *Rare and well done: some historical notes on meat and meatmen*. Chicago: Quadrangle Books, 1966.

Dugas, Vera Lea. "Texas industry, 1860–1880," *Southwestern Historical Quarterly* LIX (1955) 159–69.

Duke, Cordia Sloan, and Joe B. Frantz. *6,000 miles of fence: life on the XIT Ranch of Texas*. Austin: University of Texas Press, 1961.

Dunbar, Gary S. "Colonial Carolina cowpens." *Agricultural History* 35 (1961): 125–30.

Dupree, A. Hunter. *Science in the federal government: a history of politics and activities to 1940*. Cambridge, Mass.: The Belknap Press of the Harvard University Press, 1957.

Durham, Philip C., and Everett L. Jones. *The Negro cowboy*. New York: Dodd, Mead & Company, 1965.

Dusenberry, William. "Foot and mouth disease in Mexico, 1946–1951." *Agricultural History* 29 (1955): 82–89.

Dykstra, Robert R. *The cattle towns*. New York: Atheneum, 1970.

Eddy, Arthur J. *Ganton and company*. Chicago: McClurg, 1908.

Edminster, Lynn Ramsay. *The cattle industry and the tariff*. New York: The Macmillan Company, 1926.

Eggleston, Edward. "Husbandry in colonial times." *Century* 27 (1884): 431–49.

Elazar, Daniel J., ed. "Working conditions in Chicago in the early 20th century: testimony before the Illinois senatorial vice committee, 1913." *American Jewish Archives* 21 (1969): 149–71.

Emmett, Chris. *Shanghai Pierce, a fair likeness*. Norman: University of Oklahoma Press, 1953.

Erwin, Allen A. *The Southwest of John B. Slaughter, 1841–1922: cattleman and trail-driver of Texas, the Pecos, and Arizona*. Glendale, Calif.: The Arthur H. Clark Company, 1965.

"Farmers are raising fewer hogs; supplies of pork to stay tight." *Wall Street Journal*, September 23, 1982, p. 46.

Faulk, Odie B. "Ranching in Spanish Texas." *Hispanic American Historical Review* 45 (1965): 257–66.

Fite, George B. "The great business combination of today: the so-called beef trust." *Century* 65 (1902): 148–58.

Fite, Gilbert C. *The farmers' frontier, 1865–1900*. New York: Holt, Rinehart and Winston, 1966.

FitzGerald, D. A. *Livestock under the AAA*. Washington, D.C.: The Brookings Institution, 1935.

Fletcher, Robert H. *Free grass to fences: the Montana cattle range story*. New York: University Publishers, Incorporated, for the Historical Society of Montana, 1960.

Fletcher, Robert S. "That hard winter, 1886–1887." *Agricultural History* 4 (1930): 123–30.

Fogel, Walter. "Blacks in meatpacking: another view of the jungle." *Industrial Relations* 10 (1971): 338–53.

———. "Union impact on the retail food wages in California." *Industrial Relations* 6 (1966): 79–94.

Foss, Phillip O. *Politics and grass: the administration of the public domain*. Seattle: University of Washington Press, 1960.

———, ed. *Public land policy: proceedings of the Western Resource Conference, Fort Collins, Colorado, 1968*. Boulder: Colorado Associated University Press, 1970.

Fowler, Bertram B. *Men, meat and miracles*. New York: Julian Messner, Inc., 1952.

Fowler, Stewart H. *Beef production in the South*. Danville, Ill.: The Interstate Printers & Publishers, Inc., 1969.

———. *The marketing of livestock and meat*. Danville, Ill.: The Interstate Printers and Publishers, Inc., 1957.

Frantz, Joe B., and Julian Ernest Choate, Jr. *The American cowboy: the myth & the reality*. Norman: University of Oklahoma Press, 1955.

Freedgood, Seymour. "The spectre at Lambshead Ranch." *Fortune* 61 (1960): 123–222.

Friedmann, Karen J. "Urban food marketing in Los Angeles, 1850–1885." *Agricultural History* 54 (1980): 433–45.

Frink, Maurice, W. Turrentine Jackson, and Agnes Wright Spring. *When grass was king: contributions to the western range cattle industry study*. Boulder: University of Colorado Press, 1956.

Frissell, Toni. *The King Ranch, 1939–1944: a photographic essay*. Dobbs Ferry, N.Y.: Morgan & Morgan, 1975.

Fritz, Henry E. "The cattlemen's frontier in the trans-Mississippi West: an annotated bibliography." *Arizona and the West* 14 (1972): 45–70, 169–90.

Frozen meat: its distribution costs, acceptance, and cooking and eating qualities. Kansas State University Experiment Station Research Publication 166. 1973.

"FTC closes probe of beef industry on price fixing." *Wall Street Journal*, July 22, 1982, p. 2.

Fulgate, Francis L. "Origins of the range cattle era in south Texas." *Agricultural History* 35 (1961): 155–58.

Fulgham, Ouida J. "Roosevelt feeds the hungry: the Federal Surplus Relief Corporation." *Red River Valley Historical Review* 7 (1982): 24–32.

Furguson, Ernest. "Iowa Beef Processors plays hard ball in Siouxland." Wichita *Eagle-Beacon*, August 10, 1982, p. 3C.

Galenson, David. "The profitability of the long drive." *Agricultural History* 51 (1977): 737–58.

Gard, Wayne. *The Chisholm trail.* Norman: University of Oklahoma Press, 1954.

Garino, David P. "Ralph Shiver's pigs often die trying to avoid the cold." *Wall Street Journal,* February 16, 1982, pp. 1, 10.

Gates, Paul W. "Cattle kings in the prairies." *Mississippi Valley Historical Review* 35 (1948): 379–412.

———. *The farmer's age: agriculture, 1815–1860.* New York: Harper & Row, Publishers, 1960.

———. "Hoosier cattle kings." *Indiana Magazine of History* 44 (1948): 1–24.

———. "The promotion of agriculture by the Illinois Central Railroad, 1855–70." *Agricultural History* 5 (1931): 57–76.

Gentry, E. R. *Progressive hog raising.* Chicago: Armour & Co., 1920.

Gignilliant, John L. "Pigs, politics and protectionism: the European boycott of American pork, 1879–1891." *Agricultural History* 35 (1961): 3–12.

Gipson, Fred. *Cowhand: the story of a working cowboy.* New York: Harper & Brothers, 1953.

Goodspeed, Thomas W. *Gustavus Franklin Swift.* Chicago: University of Chicago, 1922.

Goodwyn, Frank. *Life on the King Ranch.* New York: Crowell, 1951.

Graber, Richard. *Agricultural animals and the environment.* Stillwater: Oklahoma State University Feedlot Waste Management Regional Extension Project, n.d.

Gracy, David B., II. *Littlefield lands: colonization on the Texas plains, 1912–1920.* Austin: University of Texas Press, 1968.

———. "A preliminary survey of land colonization in the panhandle-plains of Texas." *The Museum Journal* 11 (1969): 50–69.

Graebner, Norman A. "History of cattle ranching in eastern Oklahoma." *Chronicles of Oklahoma* 21 (1943): 300–11.

Grand, W. Joseph. *Illustrated history of the Union Stockyards: sketch book of familiar faces and places at the yards.* Chicago: Thomas Knapp Printing & Binding Co., 1896.

Gray, James R. *Ranch economics.* Ames: Iowa State University Press, 1968.

Gray, Lewis Cecil. *History of agriculture in the southern United States to 1860*. 2 vols. Washington, D.C.: Carnegie Institution, 1933.

Green, Donald E. *Fifty years of service to west Texas agriculture: a history of Texas Tech University's College of Agricultural Sciences, 1925–1975*. Lubbock: Texas Tech University Press, 1977.

———. *Land of the underground rain: irrigation on the Texas high plains, 1910–1970*. Austin: University of Texas Press, 1973.

———. *Panhandle pioneer: Henry C. Hitch, his ranch, and his family*. Norman: University of Oklahoma Press, 1979.

Greer, Howard C. *Accounting for a meat packing business*. Chicago: University of Chicago Press, 1943.

Gressley, Gene M. *Bankers and cattlemen*. New York: Alfred A. Knopf, 1966.

Groseclose, Everett. "Following cattle herd to market helps show why meat's so costly." *Wall Street Journal*, May 24, 1973, pp. 1, 29.

Guice, John D. W. "Cattle raisers in the old Southwest: a reinterpretation." *Western Historical Quarterly* 8 (1977): 167–87.

Guyon, Janet. "Meatpackers change jobs in face of declining pay for tedious work." *Wall Street Journal*, June 7, 1983, pp. 31, 39.

Halbert, Frederic, and Sandra Halbert. *Bitter harvest*. Grand Rapids, Mich.: William B. Eerdmans Publishing Company, 1978.

Haley, J. Evetts. *Charles Goodnight, cowman and plainsman*. Norman: University of Oklahoma Press, 1936.

———. "Driving a trail herd." *Southwest Review* 43 (1933): 384–403.

———. *George W. Littlefield, Texan*. Norman: University of Oklahoma Press, 1953.

———. "Texas fever and the Winchester quarantine." *Panhandle-Plains Historical Review* 8 (1935): 37–53.

———. *The XIT Ranch of Texas, and the early days of the Llano Estacado*. Chicago: The Lakeside Press, 1929.

Hamilton, Walton, and Irene Hill. *Antitrust in action*. Temporary National Economic Committee Monograph 16. Washington, D.C., 1940. Y4.T24:M75/16.

Hammons, Terry. *Ranching from the front seat of a Buick; the life of A. A. "Jack" Drummond*. Oklahoma City: Oklahoma Historical Society, 1982.

Hampe, Edward C., and Merle Wittenberg. *The lifeline of America: development of the food industry*. New York: McGraw-Hill Book Company, Inc., 1964.

Hanes, Bailey C. *Bill Pickett, bulldogger: the biography of a black cowboy*. Norman: University of Oklahoma Press, 1977.

Hanson, Simon G. *Argentine meat and the British market: chapters in the history of the Argentine meat industry*. Stanford: Stanford University Press, 1938.

Havins, T. R. "Texas fever." *Southwestern Historical Quarterly* 52 (1948): 147–62.

Hayes, Lauffer P., and Frank J. Raff. "The administration of the federal Food and Drug Act." *Law and Contemporary Problems* 1 (1933): 16–35.

Hayter, Earl W. "Livestock-fencing conflicts in rural America." *Agricultural History* 37 (1963): 10–20.

Henlein, Paul C. "Cattle driving from the Ohio country, 1800–1860." *Agricultural History* 28 (1954): 83–95.

———. *Cattle kingdom in the Ohio Valley, 1783–1860.* Lexington: University of Kentucky Press, 1959.

———. "Early cattle ranches of the Ohio Valley." *Agricultural History* 35 (1961): 150–54.

———. "Shifting range-feeder patterns in the Ohio Valley before 1860." *Agricultural History* 31 (1957): 1–12.

Herrick, Arthur D. *Food regulation and compliance.* 2 vols. New York: Revere Publishing Company, 1948.

Hibbard, Benjamin Horace. *A history of the public land policies.* Madison: University of Wisconsin Press, 1965.

Hicks, John D. *The populist revolt: a history of the Farmers' Alliance and the People's party.* Minneapolis: University of Minnesota Press, 1931.

Hildreth, Clifford, and F. G. Jarrett. *A statistical study of livestock production and marketing.* New York: John Wiley & Sons, Inc., 1955.

Hill, H. C. "The development of Chicago as a center for the packing industry." *Mississippi Valley Historical Review* 10 (1923): 253–73.

Hill, Lowell D., ed. *Role of government in a market economy.* Ames: Iowa State University Press, 1982.

Hill, William. "Conditions in the cattle industry." *Journal of Political Economy* 13 (1904): 1–12.

———. "Relations of packer's credit to panic and prices." *Journal of Political Economy* 16 (1908): 87–102.

Hilliard, Sam B. *Hog meat and hoecake: food supply in the old South, 1840–1860.* Carbondale: Southern Illinois University Press, 1972.

Hillman, Jimmye S., and Andrew Schmitz, eds. *International trade and agriculture: theory and policy.* Boulder, Colo.: Westview Press, 1979.

Hinman, Robert Byron, and Robert B. Harris. *The story of meat.* Chicago: Swift and Co., 1939.

Hirschauler, Herman. *The dark side of the beef trust: a treatise concerning the "canner" cow, the cold storage fowl, the diseased meats, the dopes and preservatives.* Jamestown, N.Y.: Theodore Z. Root, 1905.

Hirshman, Bill. "Dold strike ends after 34 weeks." *Wichita Eagle-Beacon,* November 13, 1982, p. 4D.

Hoffman, A. C. *Concentration in the food industries*. Temporary National Economic Committee Monograph 35. Washington, D.C., 1940. Y4.T24:M75/35.

Holden, William Currey. *The Espuela Land and Cattle Company: a study of a foreign-owned ranch in Texas*. Austin: Texas State Historical Association, 1970.

————. *A ranching saga: the lives of William Electious Halsell and Ewing Halsell*. 2 vols. San Antonio: Trinity University Press, 1976.

————. *The Spur Ranch: a study of the inclosed ranch phase of the cattle industry in Texas*. Boston: The Christopher Publishing House, 1934.

Hoy, James F. *The cattle guard: its history and lore*. Lawrence: University Press of Kansas, 1982.

Hughes, Kathleen. *Return to The Jungle: how the Reagan administration is imperiling the nation's meat and poultry inspection programs*. Washington, D.C.: Center for the Study of Responsive Law, 1983.

Hutchinson, William H. "The cowboy and the class struggle (or, never put Marx in the saddle)." *Arizona and the West* 14 (1972): 321–30.

————. "The cowboy and Karl Marx." *Pacific Historian* 20 (1976): 111–22.

Ives, J. Russell. *The livestock and meat economy of the United States*. Washington, D.C.: American Meat Institute, 1966.

Jackson, Jack. *Los mesteños: Spanish ranching in Texas, 1721–1821*. College Station: Texas A&M University Press, 1986.

Jackson, W. Turrentine. "British interests in the range cattle industry." In *When grass was king: contributions to the western range cattle industry study*, edited by Maurice Frink, W. Turrentine Jackson, and Agnes Wright Spring. Boulder: University of Colorado Press, 1968.

————. *The enterprising Scot: investors in the American West after 1873*. Edinburgh: Edinburgh University Press, 1968.

Jager, Ronald B. "The Chisholm trail's mountain of words." *Southwestern Historical Quarterly* 71 (1967): 61–68.

James, Clifford L., Edward C. Welsh, and Gordon Arneson. *Industrial concentration and tariffs*. Temporary National Economic Committee Monograph 10. Washington, D.C., 1941. Y4.T24:M75/10.

Jones, Billy M. *The search for maturity: the saga of Texas, 1875–1900*. Vol. 5 in The Saga of Texas series, edited by Seymour V. Connor. Austin: Steck-Vaughn Company, 1965.

Jones, Eliot. *The trust problem in the United States*. New York: The Macmillan Company, 1921.

Jones, Ralph F. *Longhorns north of the Arkansas*. San Antonio: The Naylor Company, 1969.

Jones, Robert Leslie. "The beef cattle industry in Ohio prior to the Civil War." *Ohio Archaeological and Historical Quarterly* 64 (1955): 168–94, 287–319.

Jordan, Terry G. "The origin and distribution of open-range cattle ranching." *Social Science Quarterly* 53 (1972): 105–21.

———. "Texan influence in nineteenth-century Arizona cattle ranching." *Journal of the West* 14 (1975):" 15–17.

———. *Trails to Texas: southern roots of western cattle ranching.* Lincoln: University of Nebraska Press, 1981.

Kane, R. James. "Populism, progressivism, and pure food." *Agricultural History* 38 (1964): 161–66.

Kelly, Darwin N. "The McNary-Haugen Bills, 1924–1928: an attempt to make the tariff effective for farm products." *Agricultural History* 14 (1940): 170–80.

Kenner, Charles. "Origins of the 'Goodnight' trail reconsidered." *Southwestern Historical Quarterly* 77 (1974): 390–394.

Knight, Ewart B., Virginia W. Plummer, and Louis Johnson, Jr. *The management and marketing practices of the small independent meat packers of Tennessee.* N.p.: Tennessee Polytechnic Institute, 1962.

Kramer, Jane. *The last cowboy.* New York: Harper & Row, Publishers, 1977.

Kujovich, Mary Yeager. "The refrigerator car and the growth of the American dressed beef industry." *Business History Review* 44 (1970): 460–82.

Kupper, Winifred. *The golden hoof: the story of the sheep of the Southwest.* New York: Alfred A. Knopf, 1945.

"Labor's pain: unionists are alarmed by high court ruling in a bankruptcy filing; decision that filing firms can avoid contracts stirs emotions—and rumors." *Wall Street Journal*, February 24, 1984, pp. 1, 10.

Laidler, Harry W. *Concentration of control in American industry.* New York: Thomas Y. Crowell Company, 1931.

Lambert, C. Roger. "The drought cattle purchase, 1934–1935: problems and complaints." *Agricultural History* 45 (1971): 85–94.

———. "Hoover and Congress debate food relief: 1930–1931." *Red River Valley Historical Review* 7 (1982): 4–13.

———. "'Slaughter of innocents' in Oklahoma: the emergency hog slaughter of 1933." *Red River Valley Historical Review* 7 (1982): 42–49.

Larmer, Forrest M. *Financing the livestock industry.* New York: The Macmillan Company, 1926.

Larsen, Lawrence H. *The urban West and the end of the frontier.* Lawrence: Regents Press of Kansas, 1978.

Larson, Eric. "Old West: at vast Nevada ranch, roped calves still bawl and still get branded." *Wall Street Journal*, January 22, 1982, pp. 1, 12.

Lea, Tom. *The King Ranch.* 2 vols. Boston: Little, Brown and Company, 1957.

Leavitt, Charles T. "Attempts to improve cattle breeds in the United States, 1790–1860." *Agricultural History* 7 (1933): 51–67.

———. "Some economic aspects of the western meat packing industry,

1830–1860." *Journal of Business of the University of Chicago* 4 (1931): 68–90.

———. "Transportation and the livestock industry in the Middle West to 1860." *Agricultural History* 8 (1934): 20–33.

Lee, Lawrence B. "American public land history: a review essay." *Agricultural History* 55 (1981): 284–99.

Leech, Harper, and John Charles Carroll. *Armour and his times.* New York: Appleton-Century-Crofts, 1938.

Leftwich, Bill. *"The cow-killers": with the Aftosa Commission in Mexico.* Austin: University of Texas Press, 1956.

Lehmann, V. W. *Forgotten legions: sheep in the Rio Grande plain of Texas.* El Paso: Texas Western Press, 1969.

Lenimer, George F. "The spread of improved cattle throughout the eastern United States to 1850." *Agricultural History* 21 (1947): 79–93.

Letwin, William. *Law and economic policy in America: the evolution of the Sherman antitrust act.* New York: Random House, 1965.

Leuchtenburg, William E. *Franklin D. Roosevelt and the New Deal, 1932–1940.* New York: Harper & Row, 1963.

Lewis, George M. *An analysis of shipments of Texas sheep and goats.* University of Texas Business Research Monograph 7. Austin, 1912.

———. *A market analysis of the cattle industry of Texas.* University of Texas Bulletin 2836. Austin, 1928.

Lincoln, Freeman. "Billy Prince's somewhat silver spoon." *Fortune* 53 (1956): 126–94.

Lippincott, Isaac. *A history of manufacturing in the Ohio Valley to the year 1860.* Chicago: University of Illinois Press, 1914.

Lippman, Thomas W. "Iowa Beef makes its move on anxious pork industry." Washington *Post,* April 18, 1982, pp. F1, 3.

Logan, Samuel H., and Gordon A. King. *Economies of scale in the slaughter plants.* University of California Research Report 260. Berkeley, 1962.

Love, Clara M. "History of the cattle industry in the Southwest." *Southwestern Historical Quarterly* 19 (1916): 370–99; 20 (1916): 1–18.

Love, Nat. *The life and adventures of Nat Love.* New ed. New York: Arno Press, 1968.

Lublin, Joann S. "Embattled unionist: effort to save pay scales in meatpacking brings Lewie Anderson many spats, not all with firms." *Wall Street Journal,* August 4, 1983, p. 42.

Lurie, Jonathan. *The Chicago Board of Trade, 1859–1905: the dynamics self-regulation.* Urbana: University of Illinois Press, 1979.

MacAvoy, Paul W. *The economic effects of regulation: the trunk line railroad cartels and the Interstate Commerce Commission before 1900.* Cambridge, Mass.: MIT Press, 1965.

McCalla, Alex F. "Protectionism in international agricultural trade, 1850–1968." *Agricultural History* 43 (1969): 329–44.

McCallum, Henry D., and Frances T. McCallum. *The wire that fenced the West.* Norman: University of Oklahoma Press, 1965.

McCormick, S. D. *An address delivered before the annual convention of the Butchers' National Protective Association, May 28, 1890, being a review of the cattle industry and showing the spoilation of the cattle pool.* N.p.: Butchers' National Protective Association, 1890.

McCoy, Joseph G. *Historic sketches of the cattle trade of the West and Southwest.* Kansas City, Mo.: Ramsey, Millett & Hudson, Printers, 1874.

McCuistion, Ed. H. *The municipal abattoir.* Texas Department of Agriculture Bulletin 51. Austin, 1916.

McDonald, Forrest, and Grady McWhiney. "The antebellum southern herdsman: a reinterpretation." *Journal of Southern History* 41 (1975): 147–66.

Macdonald, James. *Food from the far West, or American agriculture with special reference to beef production and importation of dead meat from American to Great Britain.* London: W. P. Nimmo, 1878.

McFall, Robert James. *The world's meat.* New York: Appleton-Century-Crofts, 1927.

McGovern, George, ed. *Agricultural thought in the twentieth century.* New York: The Bobbs-Merrill Company, Inc., 1967.

McGregor, Alex C. "From sheep range to agribusiness: a case history of agricultural transformation on the Columbia Plateau." *Agricultural History* 54 (1980): 11–27.

Machado, Manuel A., Jr. *Aftosa: a historical survey of foot-and-mouth disease and inter-American relationships.* Albany: State University of New York Press, 1969.

———. *The north Mexican cattle industry, 1910–1975: ideology, conflict, and change.* College Station: Texas A&M University Press, 1981.

McNall, Neil Adams. *An agricultural history of the Genesee Valley, 1790–1860.* Philadelphia: University of Pennsylvania Press, 1952.

Marcosson, Isaac F. *Adventures in interviewing.* New York: John Lane company, 1919.

Marriott, Alice. *Hell on horses and women.* Norman: University of Oklahoma Press, 1953.

Matthews, Sallie Reynolds. *Interwoven: a pioneer chronicle.* Houston: The Anson Jones Press, 1936.

Meadows, Dennis L. *Dynamics of commodity production cycles.* Cambridge, Mass.: Wright-Allen Press, Inc., 1970.

Mealor, W. Theodore, Jr., and Merle C. Prunty. "Open-range ranching in southern Florida." *Annals,* Association of American Geographers 46 (1976): 360–76.

Meyers, Albert L. *Agriculture and the national economy.* Temporary National Economic Committee Monograph 23. Washington, 1940. Y4.T24:M75/23.

Michener, James A. *Centennial.* New York: Fawcett Crest, 1976.

Mighell, Ronald L. *American agriculture: its structure and place in the economy.* New York: John Wiley & Sons, Inc., 1955.

Miller, Thomas Lloyd. *The public lands of Texas, 1519–1970.* Norman: University of Oklahoma Press, 1971.

Miner, H. Craig. *The corporation and the Indian: tribal sovereignty and industrial civilization in Indian Territory, 1865–1907.* Columbia: University of Missouri Press, 1976.

————. *Wichita: the early years, 1865–80.* Lincoln: University of Nebraska Press, 1982.

Minsky, Terri. "Gripes of Rath: workers who bought Iowa slaughterhouse regret that they did." *Wall Street Journal*, December 2, 1981, pp. 1, 10.

————. "Hog prices currently outstripping cattle, an aberration that worries pig farmers." *Wall Street Journal*, September 1, 1982, pp. 1, 12.

Morris, Betsy. "Esmark may be poised for change after a decade of major maneuvers." *Wall Street Journal*, March 1, 1984, pp. 27, 40.

Morris, Betsy, and Roy J. Harris. "ConAgra to buy Greyhound unit: Armour Food provides entry into refrigerated foods with strong brand name." *Wall Street Journal*, June 30, 1983, p. 7.

Morrisey, Richard J. "The early range cattle industry in Arizona." *Agricultural History* 24 (1950): 151–56.

————. "The northward expansion of cattle ranching in New Spain, 1550–1600." *Agricultural History* 25 (1951): 115–21.

Mosk, Sanford A. "Land policy and stock raising in the western United States." *Agricultural History* 17 (1943): 14–30.

Mothershead, Harmon Ross. *The Swan Land and Cattle Company, Ltd.* Norman: University of Oklahoma Press, 1971.

Mullendore, William Clinton. *History of the United States Food Administration, 1917–1919.* Stanford, Calif.: Stanford University Press, 1941.

Murrah, David J. *C. C. Slaughter: rancher, banker, Baptist.* Austin: University of Texas Press, 1981.

Myres, Sandra L. "The ranching frontier: Spanish institutional backgrounds of the plains cattle industry." In *Essays on the American West*, edited by Harold M. Hollingsworth and Sandra L. Myres. Austin: University of Texas Press, 1969.

————. *The Spanish ranch in Texas, 1691–1800.* El Paso: Texas Western Press, 1969.

Nall, Gary L. "The cattle-feeding industry on the Texas high plains." In *Southwestern agriculture: pre-Columbian to modern*, edited by Henry C.

Dethloff and Irvin M. May. College Station: Texas A&M University Press, 1982.

"The new cattle business." *Fortune* 61 (1980): 222, 227–28.

Neyhart, Louise A. *Giant of the yards.* Boston: Houghton Mifflin Company, 1952.

Nicholls, William H. "Market sharing in the meat packing industry." *Journal of Farm Economics* 22 (1940): 225–31.

Nimmo, Joseph, Jr. *Report of the chief of the Bureau of Statistics in regard to range and ranch cattle traffic of the United States.* Department of the Treasury Document 690. Washington, D.C., 1885. T37.2:C29.

Nolen, Russell M. "The labor movement in St. Louis from 1860 to 1890." *Missouri Historical Review* 34 (1940): 157–81.

Nordyke, Lewis. *Cattle empire: the fabulous story of the 3,000,000 acre XIT.* New York: William Morrow and Company, 1949.

Nourse, Edwin G., and Joseph G. Knapp. *The co-operative marketing of livestock.* Washington, D.C.: The Brookings Institution, 1931.

O'Brien, F. S. "The 'communist dominated' unions in the United States since 1950." *Labor History* 9 (1968): 184–209.

Oliphant, J. Orin. *On the cattle ranges of the Oregon country.* Seattle: University of Washington Press, 1968.

Oppenheimer, Harold L. *Cowboy arithmetic: cattle as an investment.* 2d ed. Danville, Ill.: The Interstate Printers & Publishers, Inc., 1964.

Orear, Leslie F., and Stephen H. Diamond. *Out of the jungle.* Chicago: Hyde Park Press, 1968.

Ornduff, Donald R. *The Hereford in America: a compilation of historic facts about the breed's background and bloodline.* Kansas City, Mo.: the author, 1957.

Osgood, Ernest Staples. *The day of the cattleman.* Minneapolis: University of Minnesota Press, 1929.

O'Shaughnessy, Lynn. "Death comes in assembly line style." *Kansas City Times,* May 11, 1982, pp. A-1, 7.

———. "Meatpacking industry would like to chain up the watchdog." *Kansas City Times,* May 10, 1982, pp. A-1, 8.

Owsley, Frank Lawrence. *Plain folk of the old South.* Baton Rouge: Louisiana State University Press, 1949.

Paarlberg, Don. *Farm and food policy: issues of the 1980s.* Lincoln: University of Nebraska Press, 1980.

Palickar, Stephen J. "The Slovaks of Chicago." *Mid-America* IV (1921), 180–96.

Paul, Allen B. *Growth of the food processing industries in Illinois from 1849 to 1947.* Chicago: University of Illinois, 1953.

Paul, Virginia. *This was cattle ranching: yesterday and today.* New York: Bonanza Books, 1973.

Peake, Ora Brooks. *The Colorado range cattle industry.* Glendale, Calif.: The Arthur H. Clark Company, 1937.

Pearce, W. M. *The Matador Land and Cattle Company.* Norman: University of Oklahoma Press, 1964.

Peffer, E. Louise. *The closing of the public domain: disposal and reservation policies, 1900–1950.* Stanford, Calif.: Stanford University Press, 1951.

Pelzer, Louis. *The cattleman's frontier: a record of the trans-Mississippi cattle industry from oxen trains to pooling companies, 1850–1890.* Glendale, Calif.: The Arthur H. Clark Company, 1936.

Perren, Richard. "The North American beef and cattle trade of Great Britain, 1870–1914." *Economic History Review* 20 (1971): 430–444.

Phelps, Dudley Maynard. *Migration of industry to South America.* New York: McGraw-Hill Book Company, 1939.

Pidgeon, Mary Elizabeth. *The employment and growth of women in slaughtering and meat packing.* Washington, D.C.: U.S. Government Printing Office, 1932. HD6093.A3.

Pierce, Bessie Louise. *A history of Chicago.* 3 vols. New York: Alfred A. Knopf, 1937, 1957.

Pope, L. S. "Animal science in the twentieth century." *Agricultural History* 54 (1980): 64–70.

Porter, K. W. "The cowkeeper dynasty of the Seminole Nation." *Florida Historical Quarterly* 30 (1952): 341–49.

———. "Negro labor in the western cattle industry, 1866–1900." *Labor History,* 10 (1969): 346–74.

Post, Lauren C. "The old cattle industry of southwestern Louisiana." *McNeese Review* 9 (1957): 43–55.

———. "The upgrading of beef cattle on the Great Plains." *California Geographer* 2 (1961): 23–30.

Powell, Fred W. *The Bureau of Animal Industry: its history, activities and organization.* Baltimore: The Johns Hopkins University Press, 1927.

Purcell, Theodore V. *Blue collar men: a pattern of dual allegiance in industry.* Cambridge, Mass.: Harvard University Press, 1960.

———. *The worker speaks his mind on company and union.* Cambridge, Mass.: Harvard University Press, 1953.

"The Pure Food Law." *Outlook* 89 (1908): 778–79.

Putnam, George E. "Joint cost in the packing industry." *Journal of Political Economy* 29 (1921), 293–303.

Ramsdell, Charles. "Espíritu Santo: an early Texas cattle ranch." *Texas Geographical Magazine* 13 (1949): 21–25.

Ranch Management Conference: proceedings. Lubbock: Texas Tech University, International Center for Arid and Semiarid Land Studies, 1967.

Randolph, Edmund. *Beef, leather and grass.* Norman: University of Oklahoma Press, 1981.

———. *Hell among the yearlings*. New York: W. W. Norton, 1955.

Rathjen, Frederick W. *The Texas panhandle frontier*. Austin: University of Texas Press, 1973.

Regier, C. C. "The struggle for food and drug legislation." *Law and Contemporary Problems* 1 (1933): 3–15.

Remington, Frederic. "Cracker cowboys of Florida." *Harper's New Monthly Magazine*, 91 (1895): 339–45.

Rhoades, E. L. *Merchandising packinghouse products*. Chicago: University of Chicago Press, 1929.

Richardson, Rupert N. *The frontier of northwest Texas, 1846–1876: advance and defense by pioneer settlers of the cross timbers and prairies*. Glendale, Calif.: The Arthur H. Clark Co., 1963.

Richthofen. Walter, Baron von. *Cattle-raising on the plains of North America*. New York: D. Appleton and Company, 1885.

Rippy, J. Fred. "British investments in Texas lands and livestock." *Southwestern Historical Quarterly* 58 (1955): 331–41.

Rollins, Philip Ashton. *The cowboy: an unconventional history of civilization on the old-time cattle range*. Rev. ed. New York: Charles Scribner's Sons, 1926.

Roosevelt, Theodore. *Ranch life and the hunting trail*. Philadelphia: Gebbie and Company, 1903.

Rosenberg, Charles E. "The Adams Act: politics and the course of scientific research." *Agricultural History* 38 (1964): 3–12.

Ross, Earle D. "The land-grant college: a democratic adaptation." *Agricultural History* 15 (1941): 26–36.

Rouse, John E. *The Crillo: Spanish cattle in the Americas*. Norman: University of Oklahoma Press, 1977.

Rowley, William D. *U.S. Forest Service grazing and rangeland: a history*. College Station: Texas A&M University Press, 1985.

Rusling, J. F. *The railroads, the stock-yards, the eveners: exposé of the great railroad ring that robs the laborer of the East and the producer of the West of $5,000,000 a year*. Washington, D.C.: Polkinhorn Printers, 1878.

Russell, Charles Edward. *The greatest trust in the world*. New York: The Ridgway-Thayer Company, Publishers, 1905.

Rust, Charles H., and Clive R. Harston. *The survival and growth potential of small meatpacking businesses in Montana*. Helena: Montana State Planning Board, 1963.

Soloutos, Theodore, and John D. Hicks. *Twentieth century populism: agricultural discontent in the Middle West, 1900–1939*. Lincoln: University of Nebraska Press, 1951.

Sandoz, Mari. *The cattlemen: from the Rio Grande across the far Marias*. New York: Hastings House, Publishers, 1958.

Savage, James W., John T. Bell, and Consul W. Butterfield. *History of*

Omaha, Nebraska, and of South Omaha. New York: Munsell & Company, 1894.

Savage, William W., Jr. *The Cherokee Strip Livestock Association.* Columbia: University of Missouri Press, 1973.

————. *The cowboy hero: his image in history & culture.* Norman: University of Oklahoma Press, 1979.

————, ed. *Cowboy life: reconstructing an American myth.* Norman: University of Oklahoma Press, 1975.

————. "Indian ranchers." In *Ranch and range in Oklahoma,* edited by Jimmy M. Skaggs. Oklahoma City: Oklahoma Historical Society, 1978.

Schlebecker, John T. *Cattle raising on the plains, 1900–1961.* Lincoln: University of Nebraska Press, 1963.

Schmidt, Louis Bernard. "Agricultural revolution in the prairie and Great Plains of the United States." *Agricultural History* 8 (1934): 169–95.

Schneidau, Robert E., and Lawrence A. Duewer, eds. *Symposium: vertical coordination in the pork industry.* Westport, Conn.: The AVI Publishing Company, 1972.

Shannon, Fred A. *The centennial years: a political and economic history of America from the late 1870s to the early 1890s.* Garden City, N.Y.: Doubleday & Company, Inc., 1967.

————. *The farmer's last frontier: agriculture, 1860–1897.* New York: Harper & Row, Publishers, 1945.

Shellenbarger, Sue. "ConAgra grows rapidly despite missteps by shrewdly acquiring and reviving firms." *Wall Street Journal,* December 12, 1982, p. 29.

————. "Iowa Beef's effort to slash labor costs at strike site may speed industry trend." *Wall Street Journal,* August 6, 1982, p. 22.

Shultz, George P., and Arnold R. Weber. *Strategies for the displaced worker confronting economic change.* New York: Harper & Row, Publishers, 1966.

Siekaniec, L. J. "The Polish colony of Sioux City." *Polish American Studies* 9 (1952): 24–27.

Simons, A[lgie] M[artin]. *Packingtown.* Chicago: Kerr & Co., 1899.

Simpson, James R., and Donald E. Farris. *The world's beef business.* Ames: Iowa State University Press, 1982.

Sims, Grover J. *Meat and meat animals in World War II.* USDA Monograph 9. Washington, D.C., 1951. A1.78:9.

Sinclair, Upton. *The autobiography of Upton Sinclair.* New York: Harcourt, Brace & World, Inc., 1962.

————. *The jungle.* New York: Doubleday, Page & Company, 1906.

Skaggs, Jimmy M. *The cattle-trailing industry: between supply and demand, 1866–1890.* Lawrence: University Press of Kansas, 1973.

————, ed. *Ranch and range in Oklahoma*. Oklahoma City: Oklahoma Historical Society, 1978.

Smith, Peter H. *Politics and beef in Argentina: patterns of conflict and change*. New York: Columbia University Press, 1969.

Smith, Wilson. "Cow college mythology and social history: a view of some centennial literature." *Agriculture History* 44 (1970): 299–310.

Sonnichsen, C. L. *Cowboys and cattle kings: life on the range today*. Norman: University of Oklahoma Press, 1950.

Sorenson, Laurel. "Chapter 11 filing by Wilson Foods roils workers' lives, tests law." *Wall Street Journal*, May 23, 1983, pp. 25, 27.

Steen, Harold K. "Grazing and environment: a history of Forest Service stock reduction policy." *Agriculture History* 49 (1975): 238–42.

Stegner, Wallace. *Beyond the hundredth meridian: John Wesley Powell and the second opening of the West*. Boston: Houghton Mifflin, 1954.

Steimel, Dirck. "Management is all to Flint Hills cow-calf producer." Wichita *Eagle-Beacon*, August 29, 1982, p. 1G.

————. "The payoff: break with grazing tradition is reaping rewards for father-son partnership in Kansas Flint Hills." Wichita *Eagle-Beacon*, September 12, 1982, 1G.

————. "Wilson and union join to fight IBP." Wichita *Eagle-Beacon*, January 29, 1984, p. 1, 7C.

Steimel, Dirck, and Angela Herrin. "Wichita's meatpacking era draws to a close: Excel Corp. last of big packers to go." Wichita *Eagle-Beacon*, May 15, 1983, pp. 1, 8–9A.

Steinbeck, John. *Of mice and men*. New York: Modern Library, 1937.

Stephens, A. Ray. *The Taft Ranch: a Texas principality*. Austin: University of Texas Press, 1964.

Stipp, David. "Bunker Hunt, down on his luck, says it's time to close business." *Wall Street Journal*, December 3, 1982, 25.

Stover, Stephen L. "Early sheep husbandry in Ohio." *Agricultural History* 36 (1962): 101–107.

————. "Ohio's sheep year, 1868." *Agricultural History* 38 (1964): 102–107.

Structure, performance and prospects of the beef chain. Paris: Organization for Economic Development, 1978.

Stuart, Alexander. "Meatpackers in stampede: fearsome Iowa Beef's access to oxydollars lends new urgency to its competitors' scramble for survival strategies." *Fortune* 103 (1981): 67–71.

Summons, Terry G. "Animal feed additives, 1940–1966." *Agricultural History* 42 (1968): 305–14.

Surface, Bill. *Roundup at the Double Diamond: the American cowboy today*. Boston: Houghton Mifflin Company, 1974.

Swanson, Wayne, and George Schultz. *Prime rip*. Englewood Cliffs, N.J.: Prentice-Hall, Inc., 1982.

Swem, Edward R. *"The significant sixty": a historical report of the progress and development of the meat packing industry, 1891–1951*. Chicago: The National Provisioner, 1952.

Swift, Helen. *My father and my mother*. Chicago: n.p., 1937.

Swift, Louis F., and Arthur Van Vlissingen, Jr. *The Yankee of the yards: the biography of Gustavus Franklin Swift*. Chicago: A. W. Shaw Company, 1927.

Swift & Co. v. U.S. 286 U.S. 106 (1932).

Talbot, Ross B. *The chicken war: an international trade conflict between the United States and the European Economic Community, 1961–64*. Ames: Iowa State University Press, 1978.

Taylor, Ross McLaury. *Brazos: an historical novel of the Southwest*. New York: Bobbs-Merrill, Inc., 1938.

Tharp, Mike. "Monte Noelke loves the sheep business, worries about future." *Wall Street Journal*, January 21, 1974, pp. 1, 22.

Thomas, James H. *The long haul: truckers, truck stops & trucking*. Memphis: Memphis State University Press, 1979.

Thompson, James Westfall. *A history of livestock raising in the United States, 1607–1860*. USDA Agricultural History Series 5. Washington, D.C., 1942. A36.133:5.

Thorelli, Hans B. *The federal antitrust policy: origination of an American tradition*. Baltimore: The Johns Hopkins University Press, 1955.

Timmons, William. *Twilight on the range: recollections of a latterday cowboy*. Austin: University of Texas Press, 1962.

Tinstman, Dale C., and Robert L. Peterson. *Iowa Beef Processors, Inc.: an entire industry revitalized*. New York: Newcomen Society in North America, 1981.

Towards a more efficient beef chain: documentation assembled for the symposium organized in Paris from 10th–13th January, 1977. Paris: Organization for Economic Development, 1977.

Towne, Charles Wayland, and Edward Norris Wentworth. *Cattle & men*. Norman: University of Oklahoma Press, 1955.

———. *Pigs: from cave to corn belt*. Norman: University of Oklahoma Press, 1950.

———. *Shepherd's empire*. Norman: University of Oklahoma Press, 1945.

Turner, Frederick Jackson. "The significance of the frontier in American history." In American Historical Association *Annual Report for 1893*. Washington, D.C.: Government Printing Office, 1894. SI4.1:893.

Tuttle, William M., Jr. "Labor conflict and racial violence: the black worker in Chicago, 1894–1919," *Labor History* X (1969), 408–32.

U.S. Bureau of the Census. *Historical statistics of the United States, colonial times to 1970.* Washington, D.C.: U.S. Government Printing Office, 1976. C3.134/2:H62/789-970/pt.1.

———. *Live stock on ranges.* Washington, D.C.: Census Bulletin, 1891. C12.3:117.

———. *Report on cattle, sheep, and swine, supplementary to enumeration of live stock on farms in 1880.* Washington, D.C.: Government Printing Office, 1884. Ill.5:3; Ill.5/A:C23.

———. "Slaughtering and meat packing." In *Manufacturers, 1905: part III, special report on selected industries.* Washington, D.C.: Government Printing Office, 1908. C3.5:M31/pt3.

U.S. Bureau of Corporations. *Report of the Commissioner of Corporations on the beef industry, 1905.* Washington, D.C.: Government Printing Office, 1905. Sen. Doc. 3, 59th Cong., special sess., ser. 4910.

U.S. Commissioner of Agriculture. *Report on the diseases of cattle in the United States.* Washington: Government Printing Office, 1871. A1.2:C29/1.

U.S. Congress, Subcommittee on Small Business. *Hearings: small business problems in the marketing of meat and other commodities: anticompetitive practices in the marketing of meat and other commodities.* Washington, D.C.: 96th Cong., 1st Sess., 1979. Y4.Sml:M46/pt.5.

———. *Electronic marketing.* Washington, D.C.: 96th Cong., 1st Sess., 1979. Y4.Sml:M46/pt.6.

———. *Monopoly effects on producers and consumers.* Washington, D.C.: 96th Cong., 1st Sess., 1980. Y4.Sml:M46/pt.7.

U.S. Department of Agriculture. *Agricultural statistics.* Washington, D.C.: United States Government Printing Office, yearly. A1.47:[date].

———. *Century of agriculture in charts and tables.* USDA Statistical Reporting Service Agriculture Handbook 318. Washington, D.C., 1966. A1.76:318.

———. *Century of service: the first 100 years of the USDA.* Washington, D.C.: Centennial Committee, USDA, 1963. A1.2:Ag8/22.

———. *Characteristics of beef cattle feedlots: California, Colorado, western corn belt.* USDA Marketing Research Report 840. Washington, D.C., 1969. A1.82:840.

———. *The lamb industry: an economic study of marketing structure, practices, and problems.* Packers and Stockyards Administration Economic Research Report 2. Washington, D.C., 1970. A96.10:2.

———. *1979 handbook of agricultural charts.* Washington, D.C.: Government Printing Office, 1979. A1.76:561.

———. *Packers and Stockyards Act, 1921, as amended: regulations, statement of general policy.* Washington, D.C.: Government Printing Office, 1971. A96.5:971.

————. *Report*. Washington, D.C.: Government Printing Office, 1849–1983. A1.1:862-982.

————. *Statistical bulletin*. Washington: United States Government Printing Office, 1923-80. A1.34:1-679.

————. *The yearbook of agriculture, 1956: animal diseases*. Washington, D.C.: Government Printing Office, n.d. A1.10:956.

————. *The yearbook of agriculture, 1962: after a hundred years—the Yearbook of agriculture*. Washington, D.C.: United States Government Printing Office, n.d. A1.10:962.

U.S. Department of Agriculture, Bureau of Animal Industry. *Annual report*. Washington, D.C.: Government Printing Office, 1884–1912. A1.1:884-912.

U.S. Department of Commerce. *Statistical abstract of the United States, 1982–83*. Washington, D.C.: Government Printing Office, 1981. C3.134:982-83.

U.S. Federal Trade Commission. *Packer consent decree: a report concerning the present status of the consent decree in the case of the United States vs. Swift & Co., et al., entered in the Supreme Court of the District of Columbia, February 27, 1920*. Sen. Doc. 219, 68th Cong., 2d Sess., 1924–25, ser. 8413.

————. *Report on the meat-packing industry*. 6 vols. Washington, D.C.: Government Printing Office, 1919. FT1.2:M46/1-6.

————. *Report on the private car lines*. 3 vols. Washington, D.C.: Government Print Office, 1920. FT1.2:P93/1-3.

Veeder, Henry. "The Federal Trade Commission and the packers." *Illinois Law Review* 15 (1921): 485–503.

Virtue, G. O. "The meat packing investigation." *Quarterly Journal of Economics* 31 (1920): 636–50.

"Vision and money: Texan turning family ranch into huge development whose skyline could someday rival downtown Dallas." Wichita *Eagle-Beacon*, November 14, 1982, p. 2G.

von Stuyvenberg, J. H., ed. *Margarine: an economic, social and scientific history, 1869–1969*. Toronto: University of Toronto Press, 1969.

Wagner, Susan. *The Federal Trade Commission*. New York: Praeger Publishers, 1971.

Wagoner, J. J. *History of the cattle industry in southern Arizona, 1540–1940*. University of Arizona Social Science Bulletin 20. Tucson, 1952.

Walker, Don D. *Clio's cowboys: studies in the historiography of the cattle trade*. Lincoln: University of Nebraska Press, 1981.

Walker, Francis. "The beef trust and the United States government." *Economic Journal* 16 (1906): 491–514.

Walsh, Margaret. "From pork merchant to meat packer: the midwestern meat industry in the mid-nineteenth century." *Agricultural History* 56 (1982): 127–37.

———. *The manufacturing frontier: pioneer industry in antebellum Wisconsin, 1830–1860.* Madison: State Historical Society of Wisconsin, 1972.

———. "Pork packing as a leading edge of midwestern industry." *Agricultural History* 11 (1977): 702–17.

———. *The rise of the midwestern meat packing industry.* Lexington: University Press of Kentucky, 1982.

———. "The spatial evolution of the midwestern pork industry, 1835–1873." *Journal of Historical Geography* 1 (1978): 1–22.

Walters, Charles, Jr. *Angry testament.* Kansas City: Halcyon House, 1969.

Wasser, C. H. "Early development of technical range management, ca. 1895–1945." *Agricultural History* 51 (1977): 63–77.

Waterloo, Claudia. "Season of stress: farm life is changed as perilous economics undermines confidence." *Wall Street Journal,* April 9, 1982, pp. 1, 13.

Webb, Walter Prescott. *The Great Plains.* New York: Ginn and Company, 1931.

Webb, Walter Prescott, and H. Bailey Carroll, eds. *The Handbook of Texas.* 2 vols. Austin: Texas State Historical Association, 1952.

Weisbord, Albert. *The story of a struggle against starvation wages and the right to organize.* Chicago: Daily Worker Pub. Co., 1926.

Weld, L. D. H. "The meat packing investigation: a reply." *Quarterly Journal of Economics* 332 (1921): 416–17.

———. *Private freight cars and American railways.* New York: Columbia University Press, 1908.

Weld, L. D. H., A. T. Kearney, and F. H. Sidney. *Economics of the packing industry.* Chicago: University of Chicago Press, 1925.

Wellford, Harrison. *Sowing the wind: a report from Ralph Nader's Center for Study of Responsive Law on food safety and the chemical harvest.* New York: Grossman Publishers, 1972.

Wellman, Paul I. *The chain.* New York: Doubleday, 1949.

———. *The trampling herd.* New York: Carrick & Evans, 1939.

Welsh, Carol Holderby. "Cattle market for the world: the Oklahoma National Stockyards." *Chronicles of Oklahoma* 60 (1982): 42–55.

Wentworth, Edward Norris. *America's sheep trails: history, personalities.* Ames: Iowa State University Press, 1948.

———. "Livestock products and the tariff." *Journal of Farm Economics* 7 (1925): 319–45.

Wentworth, Edward Norris, and Tage U. H. Ellinger. *Marketing livestock and meats.* Chicago: Armour's Livestock Bureau, 1925.

Wermiel, Stephen. "Supreme Court rules union pacts may be ignored under Chapter 11: decision, a blow to labor, seen helping companies in bankruptcy court." *Wall Street Journal*, February 23, 1984, p. 3.

Westermeir, Clifford P. "The legal status of Colorado cattlemen, 1867–1887." *The Colorado Magazine* 25 (1948): 109–18, 157–66.

Wheeler, David L. "The beef cattle industry in the old Northwest, 1803–1860." *Panhandle-Plains Historical Review* 47 (1974): 28–45.

———. "The beef cattle industry in the United States: colonial origins." *Panhandle-Plains Historical Review* 46 (1973): 54–67.

———. "The origins and development of the cattle feeding industry in the southern high plains." *Panhandle-Plains Historical Review* 49 (1976): 81–90.

Whitaker, Adelynne H. "Pesticide use in early twentieth century animal disease control." *Agricultural history* 54 (1980): 71–81.

Whitaker, James W. *Feedlot empire: beef cattle feeding in Illinois and Iowa, 1840–1900*. Ames: Iowa State University Press, 1975.

White, Bouck. *The book of Daniel Drew*. New York: Doubleday, Page & Company, 1910.

White, Wilford. "The refrigerator car and the effects upon the public of packer control of refrigerator car lines." *Southwestern Political and Social Science Quarterly* 10 (1930): 388–400.

White, William R. "Illegal fencing on the Colorado range." *The Colorado Magazine* 52 (1975): 93–113.

Whitney, Simon. *Antitrust policies: American experience in twenty industries*. 2 vols. New York: Twentieth Century Fund, 1958.

Wilcox, Clair. *Competition and monopoly in American industry*. Temporary National Economic Committee Monograph 21. Washington, D.C., 1940. Y4.T24:M75/21.

Williams, Willard F., Earl K. Bowen, and Frank C. Genovese. *Economic effects of U.S. grades for beef*. USDA Marketing Research Report 298. Washington, D.C., 1959. A1.82:298.

Williams, Willard F., and Thomas T. Stout. *Economics of the livestock-meat industry*. New York: The Macmillan Company, 1964.

Wilson, James A. "Cattlemen, packers, and government regulation: retreating individualism on the Texas range." *Southwestern Historical Quarterly* 74 (1971): 525–34.

———. "West Texas influences on the early cattle industry of Arizona." *Southwestern Historical Quarterly* 71 (1967): 37–45.

"Wilson refocuses from production to customers." Wichita *Eagle-Beacon*, August 15, 1982, pp. 9, 11G.

Wing, Jack. *The great Union Stockyards of Chicago*. Chicago: Religio-Philosophical Publishing Association, 1865.

Winter, Ralph E. "New givebacks: even profitable firms press workers to take permanent pay cuts." *Wall Street Journal,* March 6, 1984, pp. 1, 22.

Winther, Oscar Osburn, and Richard Van Orman, eds. *A classified bibliography of the periodical literature of the trans-Mississippi West (1811–1957).* Bloomington: Indiana University Press, 1964.

———. *A supplement (1957–1967).* Bloomington: Indiana University Press, 1970.

Wood, Charles L. *The Kansas beef industry.* Lawrence: Regents Press of Kansas, 1980.

———. "Science and politics in the war on cattle diseases: the Kansas experience." *Agricultural History* 54 (1980): 82–92.

Woolrich, Willis R. *The men who created cold: a history of refrigeration.* New York: Exposition Press, 1967.

Worcester, Don. *The Chisholm trail: high road of the cattle kingdom.* Lincoln: University of Nebraska Press, 1980.

Yeager, Mary. *Competition and regulation: the development of oligopoly in the meat packing industry.* Greenwich, Conn.: Jai Press, Inc., 1981.

Zeigler, Robert E. "The cowboy strike of 1883: its causes and meaning." West Texas Historical Association *Yearbook* 47 (1971): 32–46.

Zimmerman, W. D. "Live cattle trade between the United States and Great Britain, 1868–1885." *Agricultural History* 36 (1962): 46–52.

Index